MY
FIRST
MEMORY

MY
FIRST
MEMORY

Icons, thinkers and heroes
on their earliest
recollections

Edited by
BEN HOLDEN

SCRIBNER
LONDON NEW YORK TORONTO SYDNEY NEW DELHI

First published in Great Britain by Scribner, an imprint
of Simon & Schuster UK Ltd, 2019
A CBS COMPANY

Copyright © Lightbulb Pictures Ltd, 2019

SCRIBNER and design are registered trademarks of The Gale Group, Inc.,
used under licence by Simon & Schuster Inc.

The right of Ben Holden to be identified as author of
this work has been asserted in accordance with the
Copyright, Designs and Patents Act, 1988.

1 3 5 7 9 10 8 6 4 2

Simon & Schuster UK Ltd
1st Floor
222 Gray's Inn Road
London WC1X 8HB

Simon & Schuster Australia, Sydney
Simon & Schuster India, New Delhi

www.simonandschuster.co.uk
www.simonandschuster.com.au
www.simonandschuster.co.in

A CIP catalogue record for this book
is available from the British Library

Hardback ISBN: 978-1-4711-6746-1
eBook ISBN: 978-1-4711-6747-8

The author and publishers have made all reasonable efforts to contact
copyright-holders for permission, and apologise for any omissions or errors in
the form of credits given. Corrections may be made to future printings.

Typeset by M Rules
Printed and bound by CPI Group (UK) Ltd, Croydon, CR0 4YY

MIX
Paper from
responsible sources
FSC® C020471

For my parents —

Thanks for the memories.

La réalité ne se forme que dans la mémoire
(Reality only forms itself in memory)

MARCEL PROUST

Time present and time past
Are both perhaps present in time future
And time future contained in time past.

T. S. ELIOT

Contents

1. My First Memory

Introduction	3
Giacomo Casanova	31
Charles Darwin	35
Sigmund Freud	37
Edmund Gosse	40
Mark Twain	42
Maxim Gorky	44
Winston Churchill	48
Edith Wharton	50
Rudyard Kipling	54
Salvador Dalí	56
Vladimir Nabokov	58
Simone de Beauvoir	60
Laurie Lee	62
Virginia Woolf	65
Carl Jung	68
Malcolm X	73
Dodie Smith	75

Patrick Leigh Fermor 77
Paul Auster 81
Rosemary Sutcliff 84
Arthur Miller 88
Miles Davis 89
Marlon Brando 91
Doris Lessing 93
Margaret Thatcher 95
Hilary Mantel 98
Christopher Hitchens 102
Karl Ove Knausgaard 105
Stephen Hawking 108
Oliver Sacks 110
Susan Greenfield 112
Sebastian Barry 116
Melvyn Bragg 119
Nicholas Humphrey 123
Javier Marías 127
Michael Morpurgo 131

2. The Sense of a Beginning

Introduction 139
Booker T. Washington 160
Emmeline Pankhurst 165
Eleanor Roosevelt 168
Zora Neale Hurston 171
Woody Guthrie 178
Albert Einstein 181

C. S. Lewis   183
Fred Astaire   187
Gavin Maxwell   190
Martin Luther King, Jr   193
Pablo Neruda   198
Muhammad Ali   202
Luciano Pavarotti   206
The Dalai Lama   209
Rosa Parks   213
Johnny Cash   215
Paula Fox   219
Chinua Achebe   225
Sidney Poitier   228
Orhan Pamuk   232
John McGahern   237
Pelé   243
Maya Angelou   246
Usain Bolt   249
Saroo Brierley   257
Mo Farah   262
Henning Mankell   266
Bruce Springsteen   271
John Banville   275
Ursula K. Le Guin   279
Tessa Hadley   283
David Eagleman   288

3. RIGHTS OF PASSAGE

Introduction   297
Stefan Zweig   320
Walter Benjamin   324
Eva Hoffman   328
Elie Wiesel   334
Isabel Allende   341
Gillian Slovo   345
Ayaan Hirsi Ali   350
Eric R. Kandel   355
Madeleine Albright   359
Gulwali Passarlay   363
Ocean Vuong   369
George Szirtes   373
Aso Saber   376
Jade Amoli-Jackson   379
Yusra Mardini   382
Alf Dubs   386

Endnote   390
Afterword By Maurice Wren,
   Refugee Council   392
Further Reading   396
Acknowledgements   398
Copyrights And Credits   400
Index   409

PART ONE

My First Memory

Introduction

It was only once I reached the likely mid-point of my lifetime that I scrutinised first memories. Their fleeting resonance. The elusive power of innocence meeting imagination. The way a first memory is universal – we all have to start somewhere – and yet its details, however humdrum, are quintessential to the individual concerned. How it marks that first articulation of a sense of self.

I began to chase these mirages and mythologies, like an explorer prospecting for the crock-of-gold at the beginning of the rainbow. I quizzed friends and family for their earliest impressions of life; or what they imagined them to be. I scoured obsessively the lives and times of the great and the good for ghostly points of origin.

All the while, the timing of my enquiry stayed with me. Serendipity was at play, the work of Father Time and Mother Nature. I mentioned that I have reached the likely mid-point of life. While not yet over the hill, I am beginning to feel the gradient of its camber. My wife and I have watched our parents confront mortality head-on. Meanwhile, our beloved children are growing up by the second. These preoccupations prompted my wandering down Memory Lane.

The only problem is that I have forgotten my own earliest memory.

I know that I was born twenty minutes after midnight on 14 March, one hundred years to the day after Albert Einstein. Supposedly, my mum – who is not a particularly superstitious type – decided that she really didn't want me having the 13th as a birthday. She held out until midnight, soon after which I pumpkined forth.

This incipient plot thickened the following morning. My father had a key meeting with the proprietor of the newspaper that had just hired him. Not something he could miss. He was to be the new Washington Correspondent, a dream gig. Dad is punctual to a fault (growing up, our family would arrive everywhere an hour early), so he must have felt mortified to enter that boardroom not only bleary-eyed but also, what's worse, late. He had a good excuse, of course. He explained the excitement of the wee hours to the newspaper magnate: that his wife had given birth to a third son the night before, elaborating in his charming way as to why I had been a midnight child.

I can picture his face drop, however, at the response from his new employer. The guy snapped back at him: *'I was born on the thirteenth and it hasn't done me any harm.'*

Pushing forward, there follows a press image of then president Jimmy Carter reaching through an adoring crowd. It is a few weeks after my birth. We have now moved stateside. Carter is on the campaign trail near the White House and pressing the flesh of a sun-drenched DC public. It was a simpler time. The security presence is minimal. Just a pair of heavies behind aviators. Carter's daughter Amy hovers in the foreground, her back half-turned (her mother, the first lady, is curiously absent).

The president has spied a cute babe-in-arms and, sensing a photo opportunity, makes a beeline for the cherub. The Leader of the Free World beams beneficently. He lightly strokes the baby's cheek with his right index finger. Amy coos. The baby, however, is aghast at this strange man's advances. He scowls. It will undoubtedly be seconds before he recoils fully into his mother's embrace and howls blue murder, leaving the president to melt back into the folds of his retinue.

Apparently, that baby in a diaper – the one with the blond ringlets – was me.

Clearly, I can't actually remember any of these events. Yet such is our familiarity with those stories of yore told over and over and the thumbed images in family albums that we frequently feel like we do recall such happenings. Most of us cherish such nostalgia for our forgotten past lives. The truth of it all ceases to matter. We live to tell the tale again and again.

Similarly, sometimes when I can't sleep at night, I'll steal back inside my first childhood home. Among the moonlit shadows I'll lie, racking the focus of my mind's eye to eke out details. I begin to strain, as if reading in the dark. Soon enough time and space meld.

Trespassing back through that red front door, I voyage into Number 30, the home I departed aged four, having lived there for only a year or so (we had moved back to London from Washington DC by then). The whole place is insubstantial, at best. The house is without structure. Its dimensions are uneven and shifting. There are no rooms, only dilatory walls and floating floors. The colour scheme is alien. Yet distinguishing features hide tantalisingly around each invisible corner. The house has sprung to life amid the dead of night.

The adventure wakes me up, if anything. My dad – who suggested this remedy for insomnia back when I was a boy – should have told me to count sheep. Without realising it, instead he led me to construct my own private memory palace.

As with almost everything, such edifices began with the Ancient Greeks. Legend has it that in 477 BC, the poet and orator Simonides found himself the lone survivor of a banquet hall collapsing. The disaster killed all his fellow diners. Their bodies had been obliterated beyond recognition beneath the rubble. The dead needed accounting for. As the last banqueter standing, Simonides was called upon to confirm who had been present.

He ingeniously set about reconstituting the *placement* or *loci* of the feast from which he had miraculously stepped away. In his head, Simonides reconstructed the banquet hall. He walked around the table, resurrecting his fellow diners one by one. By doing so, Simonides allowed their remains to be identified via location. He also erected the first ever memory palace and, with it, the foundations for *mnemonics*, the art and craft of memory.

For centuries, his *loci method* (as it is also known) – in which familiar places are populated with distinctive imagery, by way of visual milestones – enabled orators to remember long and significant tracts. Refined by the likes of Cicero into manuals, soon memory palaces were constructed to house sermons, prayers and speeches.

In the fifteenth century, Gutenberg and the advent of books put paid to such techniques. Today, phones, computers and tablets serve as our primary memory aids, not the *loci method*. Cutting-edge mnemonics is the preserve of futurist tech-heads, robotic engineers and AI specialists, not orators or writers. Memory palaces are now ancient ruins, of archaeological and anthropological interest only.

Indeed, these edifices were already obsolete by the nineteenth century (unless you were Sherlock Holmes). Yet during that era, as their schools of psychoanalysis and functional psychology flourished, Sigmund Freud and William James would both in passing liken memories to objects stored inside the room of a house. Freud and James would offer ground-breaking theories of how memory operates, particularly Freud with his exhumations of childhood memories. They were each brilliantly ahead of their time – as befits mnemonists – and yet incongruously off the mark with this *en passant* analogy for memories. Perhaps they were simply following Augustine's lead, who wrote in the tenth book of his *Confessions*: 'When I am in this storehouse,

7

I ask that it produce what I want to recall, and immediately certain things come out.'

Memories are not, however, pieces of furniture or ornaments within some inner depository, items to be dusted off their shelf, unwrapped or moved from A to B, never changing form (as this analogy implies). Until recently, however, this was the received wisdom. Experts really believed memories to be fixed points within us, like DVDs or MPEG files that could be pulled down and replayed on demand.

On the contrary, recollection is by nature revisionist and provisional. Memories are not suspended in time, sacred cows preserved in formaldehyde. We relive our past events in the present. How I describe a vivid early memory today will differ from how I tell it twenty-five years from now. Memory lives in the moment.

I write as the beneficiary of crucial work done by a new wave of scientists and psychologists exploring the effects of subjectivity on memory. During the 1980s, these brain-boxes began to re-evaluate the norms hitherto applied to their field. Along the way, they broke memory down into three constituent systems, each with distinct functions.

Procedural memory reminds us to eat and breathe. Thanks to it, we don't forget how to ride a bike. We recall automatic functions on a quotidian basis, without a second thought.

Semantic memory links the contiguous associations that allow us to know *when and how* to perform some of those everyday tasks. It enables us to acquire and deploy skills or routines. We remember when to have breakfast and the days of the week, for two examples, courtesy of it.

Finally, there is *episodic memory*. This allows us to recall subjectively the past events of our lives. We travel through time and relive experiences. Also known as *autobiographical memory*, this is the wheelhouse for recollections of times past, the animated archive of our personal history – be it yesterday or a lifetime ago.

Episodic memory provides the foundation for this book.

When this trio combine, we become three-dimensional. Life flows. To paraphrase Descartes' clarion call to ego: I *remember*, therefore I am. Should any of the systems founder, however – as in, say, cases of Parkinson's disease for *procedural memory* or Alzheimer's disease for *semantic memory* – troubles abound. Working in concert, though, they miraculously allow us to exist as sentient human beings.

In recent decades, in addition to such new categorisations, neuroscientists have also discerned that these different functions of memory are powered by disparate parts of the brain. Put another way: remembering how to type this sentence without looking at the computer keys is coordinated by an altogether different neurological region to my misty-eyed memories of Highbury football stadium, in north London.

Moreover, that I have just written the previous sentence is currently a short-term or *primary memory*, as William James coined it. He wrote of the 'specious present', as memories are held for moments and then sifted, with only very select items being retained. I will soon forget the deed of that sentence's construction (after about 30–60 seconds, customarily). My loving memories of Arsenal's old home ground that the sentence conjures, however, are concocted of stronger stuff: namely, emotion. This renders them much longer-term or *secondary memories*. The actual recollection – the gathering back up – of these sorts of off-the-cuff remembrances James defined as: 'the knowledge of an event, or fact, of which meantime we have not been thinking, with the additional consciousness that we have thought or experienced it before'.*

Such resurfacings require *apperception*. Perception with an add-on, this is the assimilation that we each make whenever we remember days gone by. It is the echo-chamber effect of how our minds not only perceive the past but also simultaneously contextualise it within the present moment. Each time we recall something, with the very act of its retrieval, we recast the memory anew. In turn, once it has boomeranged back, the memory's own neuronal structure is itself transformed. The end result of this thought process is reassuringly called *reconsolidation*.

Looking at this another way: whenever we remember something, we are positively *living in the moment*. Tennessee Williams recognised this when he pondered:

> Has it ever struck you . . . that life is all memory, except for the one present moment that goes by you so quickly you hardly catch it going?†

Just as our mind depends on these free-flowing

* *The Principles of Psychology* (1890).
† In his play *The Milk Train Doesn't Stop Here Anymore* (1963).

confluences of past and present when making such associations, so the brain demands its different engines to fire together for memories to be summoned in the first place. It was French psychologist Théodule Ribot who, during the late nineteenth century, first postulated a cellular basis for memory functions. Scientists continue to augment his findings today. We now understand that the act of remembering is an electrifying process. Molecules blaze trails, into neurons. Synapses that are thousandths of millimetres in radius make connections between cortexes. The brain lights up and remembers itself.

This is the most basic joining of dots to describe the most complex of firmaments, as time and space conjoin within memory traces. The circuitry that must constellate for us to illuminate – or remember – something is highly intricate. The specific patterning that allows each memory to be recaptured – each unique neurological starburst – is called an 'engram'.* When we come to transcribe life stories into memoirs – or more immediately, say, with diaries – we map these hidden charts. Coleridge recognised this, marvelling at the prospect within his own notebooks:

> He looked at his own Soul
> with a Telescope. What seemed
> all irregular, he saw and
> shewed to be beautiful
> Constellations: and he added

* The term 'engram' was coined by Richard Semon, in his monograph *Die Mneme* (1904).

To the Consciousness hidden
Worlds within worlds.

The part of our brain that creates these engrams, the fountainhead from which reminiscence pours, is the *hippocampus*. It is named after the Ancient Greek word ἱππόκαμπος, meaning seahorse, whose questioning body shape it resembles (the word joins '*hippos*', meaning horse – hence hippopotamus or 'water horse' – with '*kampos*', signifying sea monster).

The *hippocampi* (we actually have two) nestle on the right and left sides of our brains, in the *medial temporal lobes*. They perch roughly above the top of our ears, about two inches inside the skull. From there, they connect with a network of cortices that in turn link to those other neurological regions that enable memory to speak. These include: the *amygdala* (after the Ancient Greek for almond and/or tonsil, the shapes of which it resembles), which joins with the front of the *hippocampus* to regulate our emotions; and at the rear of the brain – the bad boy staring out from the back of the bus – the *occipital cortex*, the lobe which allows us to map our world.

This is ground zero for our inner cartography. Yet when does Memory itself first come into view?

On average, an adult's first memories date from the age of three-and-a-quarter.* The popular explanation for this

---

* This mean average is per the study 'Fictional First Memories' (2018 – Akhtar, Justice, Morrison and Conway) which surveyed 6,641 respondents about their first memories. The mean average age for the respondents' earliest encoding of memories was 3.2 years.

is that it is only once we begin to speak that longer-term or *secondary* memories stick. This makes sense. As we come to articulate ourselves – even in the most basic of ways – we start to craft a narrative (or, at least, a prologue). Words and stories allow us to fashion (or 're-member'), when repeated, a sense of where we come from. With their acquisition, as our imaginations open and selfhood dawns, we start to make sense of the world and forge an individual path into it. Thus memory – and, with it, our life story – commences.

That is not to say that we don't remember things before we are talking, or that this is a hard-and-fast watermark for every person. We have lots of memories as young infants. Although most of us forget them all. Some grown-ups, on the other hand, claim to remember exceedingly early events and incidents from their infancy, sometimes all the way back to the womb. Salvador Dalí, for one, called his memories of intra-uterine life – extracted here – 'rare and liquid', claiming to remember the period 'as though it were yesterday'.

Steven Spielberg once remarked that he can 'always trace a movie idea back to his childhood'. The filmmaker made his name with pictures that were embedded within the child's point of view of the world – such as *E.T.* and *Close Encounters of the Third Kind*. His Americana, with its potent evocation of fear and wonder in equal measure, remains a wellspring for filmmakers today.* Spielberg also claims, revealingly,

---

* For but three obvious examples of leading American directors who have made homages to Spielberg's Amblin aesthetic: J. J. Abrams (most notably in *Super 8*); Matt Reeves (in *Let Me In*); and the Duffer Brothers (*Stranger Things*).

to be able to visualise an earliest memory from the vantage point of his pram.

Picture the scene. We're inside Cincinnati's Adath Israel synagogue. Softly lit by a twinkling chandelier, the milieu is rich with chiaroscuro. Arnold and Leah Spielberg are conveying their baby boy towards a glowing red light, burning at the end of a long blue aisle. This beacon blushes beneath a colonnaded, marble arch. It is the Ark of the Torah. On either side of the gauntlet, their chants growing louder with the procession's every step, Hasidic bearded elders sway to the rhythm of Hebrew prayer. They lean into the pram. Adult Steven would later recall how 'the old men were handing me little crackers'.*

This specific detail is a protean achievement of memory and most unusual, considering that the subject was only six months old at the time of its occurrence (when Spielberg recounted the scene to his parents – as opposed to the other way around, vouchsafing its authenticity – they pinpointed exactly when it must have happened). No wonder that Spielberg is celebrated not only for his storytelling virtuosity, but also for making connections with inner children the world over.

In both Dalí's and Spielberg's defence against the naysayers, they both went on to become famed for their potent visual imaginations (albeit in very different media). Besides, babies do remember. Newborns are able to identify their mother's voice or recognise a particular tune that was sung to them only while in the womb.

* Spielberg recalled this earliest childhood memory in an interview with Richard Corliss for *Time* magazine ('I Dream for a Living', July 1985).

Implicit memory has been shown as fully operational prior to the age of three. Studies of such infants, for example, deploy different devices and shapes designed to intrigue their subjects. As long as the circumstances and environments of these showcases are controlled and do not change (meaning that the scientist's hand puppet stays the same colour and the room in which it is on display never varies), the memories of the device usually stick.

It is at around the age of nine months that *explicit* recall – such as where a specific toy may be secreted or which adult to cling to – begins to abound. These faculties then develop rapidly, as we mature at an exponential rate, picking up new skills every day. Our brains double in size during the first year of life.

The lack of *episodic memory* ('that time Mummy gave me a new teddy'), as opposed to *semantic memory* ('if I cry, Mummy comes and comforts me'), again implies that the acquisition of skills such as basic language and spatial awareness are critical to memory consolidation. The parts of the brain that are key for humans in creating episodic memories have yet to form fully. The medial temporal lobes (those structures of our brains that are so crucial to memory, including the *hippocampus*) are simply not yet developed. Accordingly, we are unable to discern which memories are worthy of retention.

More specifically, within the hippocampus, the *dentate gyrus* is still germinating. This cluster of cells is one of the few places in the brain where *neurogenesis* – the formation of neurons – takes place. Once it begins to fire, new memories can be imbued with specific markers. We can differentiate between similar occurrences and judge circumstances better. We grow out of early infancy largely thanks to this gyrus (and, yes, now that glove puppet can change its outfit).

Until these faculties have reached maturity, though, the first landmarks of our lives are forgotten. They are washed away by *childhood amnesia* (a term coined in 1893 by psychologist Caroline Miles). Apparently, none of us is exempt from this. Daniel Schacter, professor and chair of psychology at Harvard University, is categorical: 'We remember nothing prior to the ages of two and three, and little prior to the ages of five or six.'* How, then, to account for those memories that abscond from such boundaries and overstay their welcome, like Spielberg's and Dalí's?

Other experts are more circumspect than Schacter. Professor Jonathan K. Foster, for one: 'Memories of earlier experiences before the age of four may well exist, but in a neural and/or psychological form which means that the individual can no longer access them as memories of specific experiences.'†

This is tantalising, like a transformative dream that is immediately forgotten. That they are out of reach – *and yet somewhere inside* – renders the idea of earliest memories even sweeter. They become elemental and ethereal. Tolstoy savoured this long-lostness of childhood amnesia, delighting in its paradoxical splendour:

Oh, the happy, happy, never-to-be-recalled days of

* *Searching for Memory* (1996), p. 240.
† *Memory: A Very Short Introduction* (2008).

childhood! How could one fail to love and cherish memories of such a time?*

Graham Greene – whose first memory was of sitting in a pram beside a dead dog – knew this too.

Of all my first six years I have only such random memories . . . and I cannot be sure of their time-sequence. They are significant for me because they remain, the stray symbols of a dream after the story has sunk back into the unconscious, and they cry for rescue like the survivors of a shipwreck.†

There are, though, processes available to recover such lost treasures. I had planned to undergo therapies to mine my own, in the hope of excavating that elusive first memory. Yet when I sought advice on what this might entail, experts were circumspect at best about my chances of success. I realised that I had fallen into a rabbit hole of my own making. I really should have known better. I was looking for a glib gimmick: the long-lost DVD or file that I could pull down and rewatch. Memory is never so simple.

In the 1990s, a man called George Franklin was convicted of murder in California a full twenty-one years after his alleged crime took place. The sentence was handed down following the testimony of his own daughter, Eileen. Her

* From chapter 15 of 'Childhood', translated by Rosemary Edmonds.
† From *A Sort of Life* (1971)

evidence was comprised of a series of *recovered memories.* Eileen Franklin claimed that seeing her own daughter strike a certain pose had unearthed a burial ground of memories. The sight of her young child, George's granddaughter, led Eileen to recall having seen another girl of the same age – a childhood friend – being raped and murdered by George. Her father denied the crime.

His conviction was overturned on appeal but so high-profile was the case that a tsunami of repressed memories flooded the USA. Some psychoanalysts and therapists encouraged exhumations via techniques such as *'visualisation'* and *'suggestion',* methods that supposedly dredge a patient's memory bank. The proliferation of these 'new' memories of abuse ostensibly coming to light – and the painful fallouts that ensued within families – shocked the medical establishment. A sceptical backlash against the phenomenon followed. Many such *'recovered memories',* in the absence of corroboration, came to be counter-labelled as the byproducts of *'false memory syndrome'.*

As already glimpsed, artist Salvador Dalí had an altogether purer vision of 'false memories'. Whereas *'false memory syndrome'* led to categorical recollections that destroyed whole lives, Dalí's falsities twinkle more luminously. The artist, whose most recognisable work, *The Persistence of Memory,* depicts timepieces melting away, observed:

> The difference between false memories and true ones is the same as for jewels: it is always the false ones that look the most real, the most brilliant.

Here is the sheen that adorns our most precious memories: the ones that we polish again and again, like prized gemstones, over a long passage of time. Each time we recollect those beloved memories, they become a little more corrupted by the telling. Their imperfections gleam even more pristinely.

As with so much of today's received wisdom concerning psychology, the seeds for all these theories were sown by Sigmund Freud. His own first memories follow in this collection. Observe in them the master psychoanalyst at work, as he embellishes the happenstance of childhood with layers of significance.

As regards buried memories, Freud posited that repression was a natural psychological defence mechanism, one designed to keep at bay traumatic memories from a person's awareness. His clinical reports of the conscious minds of patients hiding painful childhood truths – traumas that, unbeknown to his patients, were still influencing their daily behaviour – remain seminal.

Today, our love of storytellers who shade their protagonists with murky backstories – whether in Gothic ghost stories, Hitchcockian psycho-thrillers or sci-fi fables – in large part stems from these Freudian theories. Moreover, the manner in which hidden memories play out in such narratives – from the perspective of an 'observer' or in POV flashbacks (both of which tag us along for the ride, as reader or audience) – is also appealing for dramatists. This detached vantage point was something that Freud noted was particularly prevalent in his patients' childhood recollections. Many of the memories in this collection are rendered in just such a fashion.

Freud's colleague Carl Jung resisted many invitations to publish an autobiography. '*I know too much about the impossibility of self-portrayal*,' he explained. The requests continued nevertheless and eventually, very late in life, Jung succumbed. Having devoted his life to an exploration of the unconscious mind, though, he was hardly going to take the task of memoirist lightly.

> I have therefore weighted the matter and come to the conclusion that I shall fend off other obligations long enough to take up the very first beginnings of my life and consider them in an objective fashion. This task has proved so difficult and singular that in order to go ahead with it, I have had to promise myself that the results would not be published in my lifetime. Such a promise seemed essential in order to assure myself the necessary detachment and calm.

Even then, despite adopting this scrupulous methodology, Jung still declined to write the autobiography! He reasoned that the 'outer' manifestations that combine to form a sensible autobiography were 'phantasms' to be dismissed, while the 'inner' experiences that remain all the more 'vivid and colourful' to his mind defied explanation.

That is not to say that Jung's own early experiences all lay dormant. Some memories from his childhood had already informed his ground-breaking research: for example, the secret ceremonies and linguistics that, as a child, he had created for a mannequin hidden in the attic of the family home had helped shape his landmark theories of symbols, archetypes and the collective unconscious.

Eventually, the clamour for a life story prevailed. In the spring of 1957, at the age of eighty-two, Jung finally set about work with his assistant Aniela Jaffé. By the end of that year, and after 'long-submerged images of his childhood rose to the surface of his mind', Jung felt ready to recall his first memories on paper. The process had unsurprisingly taken on a therapeutic tone. Especially when it came to his first memories.

This autobiography is now taking a direction quite different from that I had imagined at the beginning. It has become necessary for me to write down my early memories. If I neglect to do so for a single day, unpleasant physical symptoms immediately follow. As soon as I set to work, though, they vanish and my head feels perfectly clear.

It took Jung over a year to complete the 'Early Events of My Life'. True to his word, it was only upon Jung's death, three years later in 1961, that the full manuscript of *Memories, Dreams, Reflections* was published. The earliest memories that he managed to recover feature here. Remember, however, that they are merely his 'outer memories'.

It is for all these reasons that our earliest memories remain fleeting. They glimmer beneath the surface, like Greene's 'shipwreck survivors' or fish in a springtime lake. We might catch one from time to time, if we're lucky. It can be startling when present thought hooks past experience. Such moments of *re-collection* are precious.

The most celebrated literary instance of which being, of course, Marcel Proust's 'madeleine moment', when a taste of cake prompted the most in-depth and arguably vivid retrieval of times past on record. Vladimir Nabokov, whose own first memory is catalogued here, described *À la recherche du temps perdu* in suitably glittering terms, calling it 'a treasure hunt where the treasure is time and the hiding place the past'.

More than anyone, in those seven volumes, Proust grafted language onto engrams. He rendered their triggers metaphysical and transposed them, his *'réminiscences'*, onto the page. The famous 'madeleine moment' may be rooted in his taste buds (which, by the way, themselves have a lifespan of just ten days) but its pleasure is, in his words, 'without origin'. If anywhere, it resides in Proust's intuition. Life becomes contingent. He forgets himself in memory.

Auditory cues, and indeed olfactory prompts, smells and tastes, are far more pervasive in children. Their memories – indeed, their worlds – are more turbidly sensual than those of us grown-ups. As we age, vision sees past its rival sensory modalities. It pervades our dreams and memories at their expense; this despite our sensory receptors dwelling near to those same neurological pockets so key to memory.

These extra cues to memory – sound, smell (as recalled herein by Jung with his very first memory of warm milk), taste (Proust's *involuntary memory*, prompted by his madeleine) – remain important, sure, but vision monopolises memory.

This is borne out by the prevalence of amnesia in people who suffer damage in the *occipital cortex* (remember – the cartographer at the back of the bus?). The amnesiac's inability to generate visual images can even lead to their forgetting events that took place prior to injury. Today, to remedy such conditions, various sensory devices and techniques are deployed. Other sensory prompts are stimulated – colours, tastes and such – in order to bypass visionary shortfalls and extract meanings.

The mixing of such instinctual palettes with memory is often a conduit for artists in search of their muse. After all, *synaesthesia* – the neurological condition that blends senses – has long been linked to creativity. Messiaen famously composed music in colours. Nabokov in his memoir *Speak, Memory* – which is extracted here – described his 'coloured hearing' and exceptional powers of recall. More recently, novelist A. S. Byatt has written that upon commencement of a book or story she regards her writing 'as blocks of colour'.*

As well as deep-sea metaphors, psychologists will often draw upon archaeological terminology to describe the process of piecing together cogent memories. It is another good parallel:

* Quoted in *Off the Page: Writers Talk about Beginnings, Endings and Everything in Between*, edited by Carole Burns.

after all, cultures sculpt a sense of self from the relics and revelations of civilisations past. We create museums and monuments during our present existence – so that the future might also remember our past.

Memories should be accorded the same level of care and caution. To coarsen the archaeological metaphor: each time that we relate a reminiscence of our own, we are not only reassembling a skeleton but, in the moment of its reconstruction, adding new flesh onto those bones. As Daniel Schacter adroitly puts it: 'Our sense of ourselves depends crucially on the subjective experience of remembering our pasts.'*

Psychotherapists and analysts will, for exactly this reason, often commence work with a new patient by enquiring about their first memory. Nothing can be more revealing, upfront and personal. It is an indispensable insight into a person's psychic life. Even more so than their dreams.

This truth is borne out in the extracts and essays that follow. Just as the patients recounting their earliest remembrances opens up their unconscious, so many memoirists' first memories reveal how their authors choose to be perceived. They write from the couch, as it were.

This is further complicated when the individual is a world-famous public figure. Many genuinely iconic people appear throughout this collection. Some – for instance, Winston Churchill – would even have known, while still alive, that their life stories would reverberate through

---

* *Searching for Memory*, chapter 1: 'On Remembering'.

history. When such colossi come to write their memoirs, they can't help but glorify their own legend. Ronald Reagan, for example, begins *My Early Life* in preternaturally patriotic terms. First, he links his bare bottom being smacked as a baby to a lifelong love of 'red, white and blue' (these being the colours that he exhibited during the experience) before impishly declaring that 'breast feeding was the home of the brave baby and the free bosom'.

Other accounts are included here not because of their author's historic achievements so much as their exquisite composition. Many are down-to-earth or relate humdrum happenings. They all incant songs of innocence with the voice of experience.

Arthur Miller and Doris Lessing, to name but two, attempt infantilism: in their accounts, they think like children, talk like children, return to childish ways. Taking these points of view at face value is, of course, impossible and yet we know such perspectives are common to early memories, which often tend to be 'field' or 'observer' memories, like those that Freud observed in his patients.

Perhaps all memoirs, then, to be representations of the utmost authenticity, should be written – like, for instance, J. M. Coetzee's – in the third person. That way, it is confronted head-on that the past is a foreign country and implied that there will be no land grab by narrative. The mindscape described is the estate of the author's former self. Those distant fields of experience were traversed by another person altogether. Cells have been replenished wholesale during the ensuing lifetime. Skins shed.

Edith Wharton knew perfectly well how we conceive of ourselves. She wrote of 'the little girl who eventually became me'. The pronouns in Wharton's account of her earliest memories are ghostly: 'The episode is literally the first thing *I* can remember about *her,* and therefore I date the birth of *her* identity from that day.'

Today, people toggle their 'timelines' to date how they became themselves. Traditionally, though, the best way of mitigating against ontological inconsistencies was the trusty journal or diary. A contemporaneous chronicle, it charted in the here and now what the hell just happened way back when. We recorded the present moment so that, in the future, we might revisit the past.

Writers have long relied on such props. Joan Didion, for one, has always kept notebooks (not diaries, *notebooks*). She has even published some of them. From the age of five, Didion felt compelled to write things down. Calling serial note-takers such as herself 'children afflicted apparently at birth with some presentiment of loss', Didion filled up those empty pages to illuminate the voids within. At the time of their composition, Didion hoped that the notebooks would prove 'a forgotten account with accumulated inter-est'. More constant than memory, they would be on hand 'some morning when the world seems drained of wonder'. However, she came to realise – in time – that her note-books offered up something altogether more precious. Just like Wharton's memoirs, they allowed Joan Didion – and, more's the pleasure today, her readers – to '*remember what it was to be me*'.

Iris Murdoch also kept a journal. In it, she recorded her first memory as 'my mother flying above me like a white bird'. Later in life, interestingly, Murdoch would come to forsake that notion and stake a claim for an alternative jumping-off point.

She recalled how, when she was three or four years old, she learnt to swim at the saltwater baths near Dún Laoghaire in Ireland. As little Iris paddled out, her father Wills Murdoch would call to her from across the water. He would skim paternal love to his daughter. Propelled by those calls, Iris would soon reach the other side, where Daddy waited to congratulate her.*

It is little surprise that swimming became one of Murdoch's lifelong pleasures. Even in 1997, by which time Alzheimer's disease had ravaged her majestic intellect, Murdoch and husband John Bayley would still make the pilgrimage to their special nook on the banks of the Cherwell. The rigmarole of changing into a swimming costume was by then monumental, her condition having rendered Murdoch unfamiliar and impatient with daily routines such as undressing. Bayley, though, would resolutely help her nonetheless, relenting from his task only once they had got down to her socks. Then, to the smiling astonishment of young couples abask on passing barges, the elderly swimmers would wade hand in hand through the riverbank's wild flowers, husband gently leading beloved wife. He would ease Iris's alabaster body off the summer shore and away she would slide.

* As detailed in *Iris Murdoch: A Life*, by Peter Conradi (2001).

Once in the water Iris cheers up a bit. It is almost too warm, hardly refreshing. But its old brown slow-flowing deliciousness remains, and we smile happily at each other as we paddle quietly to and fro. Water-lily leaves, with an occasional fat yellow flower, rock gently at the passage of a pleasure boat. Small bright blue dragonflies hover motionless above them. The water is deep, and cooler as we move out from the bank, but we do not go out far. Looking down I can see her muddy feet, still in their socks, moving in the brown depths. Tiny fish are inquisitively investigating her, and I can see and feel them round me too, gently palpating the bare skin.*

And so it was that, as her days neared their close, Iris Murdoch – who could no longer remember her own acclaimed life and times – still knew how to swim to the other side; in Bayley's eyewitness words, 'as naturally as a fish'. Iris's hands pushed past the currents of time and her socked feet kicked age away – a little girl again, swimming towards her father's protective embrace.

Not many first memories are so languid. Trauma will often sear a memory into being. It leaves scars.† This led C. S. Lewis to contend that 'happy childhoods are usually forgotten'. Trauma takes many forms. It can be as innocuous as a bee sting (as one eminent writer related privately, apropos

---

* *Iris: A Memoir of Iris Murdoch,* by John Bayley (1998).
† This trend is, albeit on a different level in memory, borne out by PTSD sufferers having vivid flashbacks of very traumatic experiences.

his first memory, during the curation of this volume), the sense of a parent's absence (over to you, Dr Freud), or as grave as a brush with death (for example, Patrick Leigh Fermor's shocking memory of Peace Day celebrations).

John Steinbeck claimed as his earliest memory a tour of the devastation wreaked by an earthquake in Salinas, near his childhood home. It is striking that his abiding impression should be of the aftermath and not, curiously, of the tremors themselves. Steinbeck must surely have felt their thunder. No wonder that he elsewhere mourned the 'sorrow at not being part of things in my childhood'.

I am not a psychologist, though, and would not deign to impose any such readings onto the individuals in this collection. I won't talk over them. That is not to say that these very first memories are not revealing: not only as recollections in isolation, anecdotes by which we learn more about the circumstances from which these remarkable individuals sprang, but moreover because reminiscence is a provisional act. It is the manner of their recollection (and the stories here will have been told over and over) that beguiles. Everyone's first memory is *telling*.

For this reason, the extracts and pieces gathered in the pages that now follow are ordered by date of publication. It is logical in a volume of first memories that the chronology is fashioned in line with when the recollections were made, as opposed to the era that they recount or the birthdates of their authors. As well as extracts from memoirs by titans of yesteryear, fresh recollections by some of today's brightest and wisest abound. These are brand new, specially

29

commissioned reminiscences. Original to this collection, they are all dated 2017 or 2018.

I hope that, cumulatively, these multitudinous earliest remembrances make up an atlas of recent times, as the past is converted by experience into the stories of our lives. Yet don't forget, tread with care. Memory is fallacious. Although these first memories are all illuminating, with each one offering its own apricity, they are mere refractions. The present filtering the past, they are nothing more than tricks of the light.

Giacomo Casanova (1725–1798)

And now to come to the beginning of my own existence as a thinking being. In the beginning of August in the year 1733 my organ of memory developed. I was then eight years and four months old. I remember nothing of what may have happened to me before that time. This is the incident:

I was standing in the corner of a room, leaning against the wall, holding my head, and staring at the blood which was streaming to the floor from my nose. My grandmother Marzia, whose pet I was, came to me, washed my face with cold water, and, unknown to anyone in the house, boarded a gondola with me and took me to Murano. This is a densely populated island about half an hour from Venice.

Leaving the gondola, we enter a hovel, where we find an old woman sitting on a pallet, with a black cat in her arms and five or six others around her. She was a witch. The two old women had a long conversation, of which I must have been the subject. At the end of their dialogue in the Friulian language, my grandmother gave the witch a silver ducat, whereupon she opened a chest, took me up in her arms, put me into it, shut it, and locked the lid on me, telling me not to be afraid. *It was just the way to make me afraid*, if I had been able to think; but I was in a stupor. I kept quiet, holding my handkerchief to my nose because I was still bleeding and feeling quite unperturbed by the racket I heard being made outside. I heard alternate laughter and weeping, cries, singing, and sundry thumps on the chest. It was all one to me. Finally they took me out; my blood stops flowing. After giving me numberless caresses, this strange woman undresses me, lays me on the bed, burns simples, collects the smoke from them in a sheet, wraps me in it, recites spells over me, then unwraps me and gives me five very good-tasting sweetmeats. She next rubs my temples and the back of my neck with a sweet-smelling unguent, and dresses me again. She says that my bleeding will gradually diminish, provided I tell no one what she had done to cure me, but solemnly warns me that I will lose all my blood and die if I dare reveal her mysteries to anyone. After impressing this upon me she tells me that a charming lady will visit me the following night, and that my happiness will depend upon her, if I have the strength of mind to tell no one that I received such a visit. We left and returned home.

I had scarcely gone to bed before I fell asleep without even remembering the fine visitor I was to receive. But waking several hours later, I saw, or thought I saw, a dazzlingly beautiful woman come down by the chimney, wearing a huge pannier and a dress of magnificent material, with a crown on her head set with fire. She approached slowly, looking at once majestic and kindly, sat down on my bed. From her packet she drew several small boxes, which she emptied on my head, at the same time muttering words.

After delivering a long discourse, of which I understood nothing, and kissing me, she left as she had entered, and I went back to sleep.

Coming to dress me the next morning, my grandmother was no sooner at my bedside than she commanded me to keep silence. She then impressed it on me that I would die if I dared to tell anyone what might have happened to me during the night. Those solemn adjurations from the lips of the only woman whose influence over me was absolute, and who had accustomed me to obey her every command blindly, were why I have remembered this incident; they made me seal it away in the most secret corner of my budding memory. In any case, I felt no temptation to tell the story. I did not know whether anyone would find it interesting, or to whom I might tell it. My disease had made me dull, and very poor company; people felt sorry for me and left me alone; everyone supposed that I would not live long. My father and mother never spoke to me.

After the journey to Murano and my nocturnal visit from the fairy I still bled, but less and less; my memory developed, and in less than a month I learned to read. It would be ridiculous to attribute my cure to these two absurdities, but it would be a mistake to hold that they could not contribute to it. As for the appearance of the beautiful queen, I have always believed that it was a dream, unless it was a masquerade deliberately contrived; but the remedies for the worst diseases are not always found in pharmacy. One phenomenon or another demonstrates our ignorance to us every day. I believe it is for this reason that nothing is harder

33

to find than a learned man whose mind is entirely free from superstition. There have never been wizards on this earth, but their power has always existed for those whom they have been able to cajole into believing them such.

From *History of My Life* (1792; published 1822), translated by Willard R. Trask

Giacomo Girolamo Casanova (de Seingalt) was variously a cardinal, a gambler, an alchemist, a violinist, a magician, a prison escapee, a spy and a librarian. He is perhaps best known, however, as a lover, thanks to the accounts of his numerous sexual adventures in his memoir, which was first published in a complete edition in 1960.

Charles Darwin (1809–1882)

I was born at Shrewsbury on February 12th, 1809, and my earliest recollection goes back only to when I was a few months over four years old, when we went to near Abergele for sea-bathing, and I recollect some events and places there with some little distinctness.

My mother died in July 1817, when I was little over eight years old, and it is odd that I can remember hardly anything about her except her deathbed, her black velvet gown, and her curiously constructed work-table. In the spring of this same year I was sent to a day-school in Shrewsbury, where I stayed a year. I have been told that I was much slower in learning than my younger sister Catherine, and I believe that I was in many ways a naughty boy.

By the time I went to this day-school my taste for natural history, and more especially for collecting, was well developed. I tried to make out the names of plants, and collected all sorts of things, shells, seals, franks, coins, and minerals. The passion for collecting which leads a man to be a systematic naturalist, a virtuoso, or a miser, was very strong in me, and was clearly innate, as none of my sisters or brother ever had this taste.

One little event during this year has fixed itself firmly in my mind, and I hope that it has done so from my conscience having been afterwards sorely troubled by it; it is curious as showing that apparently I was interested at this early age in the variability of plants! I told another little boy (I believe it was Leighton, who afterwards became a well-known lichenologist and botanist) that I could produce variously coloured polyanthuses and primroses by watering them with certain coloured fluids, which was of course a monstrous fable, and had never been tried by me. I may here also confess that as a little boy I was much given to inventing deliberate falsehoods, and this was always done for the sake of causing much excitement. For instance, I once gathered much valuable fruit from my father's trees and hid it in the shrubbery, and then ran in breathless haste to spread the news that I had discovered a hoard of stolen fruit.

From *The Autobiography of Charles Darwin* (1887)

Charles Darwin came from a long line of distinguished scientists, including the renowned botanist Dr Erasmus Darwin (his grandfather). Darwin's theory of 'natural selection' and ground-breaking study *On the Origin of Species* (1859) led to a profound shift in society's attitudes towards evolution, leading to its wider recognition as the basis for humankind's development as a species. To this day, Darwin's scientific discoveries and theories constitute the unifying principles behind life sciences.

Sigmund Freud (1856–1939)

In my forty-third year, when I became interested in the remnant of my own childhood memories, I recollected a scene which had come into my mind now and then over a long period – for ever, as it seemed to me – and there were reliable indications that it must date from before the end of my third year of life. I saw myself standing in tears in front of a wardrobe [in Austrian usage: *Kasten*] and demanding something, while my half-brother, twenty years older than me, was holding its door open, and then my mother suddenly came in, beautiful and slender, as if just coming home from a walk through the streets. I had used these words to describe the three-dimensional scene, but I could take it no further. I had no idea whether my brother was going to open or close the wardrobe – in the first translation of the image into words I called it a *Schrank* ['wardrobe' in standard German] – or why I was crying, or what my mother's arrival had to do with it; I was tempted to explain it to myself as a memory of my older brother's teasing me and being interrupted by our mother. Such misinterpretations of a remembered childhood scene are not at all unusual; we remember a situation, but it is unfocused, and we do not know exactly where the psychic emphasis lies. My analytical investigations led me to an entirely unexpected interpretation of this image. I had been missing my mother, and began to suspect that she might be shut up in the wardrobe – the *Schrank* or *Kasten* – so I asked my brother to open it. When he did and I could see that my mother was not inside, I began screaming; that was the part I remembered, along with my mother's appearance immediately afterwards, which calmed my fears and longings. But what made me, as a child, think of looking for my absent mother in the wardrobe? Some of my dreams from the same period relate vaguely to a nursemaid of whom I had certain other memories, for instance that she consistently used to make me hand over to her the small change people gave me as presents, a detail which itself could claim to figure as a screen memory for later events. This time, I decided to facilitate the task of interpretation, and I asked my now elderly mother about the nursemaid. I learned a good deal, including the fact that this clever but dishonest character had stolen from the household on a large scale while my mother was lying in, and my half-brother had insisted on bringing legal charges against her. This information, casting a sudden bright light on my childhood memory, helped me to understand it. The nursemaid's sudden disappearance had affected me quite deeply, and in fact I had turned to that same brother to ask where she was, probably because I had noticed that he had something to do with her removal from the household. Evasively playing on words, as he commonly did, he had told me that she was 'in the clink' [German: *eingekastelt*, a colloquial expression for 'in jail']. I understood this answer in a purely childish way [as meaning 'in the wardrobe' – *Kasten*] and asked no more questions, since there seemed no more to learn. When my mother went out a little later I was anxious, fearing that my bad brother had shut her up too, just like the nursemaid, and I made him open the wardrobe for me. And now I also understand why my mother's slender figure, which seemed to have been just restored, featured so prominently in my visual version of this childhood scene; I am two and a half years older than my sister, who was born at this time, and when I was three years old my half-brother left our household.

From *The Psychopathology of Everyday Life* (1901)

Sigmund Freud was born in Freiberg, Moravia, but would spend much of his life in Vienna. It was there that he developed his theories of infantile sexuality and wrote his seminal work, *The Interpretation of Dreams* (1899). His further publications included *Beyond the Pleasure Principle* (1920) and *The Ego and the Id* (1923). Psychoanalysis – the school of thought that Freud founded – was later banned by the Nazi regime. In 1938, when the Nazis annexed Austria, Freud fled to London. He died the following year in Hampstead.

Edmund Gosse (1849–1928)

Out of the darkness of my infancy there comes only one flash of memory. I am seated alone, in my baby-chair, at a dinner-table set for several people. Somebody brings in a leg of mutton, puts it down close to me, and goes out. I am again alone, gazing at two low windows, wide open upon a garden. Suddenly, noiselessly, a large, long animal (obviously a greyhound) appears at one window-sill, slips into the room, seizes the leg of mutton and slips out again. When this happened I could not yet talk. The accomplishment of speech came to me very late, doubtless because I never heard young voices. Many years later, when I mentioned this recollection, there was a shout of laughter and surprise:

'That, then, was what became of the mutton! It was not you, who, as your Uncle A. pretended, ate it all up, in the twinkling of an eye, bone and all!'

I suppose that it was the startling intensity of this incident which stamped it upon a memory from which all other impressions of this early date have vanished.

From *Father and Son* (1907)

Edmund Gosse is best remembered today for his memoir *Father and Son* (extracted here), which recounts his relationship with his puritanical and domineering father Philip. It describes Gosse's escape from an often unhappy childhood into the world of books. Gosse would go on to write many literary critical works, notably *Seventeenth-Century Studies* (1883), as well as serve as the librarian to the House of Lords.

Mark Twain (1835–1910)

Recently someone in Missouri has sent me a picture of the house I was born in. Heretofore I have always stated that it was a palace, but I shall be more guarded, now.

I remember only one circumstance connected with my life in it. I remember it very well, though I was but two and a half years old at the time. The family packed up everything and started in wagons for Hannibal, on the Mississippi, thirty miles away. Toward night, when they camped and counted up the children, one was missing. I was the one. I had been left behind. Parents ought always to count the children before they start. I was having a good enough time playing by myself until I found that the doors were fastened and that there was a grisly deep silence brooding over the place. I knew, then, that the family were gone, and that they had forgotten me. I was well frightened, and I made all the noise I could, but no one was near and it did no good. I spent the afternoon in captivity and was not rescued till the gloaming had fallen and the place was alive with ghosts.

From *Autobiography of Mark Twain* (1907)

Mark Twain was the pseudonym of Samuel Langhorne Clemens. This pen name was adopted by Clemens after his time as a river-boat pilot: 'mark twain' being the call sounded when a river runs as shallow as 'the mark of two fathoms'.

Twain's two great masterpieces — *The Adventures of Tom Sawyer* (1876) and *The Adventures of Huckleberry Finn* (1884) — were inspired by his childhood experiences on the Mississippi frontier.

Maxim Gorky (1868–1936)

In a narrow, darkened room, my father, dressed in a white and unusually long garment, lay on the floor under the window. The toes of his bare feet were curiously extended, and the fingers of the still hands, which rested peacefully upon his breast, were curved; his merry eyes were tightly closed by the black disks of two copper coins; the light had gone out of his still face, and I was frightened by the ugly way he showed his teeth.

My mother, only half clad in a red petticoat, knelt and combed my father's long, soft hair, from his brow to the nape of his neck, with the same black comb which I loved to use to tear the rind of water-melons; she talked unceasingly in her low, husky voice, and it seemed as if her swollen eyes must be washed away by the incessant flow of tears.

Holding me by the hand was my grandmother, who had a big, round head, large eyes, and a nose like a sponge – a dark, tender, wonderfully interesting person. She also was weeping, and her grief formed a fitting accompaniment to my mother's, as, shuddering the while, she pushed me towards my father; but I, terrified and uneasy, obstinately tried to hide myself against her. I had never seen grown-up people cry before, and I did not understand the words which my grandmother uttered again and again:

'Say good-bye to daddy. You will never see him again. He is dead — before his time.'

I had been very ill, had only just left my bed in fact, and I remember perfectly well that at the beginning of my illness my father used to merrily bustle about me. Then he suddenly disappeared and his place was taken by my grandmother, a stranger to me.

'Where did you come from?' I asked her.

'From up there, from Nijni,' she answered; 'but I did not walk here, I came by boat. One does not walk on water, you little imp.'

This was ludicrous, incomprehensible, and untrue; upstairs there lived a bearded, gaudy Persian, and in the cellar an old, yellow Kalmuck who sold sheepskins. One could get upstairs by riding on the banisters, or if one fell that way, one could roll. I knew this by experience. But where was there room for water? It was all untrue and delightfully muddled.

'And why am I a little imp?'

'Why? Because you are so noisy,' she said, laughing.

She spoke sweetly, merrily, melodiously, and from the very first day I made friends with her; all I wanted now was for her to make haste and take me out of that room.

My mother pressed me to her; her tears and groans created in me a strange feeling of disquietude. It was the first time I had seen her like this. She had always appeared

45

a stern woman of few words; neat, glossy, and strongly built like a horse, with a body of almost savage strength, and terribly strong arms. But now she was swollen and palpitating, and utterly desolate. Her hair, which was always coiled so neatly about her head, with her large, gaily trimmed cap, was tumbled about her bare shoulders, fell over her face, and part of it which remained plaited, trailed across my father's sleeping face. Although I had been in the room a long time she had not once looked at me; she could do nothing but dress my father's hair, sobbing and choking with tears the while.

Presently some swarthy gravediggers and a soldier peeped in at the door.

The latter shouted angrily:

'Clear out now! Hurry up!'

The window was curtained by a dark shawl, which the wind inflated like a sail. I knew this because one day my father had taken me out in a sailing-boat, and without warning there had come a peal of thunder. He laughed, and holding me against his knees, cried, 'It is nothing. Don't be frightened!'

Suddenly my mother threw herself heavily on the floor, but almost at once turned over on her back, dragging her hair in the dust; her impassive, white face had become livid, and showing her teeth like my father, she said in a terrible voice, 'Close the door! . . . Alexis . . . go away!'

Thrusting me on one side, grandmother rushed to the door crying:

'Friends! Don't be frightened; don't interfere, but go

46

away, for the love of Christ. This is not cholera but childbirth . . . I beg of you to go, good people!'

I hid myself in a corner behind a box, and thence I saw how my mother writhed upon the floor, panting and gnashing her teeth; and grandmother, kneeling beside her, talked lovingly and hopefully.

'In the name of the Father and of the Son . . . ! Be patient, Varusha! Holy Mother of God! . . . Our Defence . . . !'

I was terrified. They crept about on the floor close to my father, touching him, groaning and shrieking, and he remained unmoved and actually smiling. This creeping about on the floor lasted a long time; several times my mother stood up, only to fall down again, and grandmother rolled in and out of the room like a large, black, soft ball. All of a sudden a child cried.

'Thank God!' said grandmother. 'It is a boy!' And she lighted a candle.

I must have fallen asleep in the corner, for I remember nothing more.

From *My Childhood* (1913), translated by Gertrude M. Foakes

Maxim Gorky (the pseudonym of Aleksei Maksimovich Peshkov) was born in Nizhny Novgorod. As well as a novelist and playwright, Gorky was a pedlar, scullery boy, gardener, dock hand, tramp and nomad. This varied life was described in his autobiographical trilogy, of which *My Childhood* constitutes the first book.

Winston Churchill (1874–1965)

When does one first begin to remember? When do the waving lights and shadows of dawning consciousness cast their print upon the mind of a child? My earliest memories are of Ireland. I can recall scenes and events in Ireland quite well, and sometimes simply, even people. Yet I was born on November 30, 1874, and I left Ireland early in the year 1879. My father had gone to Ireland as secretary to his father, the Duke of Marlborough, appointed Lord-Lieutenant by Mr. Disraeli in 1876. We lived in a house called 'The Little Lodge', about a stone's throw from the Viceregal. Here I spent nearly three years of childhood. I have clear and vivid impressions of some events. I remember my grandfather, the Viceroy, unveiling the Lord Gough statue in 1878. A great black crowd, scarlet soldiers on horseback, string pulling away a brown shiny sheet, the old Duke, the formidable grandpapa, talking loudly to the crowd. I recall even a phrase he used: 'and with a withering volley he shattered the enemy's line'. I quite understood that he was speaking about war and fighting and that a 'volley' meant what the black-coated soldiers (Riflemen) used to do with loud bangs so often in the Phoenix Park where I was taken for my morning walks. This, I think, is my first coherent memory.

From *My Early Life* (1930)

Sir Winston Churchill was born at Blenheim Palace, a descendant of the Duke of Marlborough. He served as prime minister from 1940–45, and again 1951–55, relinquishing office at the age of eighty-one.

In 1953 he was awarded the Nobel Prize in Literature. Following his death in 1965, Churchill was given a state funeral.

Edith Wharton (1862–1937)

It was on a bright day of midwinter, in New York. The little girl who eventually became me, but as yet was neither me nor anybody else in particular, but merely a soft anonymous morsel of humanity – this little girl, who bore my name, was going for a walk with her father. The episode is literally the first thing I can remember about her, and therefore I date the birth of her identity from that day.

She had been put into her warmest coat, and into a new and very pretty bonnet, which she had surveyed in the glass with considerable satisfaction. The bonnet (I can see it today) was of white satin, patterned with a pink and green plaid in raised velvet. It was all drawn into close gathers, with a *bavolet* in the neck to keep out the cold, and thick ruffles of silky *blonde* lace under the brim in front. As the air was very cold a gossamer veil of the finest white Shetland wool was drawn about the bonnet and hung down over the wearer's round red cheeks like the white paper filigree over a Valentine; and her hands were encased in white woollen mittens.

One of them lay in the large safe hollow of her father's bare hand; her tall handsome father, who was so warm-blooded that in the coldest weather he always went out without gloves, and whose head, with its ruddy complexion and intensely blue eyes, was so far aloft that when she walked beside him she was too near to see his face. It was always an event in the little girl's life to take a walk with her father, and more particularly so today, because she had on her new winter bonnet, which was so beautiful (and so becoming) that for the first time she woke to the importance of dress, and of herself as a subject for adornment — so that I may date from that hour the birth of the conscious and feminine *me* in the little girl's vague soul.

The little girl and her father walked up Fifth Avenue: the old Fifth Avenue with its double line of low brownstone houses, of a desperate uniformity of style, broken only — and surprisingly — by two equally unexpected features: the fenced-in plot of ground where the old Miss Kennedy's cows were pastured, and the truncated Egyptian pyramid which so strangely served as a reservoir for New York's water supply. The Fifth Avenue of that day was a placid and uneventful thoroughfare, along which genteel landaus, broughams and victorias, and more countrified vehicles of the 'carry-all' and 'surrey' type, moved up and down at decent intervals and a decorous pace. On Sundays after church the fashionable of various denominations paraded there on foot, in gathered satin bonnets and tall hats; but at other times it presented long stretches of empty pavements, so that the little girl, advancing at her father's side was able to see at a considerable distance the approach of another pair of legs, not

51

as long but considerably stockier than her father's. The little girl was so very little that she never got much higher than the knees in her survey of grown-up people, and would not have known, if her father had not told her, that the approaching legs belonged to her cousin Henry. The news was very interesting, because in attendance on her cousin Henry was a small person, no bigger than herself, who must obviously be Cousin Henry's little boy Daniel, and therefore somehow belong to the little girl. So when the tall legs and the stocky ones halted for a talk, which took place somewhere high up in the air, and the small Daniel and Edith found themselves face to face close to the pavement, the little girl peered with interest at the little boy through the white woollen mist over her face. The little boy, who was very round and rosy, looked back with equal interest; and suddenly he put out a chubby hand, lifted the little girl's veil, and boldly planted a kiss on her cheek. It was the first time – and the little girl found it very pleasant.

This is my earliest definite memory of anything happening to me; and it will be seen that I was wakened to conscious life by the two tremendous forces of love and vanity.

From *A Backward Glance* (1934)

Edith Wharton, née Jones, was the only daughter of a prominent New York landowner. Her reputation as a novelist was established in 1905 with the publication of *The House* *of Mirth*. Later notable novels included *Ethan Frome* (1911) and *The Age of Innocence* (1920), for which she received the Pulitzer Prize. Wharton was appointed Chevalier of the Legion of Honour for her work combating tuberculosis in France during the First World War.

Rudyard Kipling (1865–1936)

My first impression is of daybreak, light and colour and golden and purple fruits at the level of my shoulder. This would be the memory of early morning walks to the Bombay fruit market with my *ayah* and later with my sister in her perambulator, and of our returns with our purchases piled high on the bows of it. Our *ayah* was a Portuguese Roman Catholic who would pray – I beside her – at a wayside Cross. Meeta, my Hindu bearer, would sometimes go into little Hindu temples where, being below the age of caste, I held his hand and looked at the dimly-seen, friendly Gods.

Our evening walks were by the sea in the shadow of palm-groves, which, I think, were called the Mahim Woods. When the wind blew the great nuts would tumble, and we fled – my *ayah* and my sister in her perambulator – to the safety of the open. I have always felt the menacing darkness of tropical eventides, as I have loved the voices of night-winds through palm or banana leaves, and the song of the tree-frogs.

There were far-going Arab dhows on the pearly waters, and gaily dressed Parsees wading out to worship the sunset. Of their creed I knew nothing, nor did I know that near our little house on the Bombay Esplanade were the Towers of Silence, where their Dead are exposed to the waiting vultures on the rim of the towers, who scuffle and spread wings when they see the bearers of the Dead below. I did not understand my Mother's distress when she found 'a child's hand' in our garden, and said I was not to ask questions about it. I wanted to ask questions about it. But my *ayah* told me.

From *Something of Myself* (1937)

Rudyard Kipling was the first English-language writer to receive the Nobel Prize in Literature, in 1907, aged forty-two. He remains the youngest ever recipient of the award.

Although his values and aesthetics divide opinion – Henry James called him 'the most complete man of genius', while George Orwell criticised him as a 'jingo imperialist' – Kipling's works, such as *The Jungle Book* (1894) and *Kim* (1901), continue to endure. His poem 'If' was voted the nation's favourite by the British public in a 1995 BBC survey.

Salvador Dalí (1904–1989)

I presume that my readers do not at all remember, or remember only very vaguely, that highly important period of their existence which anteceded their birth and which transpired in their mother's womb. But I – yes, I remember this period, as though it were yesterday . . .

Allow me to begin with a short general description: the intra-uterine paradise was the colour of hell, that is to say, red, orange, yellow and bluish, the colour of flames, of fire; above all it was soft, immobile, warm, symmetrical, double gluey. Already at that time all pleasure, all enchantment for me was in my eyes, and the most splendid, the most striking vision was that of a pair of eggs fried in a pan, without the pan; to this is probably due that perturbation and that emotion which I have since felt, the whole rest of my life, in the presence of this ever-hallucinatory image. The eggs, fried in the pan, without the pan, which I saw before my birth were grandiose, phosphorescent and very detailed in all the folds of their bluish whites. These two eggs would approach (toward me), recede, move toward the left, toward the right, upward, downward; they would attain the iridescence and the intensity of mother-of-pearl fires, only to diminish progressively and at last vanish. The fact that I am still able today to reproduce at will a similar image, though much feebler, and shorn of all the grandeur and the magic of that time, by subjecting my pupils to a strong pressure of my fingers, makes me interpret this fulgurating image of the eggs as being a phosphene, originating in similar pressures: those of my fists closed on my orbits, which is characteristic of the foetal posture. It is a common game among all children to press their eyes in order to see circles of colours *'which are sometimes called angels'*. The child would then be seeking to reproduce visual memories of his embryonic period, pressing his already nostalgic eyes till they hurt in order to extract from them the longed-for lights and colours, in order approximately to see again the divine aureole of the spectral angels perceived in his lost paradise.

From *The Secret Life of Salvador Dalí* (1942), translated by Haakon M. Chevalier

Salvador Dalí's full name was Salvador Domingo Felipe Jacinto Dalí i Domènech, Marquis of Dalí de Púbol. He was a Catalan painter who also produced works of photography, film and sculpture. A leading light of the surrealist movement, Sigmund Freud's theories of the unconscious mind were influential on his artistic development. Dalí's most notable works include *The Persistence of Memory* (1931) and *The Metamorphosis of Narcissus* (1937). The sunburnt landscapes that serve as backdrops for these and his other works were inspired by those Dalí remembered from his boyhood.

Vladimir Nabokov (1899–1977)

How small the cosmos (a kangaroo's pouch would hold it), how paltry and puny in comparison to human conscious- ness, to a single individual recollection, and its expression in words! I may be inordinately fond of my earliest impres- sions, but then I have reason to be grateful to them. They led the way to a veritable Eden of visual and tactile sensations. One night, during a trip abroad, in the fall of 1903, I recall kneeling on my (flattish) pillow at the window of a sleeping car (probably on the long-extinct Mediterranean Train de Luxe, the one whose six cars had the lower part of their body painted in umber and the panels in cream) and seeing with an inexplicable pang, a handful of fabulous lights that beckoned to me from a distant hillside, and then slipped into a pocket of black velvet: diamonds that I later gave away to my characters to alleviate the burden of my wealth. I had probably managed to undo and push up the tight tooled blind at the head of my berth, and my heels were cold, but I still kept kneeling and peering. Nothing is sweeter or stranger than to ponder those first thrills. They belong to the har- monious world of a perfect childhood and, as such, possess a naturally plastic form in one's memory, which can be set down with hardly any effort; it is only starting with the recollections of one's adolescence that Mnemosyne begins to get choosy and crabbed . . . But even so, the individual mystery remains to tantalize the memoirist. Neither in environment nor in heredity can I find the exact instrument that fashioned me, the anonymous roller that pressed upon my life a certain intricate watermark whose unique design becomes visible when the lamp of art is made to shine through life's foolscap.

From *Speak, Memory* (1947)

Vladimir Nabokov, born in St Petersburg, was a trilingual child who could read English before either his native Russian or French. He developed a passion for Lepidoptera at the age of seven, which continued for the rest of his life (and included various discoveries, such as the butterfly now known as Nabokov's Pug).

He moved to the United States in 1940, after which he published many of his best-known works, including *Lolita* (1955), *Pale Fire* (1962) and *Ada or Ardor* (1969).

Simone de Beauvoir (1908–1986)

I was born at four o'clock in the morning on the 9th of January 1908 in a room fitted with white-enamelled furniture and overlooking the Boulevard Raspail. In the family photographs taken the following summer can be seen ladies in long dresses and ostrich-feathered hats and gentlemen wearing boaters and panamas, all smiling at a baby: they are my parents, my grandfather, uncles, aunts; and the baby is me. My father was thirty, my mother twenty-one, and I was their first child. I turn the page: here is a photograph of Mama holding in her arms a baby who isn't me; I am wearing a pleated skirt and a tam-o'-shanter; I am two and a half, and my sister has just been born. I was, it appears, very jealous, but not for long. As far back as I can remember, I was always proud of being the elder: of being first. Disguised as Little Red Riding Hood and carrying a basket full of goodies, I felt myself to be much more interesting than an infant bundled up in a cradle. I had a little sister: that doll-like creature didn't have me.

I retain only one confused impression from my earliest years: it is all red, and black, and warm. Our apartment was red: the upholstery was of red moquette, the Renaissance dining-room was red, the figured silk hangings over the stained-glass doors were red, and the velvet curtains in Papa's study were red too. The furniture in this awful sanctum was made of black pearwood; I used to creep into the knee-hole under the desk and envelop myself in its dusty gloom; it was dark and warm, and the red of the carpet rejoiced my eyes. That is how I seem to have passed the early days of infancy. Safely ensconced, I watched, I touched, I took stock of the world.

From *Memoirs of a Dutiful Daughter* (1958), translated by James Kirkup

Simone de Beauvoir famously wrote 'One is not born a woman: one becomes a woman' in her landmark study of women's social situation, *The Second Sex* (1949). One of the first feminist tracts, it was followed in 1954 by her novel *Les Mandarins*, which won the Prix Goncourt, and later by various other works of memoir and fiction. These writings formed a key contribution to the existentialist movement of the mid-twentieth century, alongside those of her companion Jean-Paul Sartre.

Laurie Lee (1914–1997)

I was set down from the carrier's cart at the age of three; and there with a sense of bewilderment and terror my life in the village began.

The June grass, amongst which I stood, was taller than I was, and I wept. I had never been so close to grass before. It towered above me and all around me, each blade tattooed with tiger-skins of sunlight. It was knife-edged, dark, and a wicked green, thick as a forest and alive with grasshoppers that chirped and chattered and leapt through the air like monkeys.

I was lost and didn't know where to move. A tropic heat oozed up from the ground, rank with sharp odours of roots and nettles. Snow-clouds of elder-blossom banked in the sky, showering upon me the fumes and flakes of their sweet and giddy suffocation. High overhead ran frenzied larks, screaming, as though the sky were tearing apart.

For the first time in my life I was out of sight of humans. For the first time in my life I was alone in a world whose behaviour I could neither predict nor fathom: a world of birds that squealed, of plants that stank, of insects that sprang about without warning. I was lost and I did not

62

expect to be found again. I put back my head and howled, and the sun hit me smartly on the face, like a bully.

From this daylight nightmare I was awakened, as from many another, by the appearance of my sisters. They came scrambling and calling up the steep rough bank, and parting the long grass found me. Faces of rose, familiar, living; huge shining faces hung up like shields between me and the sky; faces with grins and white teeth (some broken) to be conjured like genii with a howl, brushing off terror with their broad scoldings and affection. They leaned over me – one, two, three – their mouths smeared with redcurrants and their hands dripping with juice.

'There, there, it's all right, don't you wail any more. Come down 'ome and we'll stuff you with currants.'

And Marjorie, the eldest, lifted me into her long brown hair, and ran me jogging down the path and through the steep rose-filled garden, and set me down on the cottage doorstep, which was our home, though I couldn't believe it.

That was the day we came to the village, in the summer of the last year of the First World War. To a cottage that stood in a half-acre of garden on a steep bank above a lake; a cottage with three floors and a cellar and a treasure in the walls, with a pump and apple trees, syringa and strawberries, rooks in the chimneys, frogs in the cellar, mushrooms in the ceiling, and all for three and sixpence a week.

I don't know where I lived before then. My life began on the carrier's cart which brought me up the long slow hills to the village, and dumped me in the high grass, and lost me. I had ridden wrapped in a Union Jack to protect me from the sun, and when I rolled out of it, and stood piping loud among the buzzing jungle of that summer bank, then, I feel, I was born. And to all the rest of us, the whole family of eight, it was the beginning of life.

From *Cider with Rosie* (1959)

Laurie Lee – born in Stroud, Gloucestershire – is best remembered for his evocations of an English rural childhood, as well as his accounts of youthful travels and service in the Spanish Civil War. The autobiographical trilogy of books recounting these experiences was published in one volume as *Red Sky at Sunrise (1992)*.

Virginia Woolf (1882–1941)

I begin: the first memory.

This was of red and purple flowers on a black ground – my mother's dress; and she was sitting either in a train or in an omnibus, and I was on her lap. I therefore saw the flowers she was wearing very close; and can still see purple and red and blue, I think, against the black; they must have been anemones, I suppose. Perhaps we were going to St Ives; more probably, for from the light it must have been evening, we were coming back to London. But it is more convenient artistically to suppose that we were going to St Ives, for that will lead to my other memory, which also seems to be my first memory, and in fact is the most important of all my memories. If life has a base that it stands upon, if it is a bowl that one fills and fills and fills – then my bowl without a doubt stands upon this memory. It is of lying asleep, half awake, in bed in the nursery at St Ives. It is of hearing the waves breaking, one, two, one, two, and sending a splash of water over the beach; and then breaking, one, two, one, two, behind a yellow blind. It is of hearing the blind draw its little acorn across the floor as the wind blew the blind out. It is of lying and hearing this splash and seeing this light, and feeling, it is almost impossible that I should be here; of feeling the purest ecstasy I can conceive . . .

But of course there was one external reason for the intensity of this first impression: the impression of the waves and the acorn on the blind; the feeling, as I describe it sometimes to myself, of lying in a grape and seeing through a film of semi-transparent yellow – it was due partly to the many months we spent in London. The change of nursery was a great change. And there was the long train journey; and the excitement. I remember the dark; the lights; the stir of the going up to bed.

But to fix my mind upon the nursery – it had a balcony; there was a partition, but it joined the balcony of my father's and mother's bedroom. My mother would come out onto her balcony in a white dressing gown. There were passion flowers growing on the wall; they were great starry blossoms, with purple streaks, and large green buds, part empty, part full.

If I were a painter I should paint these first impressions in pale yellow, silver, and green. There was the pale yellow blind; the green sea; and the silver of the passion flowers. I should make a picture that was globular; semi-transparent. I should make a picture of curved petals; of shells; of things that were semi-transparent; I should make curved shapes, showing the light through, but not giving a clear outline. Everything would be large and dim; and what was seen would at the same time be heard; sounds would come through this petal or leaf – sounds indistinguishable from sights . . . When I think of the early morning in bed I also hear the caw of rooks falling from a great height. The sound seems to fall through an elastic, gummy air; which holds it up; which prevents it from being sharp and distinct. The quality of the air above Talland House seemed to suspend sound, to let it sink down slowly, as if it were caught in a blue gummy veil. The rooks cawing is part of the waves breaking – one, two, one, two – and the splash as the wave drew back and then it gathered again, and I lay there half awake, half asleep, drawing in such ecstasy as I cannot describe.

From *Moments of Being* (published 1976)

Virginia Woolf's ground-breaking modernist novels include *Jacob's Room* (1922, published by her and Leonard Woolf's Hogarth Press), *Mrs Dalloway* (1925), *To the Lighthouse* (1927) and *The Waves* (1931). Shortly after finishing her novel *Between the Acts* (1941), suffering from severe mental health issues, Woolf drowned herself in the river beside her and Leonard's Sussex country home, Monk's House.

Carl Jung (1875–1961)

My memories begin with my second or third year. I recall the vicarage, the garden, the laundry house, the church, the castle, the Falls, the small castle of Wörth, and the sexton's farm. These are nothing but islands of memory afloat in a sea of vagueness, each by itself, apparently with no connection between them.

One memory comes up which is perhaps the earliest of my life, and is indeed only a rather hazy impression. I am lying in a pram, in the shadow of a tree. It is a fine, warm summer day, the sky blue, the golden sunlight darting through green leaves. The hood of the pram has been lifted up. I have just awakened to the glorious beauty of the day, and have a sense of indescribable well-being. I see the sun glittering through the leaves and blossoms of the bushes. Everything is wholly wonderful, colourful, and splendid.

Another memory: I am sitting in our dining-room, on the west side of the house, perched in a high chair and spooning up warm milk with bits of broken bread in it. The milk has a pleasant taste and a characteristic smell. It was the moment when, so to speak, I became conscious of smelling. This memory, too, goes very far back.

Still another: a lovely summer evening. An aunt said to me, 'Now I am going to show you something.' She took me out in front of the house, on the road to Dachsen. On the far horizon the chain of Alps lay bathed in glowing sunset reds. The Alps could be seen very clearly that evening. 'Now look over there' – I can hear her saying to me in Swiss dialect – 'the mountains are all red.' For the first time I consciously saw the Alps. Then I was told that the next day the village children would be going on a school outing to the Uetliberg, near Zürich. I wanted so much to go too. To my sorrow, I was informed that children as small as I could not go along, there was nothing to be done about it. From then on the Uetliberg and Zürich became an unattainable land of dreams, near to the glowing, snow-covered mountains.

From a somewhat later period comes another memory. My mother took me to the Thurgau to visit friends, who had a castle on Lake Constance. I could not be dragged away from the water. The waves from the steamer washed up to the shore, the sun glistened on the water, and the sand under the water had been curled into little ridges by the waves. The lake stretched away and away into the distance. This expanse of water was an inconceivable pleasure to me, an incomparable splendour. At that time the idea became fixed in my mind that I must live near a lake; without water, I thought, nobody could live at all.

Still another memory comes up; strangers, bustle, excitement. The maid comes running and exclaims, 'The fishermen have found a corpse – came down the Falls – they want to put it in the wash-house!' My father says, 'Yes, yes.' I want to see the dead boy at once. My mother holds me back and sternly forbids me to go into the garden. When all the men had left, I quickly stole into the garden. But the door was locked. I went around the house; at the back there was an open drain running down the slope, and I saw blood and water trickling out. I found this extraordinarily interesting. At that time I was not yet four years old.

Yet another image: I am restive, feverish, unable to sleep. My father carries me in his arms, paces up and down, singing his old student songs. I particularly remember one I was especially fond of and which always used to soothe me, *'Alles schweige, jeder neige . . .'* The beginning went something like that. To this day I can remember my father's voice, singing over me in the stillness of the night.

I was suffering, so my mother told me afterwards, from general eczema. Dim intimations of trouble in my parents' marriage hovered around me. My illness, in 1878, must have been connected with a temporary separation of my parents. My mother spent several months in a hospital in Basel, and presumably her illness had something to do with the difficulty in the marriage. An aunt of mine, who was a spinster and some twenty years older than my mother, took care of me. I was deeply troubled by my mother's being away. From then on, I always felt mistrustful when the word 'love' was spoken. The feeling I associated with 'woman' was for a long time that of innate unreliability. 'Father', on the other hand, meant reliability and – powerlessness. That is the handicap I started off with. Later, these early impressions were revised: I have trusted men friends and been disappointed by them, and I have mistrusted women and was not disappointed.

While my mother was away, our maid, too, looked after me. I still remember her picking me up and laying my head against her shoulder. She had black hair and an olive complexion, and was quite different from my mother. I can see, even now, her hairline, her throat, with its darkly pigmented skin, and her ear. All this seemed to me very strange and yet strangely familiar. It was as though she belonged not to my family but only to me, as though she were connected in some way with other mysterious things I could not understand. This type of girl later became a component of my anima.* The feeling of strangeness which she conveyed, and yet of having known her always, was a characteristic of that figure which later came to symbolise for me the whole essence of womanhood.

From the period of my parents' separation I have another memory image: a young, very pretty and charming girl with blue eyes and fair hair is leading me, on a blue autumn day, under golden maple and chestnut trees along the Rhine below the Falls, near Wörth castle. The sun is shining through the foliage, and yellow leaves lie on the ground. This girl later became my mother-in-law. She admired

---

* *Anima* (/*Animus*) can be defined here – per the glossary of definitions in Jung's own autobiography, itself compiled by his friend, assistant and editor Aniela Jaffé – as the personification of the feminine nature of a man's unconscious. Referring to the fact that the smaller number of contrasexual genes in a person produces a corresponding contrasexual character, it can also be applied to the masculine nature of a woman's unconscious.

my father. I did not see her again until I was twenty-one years old.

These are my outward memories.

From *Memories, Dreams, Reflections* (1961), translated by Richard and Clara Winston

Carl Jung was born in Switzerland and studied at the University of Zurich. Initially regarded by Freud as his heir apparent, Jung broke from his older colleague in 1914. This schism in their schools of thought continues to reverberate today. Jung went on to found his own school of study: 'analytic psychology'. He travelled the world to pursue his studies of myth and symbolism.

Just as his autobiography would have to wait until after his death to reach print, various written works by Jung remain unpublished to this day.

Malcolm X (1925–1965)

Shortly after Yvonne [Malcolm X's youngest sister] was born came the nightmare night in 1929, my earliest vivid memory. I remember being suddenly snatched awake into a frightening confusion of pistol shots and shouting and smoke and flames. My father had shouted and shot at the two white men who had set the fire and were running away. Our home was burning down around us. We were lunging and bumping and tumbling all over each other to escape. My mother, with the baby in her arms, just made it into the yard before the house crashed in, showering sparks. I remember we were outside in the night in our underwear, crying and yelling our heads off. The white police and firemen came and stood around watching as the house burned down to the ground.

From *The Autobiography of Malcolm X* (1965), written with Alex Haley

Malcolm X was born Malcolm Little, in Omaha, Nebraska. His father – a Baptist lay preacher and outspoken activist for African Americans – died when Malcolm was just six years old, ostensibly in a car accident but, by all accounts, the murder victim of white supremacists. Subsequently, when he was thirteen, Malcolm's mother was placed in a mental hospital.

Malcolm changed Little to X as a rejection of the surname given to his family by the 'white slavemaster'. He went on to become a minister of the Islamic faith and civil rights activist. He was assassinated in 1965, aged thirty-nine.

Dodie Smith (1896–1990)

When widowed, my mother brought me to live with her family in Old Trafford, then a pleasant suburb a few miles from Manchester. The household consisted of my grandfather and grandmother, William and Margaret Furber; my uncles Harold, Arthur and Eddie; my aunts, Madge and Bertha, and a maid. They lived in a tall, narrow house called Heathcliffe which must have been pretty full even before my mother and I arrived.

I have three recollections of Heathcliffe. The first, which is my earliest memory, is of an attic with a skylight known as the blue room. For some unknown reason the skylight fascinated me and I would croon, 'Blue room, blue room', until my devoted grandmother carried me up the many stairs. And, having glanced once at the skylight, I would immediately lose interest in it; only to start asking to be carried up again as soon as we got downstairs. The second memory is of the tray of my high-chair, in which I frequently made a pudding of my food. I would then hold my hands away from it and murmur, 'Sticky, sticky' with great disgust, until someone cleared up the mess.

My last memory of Heathcliffe is on the day we moved

to our next home, Kingstone House. Late in the afternoon I was dressed in a little fawn coat known as my shooting-jacket and put to sit on the grand piano, while all around me were men carrying out furniture. At last they took everything but the piano and I was quite alone. It was beginning to get dark and it suddenly occurred to me that I might be left behind. But almost instantly I knew that I was far too valuable and, knowing this, I allowed myself to play with the idea, scaring myself pleasantly. This is my first memory of using my imagination. I must have been little over two.

From *Look Back with Love* (1974)

Dodie Smith's father Ernest, a bank manager, died when she was just two. She and her mother then moved to Old Trafford, Manchester, to live with her grandparents. An acclaimed playwright, Smith is best remembered today for her novels for children, particularly *I Capture the Castle* (1948) and *The Hundred and One Dalmatians* (1956).

Patrick Leigh Fermor (1915–2011)

In the second year of World War I, soon after I was born, my mother and sister sailed away to India (where my father was a servant of the Indian Government) and I was left behind so that one of us might survive if the ship were sunk by a submarine. I was to be taken out when the oceans were safer, and, failing this, remain in England until the war had reached its quick and victorious end. But the war was long and ships scarce; four years passed; and during the interim, on a temporary footing which perforce grew longer, I remained in the care of a very kind and very simple family. This period of separation was the opposite of the ordeal Kipling describes in *Baa Baa Black Sheep*. I was allowed to do as I chose in everything. There was no question of dis-obeying orders: none were given; still less was there ever a stern word or an admonitory smack. This new family, and a background of barns, ricks and teazles, clouded with spinneys and the undulation of ridge and furrow, were the first things I can remember setting eyes on: and I spent these important years, which are said to be such formative ones, more or less as a small farmer's child run wild: they have left a memory of complete and unalloyed bliss.

I must go back fourteen years [from eighteen], to the first complete event I can remember. I was being led by Margaret, the daughter of the family who were looking after me, across the fields in Northamptonshire in the late afternoon of June 18th 1919. It was Peace Day, and she was twelve, I think, and I was four. In one of the water-meadows, a throng of villagers had assembled around an enormous bonfire all ready for kindling, and on top of it, ready for burning, were dummies of the Kaiser and the Crown Prince. The Kaiser wore a real German spiked-helmet and a cloth mask with huge whiskers; Little Willy was equipped with a cardboard monocle and a busby made of a hearthrug, and both had real German boots. Everyone lay on the grass, singing *It's a long, long trail a-winding*, *The only girl in the world* and *Keep the home fires burning*; then, *Goodbyee, don't cryee*, and *K-K-K-Katie*. We were waiting till it was dark enough to light the bonfire. (An irrelevant remembered detail: when it was almost dark, a man called Thatcher Brown said 'Half a mo!' and, putting a ladder against the stack, he climbed up and pulled off the boots, leaving tufts of straw bursting out below the knees. There were protestations: 'Too good to waste,' he said.) At last someone set fire to the dry furze at the bottom and up went the flames in a great blaze. Everyone joined hands and danced around it, singing *Mademoiselle from Armentières* and *Pack up your troubles in your old kitbag*. The whole field was lit up and when the flames reached the two dummies, irregular volleys of bangs and cracks broke out; they must have been stuffed with fireworks. Squibs and stars showered into the night. Everyone clapped and cheered, shouting: 'There goes Kaiser

78

Bill!' For the children there, hoisted on shoulders like me, it was a moment of ecstasy and terror. Lit by the flames, the figures of the halted dancers threw concentric spokes of shadow across the grass. The two dummies above were beginning to collapse like ghostly scarecrows of red ash. Shouting, waving sparklers and throwing fire-crackers, boys were running in and out of the ring of gazers when the delighted shrieks changed to a new key. Screams broke out, then cries for help. Everyone swarmed to a single spot, and looked down. Margaret joined them, then rushed back. She put her hands over my eyes, and we started running. When we were a little way off, she hoisted me piggy-back, saying, *'Don't look back!'* She raced on across the dark fields and between the ricks and over the stiles as fast as she could run. But I did look back for a moment, all the same; the abandoned bonfire lit up the crowd which had assembled under the willows. Everything, somehow, spelt disaster and mishap. When we got home, she rushed upstairs, undressed me and put me into her bed and slipped in, hugging me to her flannel nightdress, sobbing and shuddering and refusing to answer questions. It was only after an endless siege that she told me, days later, what had happened. One of the village boys had been dancing on the grass with his head back and a Roman candle in his mouth. The firework had slipped through his teeth and down his throat. They rushed him in agony – 'spitting stars', they said – down to the brook. But it was too late . . .

From *A Time of Gifts* (1977)

In December of 1933, at the age of eighteen, **Patrick Leigh Fermor** set out to walk across Europe. He reached Istanbul in 1935. During the Second World War, he served in occupied Crete and was later awarded the DSO for leading a successful operation to kidnap a German general.

He went on to write landmark travel books and novels – but it was only towards the end of his life that Leigh Fermor recounted those youthful adventures. These excerpts are taken from the first of three volumes charting that trans-European odyssey, *A Time of Gifts*, widely considered to be his masterpiece.

Paul Auster (1947–)

I think of it sometimes: how I was conceived in that Niagara Falls resort for honeymooners. Not that it matters where it happened. But the thought of what must have been a passionless embrace, a blind, dutiful groping between chilly hotel sheets, has never failed to humble me into an awareness of my own contingency. Niagara Falls. Or the hazard of two bodies joining. And then me, a random homunculus, like some dare-devil in a barrel, shooting over the falls.

A little more than eight months later, on the morning of her twenty-second birthday, my mother woke up and told my father that the baby was coming. Ridiculous, he said, that baby's not due for another three weeks – and promptly went off to work, leaving her without a car.

She waited. Thought maybe he was right. Waited a little more, then called a sister-in-law and asked to be driven to the hospital. My aunt stayed with my mother throughout the day, calling my father every few hours to ask him to come. Later, he would say, I'm busy now, I'll get there when I can.

At a little past midnight I poked my way into the world, ass first, no doubt screaming.

My mother waited for my father to show up, but he did

not arrive until the next morning – accompanied by his mother, who wanted to inspect grandchild number seven. A short, nervous visit, and then off again to work.

She cried, of course. After all, she was young, and she had not expected it to mean so little to him. But he could never understand such things. Not in the beginning, and not in the end. It was never possible for him to be where he was. For as long as he lived, he was somewhere else, between here and there. But never really here. And really there . . .

Earliest memory: his absence. For the first years of my life he would leave for work early in the morning, before I was awake, and come home long after I had been put to bed. I was my mother's boy, and I lived in her orbit. I was a little moon circling her gigantic earth, a mote in the sphere of her gravity, and I controlled the tides, the weather, the forces of feeling. His refrain to her was: Don't fuss so much, you'll spoil him. But my health was not good, and she used this to justify the attention she lavished on me. We spent a lot of time together, she in her loneliness and I in my cramps, waiting patiently in doctors' offices for someone to quell the insurrection that continually raged in my stomach. Even then, I would cling to these doctors in a desperate sort of way, wanting them to hold me. From the very beginning, it seems, I was looking for my father, looking frantically for anyone who resembled him.

From *The Invention of Solitude* (1982)

Paul Auster was born in Newark, New Jersey. His novel *4 3 2 1* (2017) was shortlisted for the 2017 Man Booker Prize. His other books include *The New York Trilogy* (1987), *Moon Palace* (1989), *The Book of Illusions* (2002), *Sunset Park* (2010) and *Winter Journal* (2012). He has been awarded the Prince of Asturias Award for Literature, the Prix Médicis Étranger, an Independent Spirit Award and the Premio Napoli.

Rosemary Sutcliff (1920–1992)

For some years, I thought that I could remember being born. Later, I realised that I only remembered what I had been told about being born – by my mother, who was of the stuff that minstrels are made, but singularly unaware of the effect that her stories might have on a small daughter who believed implicitly in every word she uttered. So then, my birth-memory, via my mother, was of being brought by the stork in the middle of a desperate snowstorm. I was really intended for Mrs McPhee who lived next door, and who had, said my mother, made ready whole drawers full of baby-clothes including tiny kilts, and decided to call me Jeannie; but in the appalling snow he lost his way and came knocking on our door, begging to be taken in for the night, failing which he would have to go to the police, and I would be put in an orphanage. It was a *very* bad storm, and my teeth were chattering; so my mother took pity on us and let us come in and sit by the fire and gave us both hot cocoa, after which the stork departed, leaving me behind and promising to come back for me next day. He never came, and so there I still was, with Mummy and Daddy, two or three years later. I was a trusting child, or possibly just plain gullible. I never thought to wonder why, if the story were true, I had not merely been handed over the garden fence to my rightful owners next morning. Nor did it occur to me that at age zero, I would have been unlikely to have teeth to chatter.

It was a grief to me that I did not truly belong to my parents, but presumably I was unable to make this known; and when I was nearly four, and somebody said to me, in my mother's presence, 'What's your name, little girl?' to which I replied in a voice quivering with emotion, 'I'm really little Jeannie McPhee, but I'm living with Daddy and Mummy just now,' my mother was the world's most surprised and horrified woman. But she never learned.

Though that particular account of my birth was apocryphal, there seem to have been quite a few genuine dramas attached to the event. The doctor said I was due to arrive on Christmas Eve; my mother said I was coming on December 14th and on the 14th I came. Having a kind of two-thirds belief in horoscopes, I have sometimes wondered what effect that has had on my life and on the kind of person I am. I *was* born in a blizzard, and we had run out of coal and my father had to go next door, presumably to the McPhees', to borrow some in a wheelbarrow; and when next day the coalman did arrive, his horse fell down under the bedroom window.

I don't, then, actually remember being born; but I do have a genuine first memory that goes back to the time when I was eighteen months old. We were staying with my dear uncle Harold, whose home, when he was not in India, was still at Poole in Dorset; and my mother had me out in my pram in Poole Park. We came trundling along a path between big dark evergreen bushes reaching to the sky. The path turned a corner, and the bushes fell back forming a small open space in which were wire-netting cages containing large birds which look in my memory like golden pheasants. I did not so much mind the pheasants but there was another cage holding captive a restless revolving red squirrel, at sight of which all the woes of the world, all sins and sorrows, all injustice, all man's inhumanity to man came crashing in one great engulfing wave over my eighteen-month-old head, which was not yet ready to cope with it. I took one look, and broke into a roar of grief and fury which nothing would console or quieten, until I had been smartly trundled out of the gardens.

Afterwards we both forgot about the whole thing until after I was grown up, when something, I have no idea what, triggered the old memory, and back came the pictures. I described the incident to my mother. Had it ever happened, or was I inventing it? My mother thought – and remembered also; all too vividly. It had been *dreadful*, she said. I had gone on and on, and she hadn't been able to slap me because she had actually agreed with me entirely, and her mother, my grandmother, had hated things in cages so much that she had vowed to vote for any government that would abolish menageries and travelling circuses; and my face had been *purple*, and it had taken the gift of a green balloon to silence me at last; and I knew how much she disapproved of bribery. She added that I couldn't have been more than eighteen months old because after that we were never in Poole Park again until I was seven.

Which is how I know that, unlike the stork saga, it was a genuine memory.

From *Blue Remembered Hills* (1983)

In an interview given towards the end of her life, **Rosemary Sutcliff** stated that her books 'are for children of all ages, from nine to ninety'. Indeed, Sutcliff herself only learnt to read at the age of nine. Her output as an author was prolific and she was still writing on the morning of her death.

Sutcliff's many works notably include *The Eagle of the Ninth* (1954), the first of a series of novels for younger readers set in Roman Britain.

Arthur Miller (1915–2005)

The view from the floor is of a pair of pointy black calf-height shoes, one of them twitching restlessly, and just above them the plum-colored skirt rising from the ankles to the blouse, and higher still the young round face and her ever-changing tones of voice as she gossips into the wall telephone with one of her two sisters, something she would go on doing the rest of her life until one by one they peeled off the wire and vanished into the sky. Now she bends over and tries to move me clear of her foot. But I must lie on her shoe, and from far up above through skirt and darkness I hear her laughing pleasantly at my persistence.

From *Timebends* (1987)

The landmark plays written by **Arthur Miller** include *All My Sons* (1947), *Death of a Salesman* (1949 – winner of the Pulitzer Prize), *The Crucible* (1953) and *A View from the Bridge* (1955). The last of these was revised in 1956, the same year that Miller refused to identify people he had seen at a writers' meeting to the Committee on Un-American Activities.

Miles Davis (1926–1991)

The very first thing I remember in my early childhood is a flame, a blue flame jumping off a gas stove somebody lit. It might have been me playing around with the stove. I don't remember who it was. Anyway, I remember being shocked by the whoosh of the blue flame jumping off the burner, the suddenness of it. That's as far back as I can remember; any further back than this is just fog, you know, just mystery. But that stove flame is as clear as music in my mind. I was three years old.

I saw that flame and felt that hotness of it close to my face. I felt fear, real fear, for the first time in my life. But I remember it also like some kind of adventure, some kind of weird joy, too. I guess that experience took me someplace in my head I hadn't been before. To some frontier, the edge, maybe, of everything possible. I don't know; I never tried to analyse it before. The fear I had was almost like an invitation, a challenge to go forward into something I knew nothing about. That's where I think my personal philosophy of life and my commitment to everything I believe in started, with that moment. I don't know, but I think it might be true. Who knows? What the fuck did I know about anything back then? In my mind I have always believed and thought since then that my motion had to be forward, away from the heat of that flame.

From *Miles*, written with Quincy Troupe (1989)

Miles Davis, a trumpeter and composer, was among the most influential musicians of the twentieth century. He pioneered the movement known as 'cool jazz' and his album *Kind of Blue* (1959) is held to be the most popular jazz recording ever produced.

Marlon Brando (1924–2004)

As I stumble back across the years of my life trying to recall what it was about, I find that nothing is really clear. I suppose the first memory I have was when I was too young to remember how young I was. I opened my eyes, looked around in the mouse-colored light and realized that Ermi was still asleep, so I dressed myself as best I could and went down the stairs, left foot first on each step. I had to scuff my way to the porch because I couldn't buckle my sandals. I sat on the one step in the sun at the dead end of Thirty-Second Street and waited. It must have been spring because the big tree in front of the house was shedding pods with two wings like a dragonfly. On days when there wasn't any wind, they would spin around in the air as they drifted softly to the ground.

I watched them float all the way down, sitting with my neck craned back until my mouth opened and holding out my hand just in case, but they never landed on it. When one hit the ground I'd look up again, my eyes darting, waiting for the next magical event, the sun warming the yellow hairs on my head.

Waiting like that for the next magic was as good a

moment as any other that I can remember in the last sixty-five years.

From *Songs My Mother Taught Me*, with Robert Lindsey (1994)

Marlon Brando won the Academy Award for Best Actor for his performances in *On the Waterfront* (1954) and *The Godfather* (1972). His other acclaimed roles include those of Stanley Kowalski in *A Streetcar Named Desire* (1951) and Colonel Kurtz in *Apocalypse Now* (1979). In 1999, *Time* magazine named Brando one of its 'Most Important People of the Century'.

Doris Lessing (1919–2013)

A tiny thing among trampling, knocking careless giants who smell, who lean down towards you with great ugly hairy faces, showing big dirty teeth. A foot you keep an eye on, while trying to watch all the other dangers as well, is almost as big as you are. The hands they use to grip you can squeeze the breath half out of you. The rooms you run about in, the furniture you move along, windows, doors, are vast, nothing is your size, but one day you will grow tall enough to reach the handle of the door, or the knob on a cupboard. These are the real childhood memories and any that have you level with grown-ups are later inventions. An intense physicality, that is the truth of childhood.

My first memory is before I was two, and it is of an enormous dangerous horse towering up, up, and on it is my father still higher, his head and shoulders somewhere in the sky. There he sits with his wooden leg always there under his trousers, a big hard slippery hidden thing. I am trying not to cry, while being lifted up in tight squeezing hands, and put in front of my father's body, told to grip the front of the saddle, a hard jutting edge I must stretch my fingers to hold. I am inside the heat of horse, the smell of horse, the smell of my father, all hot pungent smells. When the horse moves it is a jerking jolting motion and I lean back my head and shoulders into my father's stomach and feel there the hard straps of the wooden-leg harness. My stomach is reeling because of the swoop up from the ground now so far below me. Now, that is a real memory, violent, smelly – physical.

From *Under My Skin* (1994)

Doris Lessing was born to British parents in Iran, where she lived for her first six years. Her works include the sequence of five novels collectively entitled *Children of Violence* (1952–69) as well as *The Golden Notebook* (1962) and *The Good Terrorist* (1985). Lessing was awarded the Nobel Prize in Literature in 2007, becoming the oldest ever recipient of the award.

Margaret Thatcher (1925–2013)

My first distinct memory is of traffic. I was being pushed in a pram through the town to the park on a sunny day, and I must have encountered the bustle of Grantham on the way. The occasion stays in my mind as an exciting mixture of colour, vehicles, people and thunderous noise – yet, perhaps paradoxically, the memory is a pleasant one. I must have liked this first conscious plunge into the outside world.

As for indistinct memories, most of us probably recall our earliest years as a sort of blur. Mine was an idyllic blur in which the sun was always shining through the leaves of the lime tree into our living room and someone – my mother, my sister, one of the people working in the shop – was always nearby to cuddle me or pacify me with a sweet. Family tradition has it that I was a very quiet baby, which my political opponents might have some difficulty in believing. But I had not been born into a quiet family . . .

Perhaps the biggest excitement of my early years was a visit to London when I was twelve years old. I came down by train in the charge of a friend of my mother's, arriving at King's Cross, where I was met by the Rev. Skinner and his wife, two family friends who were going to look after me. The first impact of London was overwhelming: King's Cross itself was a giant bustling cavern; the rest of the city had all the dazzle of a commercial and imperial capital. For the first time in my life I saw people from foreign countries, some in the traditional and native dress of India and Africa. The sheer volume of traffic and of pedestrians was exhilarating; they seemed to generate a sort of electricity. London's buildings were impressive for another reason: begrimed with soot, they had a dark imposing magnificence which constantly reminded me that I was at the centre of the world.

I was taken by the Skinners to all the usual sites. I fed the pigeons in Trafalgar Square; I rode the Underground – a slightly forbidding experience for a child; I visited the Zoo, where I rode on an elephant and recoiled from the reptiles – an early portent of my relations with Fleet Street; I was disappointed by Oxford Street, which was much narrower than the boulevard of my imagination; made a pilgrimage to St Paul's, where John Wesley had prayed on the morning of his conversion; and of course, to the Houses of Parliament and Big Ben, which did not disappoint at all; and I went to look at Downing Street, but unlike the young Harold Wilson did not have the prescience to have my photograph taken outside No. 10.

From *The Path to Power* (1995)

Margaret Thatcher served as prime minister of the United Kingdom from 1979 to 1990. She was the longest-serving British prime minister of the twentieth century and the first woman to have been appointed to the role.

Hilary Mantel (1952–)

Before I went to school there was a time when I was happy, and I want to write down what I remember about that time. The story of my own childhood is a complicated sentence that I am always trying to finish, to finish and put behind me. It resists finishing, and partly this is because words are not enough; my early world was synesthetic, and I am haunted by the ghosts of my own sense impressions, which re-emerge when I try to write, and shiver between the lines.

We are taught to be chary of early memories. Sometimes psychologists fake photographs in which a picture of their subject, in his or her childhood, appears in an unfamiliar setting, in places or with people whom in real life they have never seen. The subjects are amazed at first but then – in proportion to their anxiety to please – they oblige by producing a 'memory' to cover the experience that they have never actually had. I don't know what this shows, except that psychologists have persuasive personalities, that some subjects are imaginative, and that we are all told to trust the evidence of our senses, and we do it: we trust the objective fact of the photograph, not our subjective bewilderment. It's a trick, it isn't science; it's about our present, not about our past. Though my early memories are patchy, I think they are not, or not entirely, a confabulation, and I believe this because of their over-whelming sensory power; they come complete, not like the groping, generalised formulations of the subjects fooled by the photograph. As I say 'tasted', I taste, and as I say 'I heard', I hear: I am not talking about a Proustian moment, but a Proustian cine-film. Anyone can run these ancient newsreels, with a bit of preparation, a bit of prac-tice; maybe it comes easier to writers than to many people, but I wouldn't be sure about that. I wouldn't agree either that it doesn't matter what you remember, but only what you think you remember. I have an investment in accuracy; I would never say, 'It doesn't matter, it's history now.' I know, on the other hand, that a small child has a strange sense of time, where a year seems a decade, and everyone over the age of ten seems grown-up and of an equal age; so although I feel sure of what happened, I am less sure of the sequence and the dateline. I know, too, that once a family has acquired a habit of secrecy, memories begin to distort, because its members confabulate to cover the gaps in the facts; you have to make some sort of sense of what's going on around you, so you cobble together a narrative as best you can. You add to it, and reason about it, and the distortions breed distortions.

Still, I think people can remember: a face, a perfume: one true thing or two. Doctors used to say babies didn't feel pain; we know they were wrong. We are born with our sensibilities; perhaps we are conceived that way. Part of our difficulty in trusting ourselves is that in talking of memory we are inclined to use geological metaphors. We talk about buried parts of our past and assume the most distant in time are the hardest to reach: that one has to prospect for them with the help of a hypnotist, or psychotherapist. I don't think memory is like that: rather that it is like St Augustine's 'spreading limitless room'. Or a great plain, a steppe, where all the memories are laid side by side, at the same depth, like seeds under the soil . . .

This is the first thing I remember. I am sitting up in my pram. We are outside, in the park called Bankswood. My mother walks backwards. I hold out my arms because I don't want her to go. She says she's only going to take my picture. I don't understand why she goes backwards, back and aslant, tacking to one side. The trees overhead make a noise of urgent conversation, too quick to catch; the leaves pat, the sky moves, the sun peers down at me. Away and away she goes, till she comes to a halt. She raises her arm and partly hides her face. The sky and trees rush over my head. I feel dizzied. The entire world is sound, movement. She moves towards me, speaking. The memory ends.

The memory exists now in black and white, because when I was older I saw Bankswood pictures: this photograph or similar ones, perhaps taken that day, perhaps weeks earlier, or weeks later. In the nineteen-fifties photographs often didn't come out at all, or were so fuzzy that they were thrown away. What remains as a memory, though the colour has bled away, is the fast scudding of clouds and the rush of sounds over my head, the wind in the trees: as if the waters of life have begun to flow.

From *Giving Up the Ghost* (2003)

Hilary Mantel is the only female novelist to have twice been awarded the Man Booker Prize, first for the 2009 novel *Wolf Hall*, a fictional account of Thomas Cromwell's rise to power in the court of Henry VIII, and then for *Bring Up the Bodies* (2012), the second instalment of her Cromwell trilogy. She was appointed DBE in 2014.

Christopher Hitchens (1949–2011)

Whatever one's ontology may be, it will always seem tempting to believe that everything must have a first cause or, if nothing quite as grand as that, at the very least a definite beginning. And on that point I have no vagueness or indecision. I do know a little of how I came to be in two minds. And *this* is how it begins with me:

I am standing on a ferry-boat that is crossing a lovely harbor. I have since learned many versions and variations of the word 'blue,' but let's say that a brilliant if slightly harsh sunshine illuminates a cerulean sky-vault and an azure sea and also limns the way in which these two textures collide and reflect. The resulting tinge of green is in lambent contrast with the darker vegetation on the hillsides and makes an almost blinding combination when, allied with those discrepant yet melding blues, it hits the white buildings that reach down to the edge of the water. As a flash of drama and beauty and seascape and landscape, it's as good an inaugural memory as one could wish.

Since this little voyage is occurring in about 1952 and I have been born in 1949, I have no means of appreciating that this is the Grand Harbor of Valletta, the capital of the tiny island-state of Malta and one of the finest Baroque and Renaissance cities of Europe. A jewel set in the sea between Sicily and Libya, it has been for centuries a place of the two-edged sword between the Christian and Muslim worlds. Its population is so overwhelmingly Roman Catholic that there are, within the walled city, a great plethora of ornate churches, the cathedral being decorated by the murals of Caravaggio himself, that seductive votary of the higher wickedness. The island withstood one of the longest Turkish sieges in the history of 'Christendom.' But the Maltese tongue is a dialect version of the Arabic spoken in the Maghreb and is the only Semitic language to be written in a Latin script. If you happen to attend a Maltese Catholic church during Mass, you will see the priest raising the Communion Host and calling on 'Allah,' because this after all is the local word for 'god.' My first memory, in other words, is of a ragged and jagged, but nonetheless permeable and charming, frontier between two cultures and civilizations.

I am, at this stage, far too secure and confident to register anything of the kind. (If I speak a few phrases of Maltese, it is not with a view to becoming bilingual or multicultural but in order to address my priest-ridden nannies and the kitchen maids with their huge broods of children. This was the place where I first learned to see a picture of Catholicism as one of plump shepherds and lean sheep.)* Malta is effectively a British colony – its most heroic recent chapter the

* Hitchens here notes: 'Everything about Christianity is contained in the pathetic image of "the flock."'

withstanding of a hysterical aerial bombardment by Hitler and Mussolini – and it has remained a solid possession of the Royal Navy, in which my father proudly serves, ever since the Napoleonic Wars. Much more to the immediate point, I am standing on the deck of this vessel in company with my mother, who holds my hand when I desire it and also lets me scamper off to explore if I insist.

So, all things being considered, not too shaky a start. I am well-dressed and well-fed, with a full head of hair and a slender waist, and operating in a context of startling architectural and natural beauty, and full of *brio* and self-confidence, and on a boat in the company of a beautiful woman who loves me.

From *Hitch-22* (2010)

One of his time's most influential public intellectuals, **Christopher Hitchens'** many books included works on Thomas Jefferson, Thomas Paine, George Orwell, Mother Teresa, Henry Kissinger and Bill Clinton, as well as the international bestseller, *God Is Not Great* (2007).

Karl Ove Knausgaard (1968–)

Memory is not a reliable quantity in life. And it isn't for the simple reason that memory doesn't prioritise the truth. It is never the demand for truth that determines whether memory recalls an action accurately or not. It is self-interest which does. Memory is pragmatic, it is sly and artful, but not in any hostile or malicious way; on the contrary, it does everything it can to keep its host satisfied. Something pushes a memory into the great void of oblivion, something distorts it beyond recognition, something misunderstands it totally, and this something is as good as nothing, recalls it with sharpness, clarity and accuracy. That which is remembered accurately is never given to you to determine.

In my case, any memory of my first six years is virtually non-existent. I remember hardly anything. I have no idea who took care of me, what I did, who I played with, it has all completely gone, the years 1969–1974 are a great big hole in my life. The little I can muster is of scant value: I am standing on a wooden bridge in a sparse high-altitude forest, beneath me rushes a torrent, the water is green and white, I am jumping up and down, the bridge is swaying and I am laughing. Beside me is Geir Prestbakmo, a boy from the neighbourhood, he is jumping up and down and laughing too. I am sitting on the rear seat of a car, we are waiting at the lights, dad turns and says we are in Mjøndalen. We are going to an IK Start game, I've been told, but I can't remember a thing about the trip there, the football match or the journey home. I am walking up the hill outside the house pushing a big plastic lorry; it is green and yellow and gives me an absolutely fantastic feeling of riches and wealth and happiness.

That is all. That is my first six years.

But these are canonised memories, already established at the age of seven or eight, the magic of childhood: my very first memories! However, there are other kinds of memories. Those which are not fixed and cannot be evoked by will, but which at odd moments let go, as it were, and rise into my consciousness of their own accord and float around there for a while like transparent jellyfish, roused by a certain smell, a certain taste, a certain sound . . . these are always accompanied by an immediate, intense feeling of happiness. Then there are the memories associated with the body, when you do something you used to do: shield your eyes from the sun with your arm, catch a ball, run across a meadow with a kite in your hand and your children hard on your heels. There are memories that accompany emotions: sudden anger, sudden tears, sudden fear, and you are where you were, as if hurled back inside yourself, propelled through the age at breakneck speed. And then there are the memories associated with a landscape, for landscape in childhood is not like the landscape that follows later; they are charged in very different ways. In that landscape every rock, every tree had a meaning, and because everything was seen for the first time and because it was seen so many times, it was anchored in the depths of your consciousness, not as something vague or approximate, the way the landscape outside a house appears to an adult if they close their eyes and it has to be summoned forth, but as something with immense precision and detail. In my mind I only have to open the door and go outside for the images to come streaming towards me. The shingle in the driveway, almost bluish in colour in the summer. Oh, that alone, the driveways of childhood! And the 1970s cars parked in them! VW Beetles, Citroën DS 21s, Ford Taunuses, Granadas, Consuls, Opel Asconas, Kadetts, Ladas, Volvo Amazons . . .

From *Boyhood Island* (2010), translated by Don Bartlett

Karl Ove Knausgaard has been called 'the Norwegian Proust'. His first novel, *Out of the World* (1998), was the first ever debut to win the Norwegians' Critics Prize. Knausgaard's *My Struggle* series of six novels (2009–11) – of which *Boyhood Island* is the third instalment – has been widely acclaimed as a masterpiece.

Stephen Hawking (1942–2018)

I was born on January 8 1942, exactly three hundred years after the death of Galileo. I estimate, however, that about two hundred other babies were also born that day. I don't know whether any of them was later interested in astronomy . . .

My earliest memory is of standing in the nursery of Byron House School in Highgate and crying my head off. All around me, children were playing with what seemed like wonderful toys, and I wanted to join in. But I was only two and a half, this was the first time I had been left with people I didn't know, and I was scared. I think my parents were rather surprised at my reaction, because I was their first child and they had been following child development textbooks that said that children ought to be ready to start making social relationships at two. But they took me away that awful morning and didn't send me back to Byron House for another year and a half.

At that time, during and just after the war, Highgate was an area in which a number of scientific and academic people lived. (In another country they would have been called intellectuals, but the English have never admitted to having any intellectuals.) All these parents sent their children to Byron House School, which was a very progressive school for those times.

I remember complaining to my parents that the school wasn't teaching me anything.

From *My Brief History* (2013)

Stephen Hawking was the Lucasian Professor of Mathematics at the University of Cambridge (the chair once held by Isaac Newton) between 1979 and 2009. The author of *A Brief History of Time* (1988), an international bestseller, Hawking contracted motor neurone disease in 1963 and was given two years to live. Yet he endured for many decades more, coming to be popularly regarded as the most brilliant theoretical physicist since Albert Einstein.

Oliver Sacks (1933–2015)

I have a vivid memory from about the age of two of pulling the tail of our chow, Peter, while he was gnawing a bone under the hall table, of Peter leaping up and biting me in the cheek, and of my being carried, howling, into my father's surgery in the house, where a couple of stitches were put in my cheek.

There is an objective reality here: I was bitten on the cheek by Peter when I was two, and still bear the scar of this. But do I actually remember it, or was I told about it, subsequently constructing a 'memory' that became more and more firmly fixed in my mind by repetition? The memory seems intensely real to me, and the fear associated with it is certainly real, for I developed a fear of large animals after this incident – Peter was almost as large as I was at two – a fear that they would suddenly attack or bite me . . .

We, as human beings, are landed with memory systems that have fallibilities, frailties, and imperfections – but also great flexibility and creativity. Confusion over sources or indifference to them can be a paradoxical strength: if we could tag the sources of all our knowledge, we would be overwhelmed with often irrelevant information.

Indifference to source allows us to assimilate what we read, what we are told, what others say and think and write and paint, as intensely and richly as if they were primary experiences. It allows us to see and hear with other eyes and ears, to enter into other minds, to assimilate the art and science and religion of the whole culture, to enter into and contribute to the common mind, the general commonwealth of knowledge. This sort of sharing and participation, this communion, would not be possible if all our knowledge, our memories, were tagged and identified, seen as private, exclusively ours. Memory is dialogic and arises not only from direct experience but from the intercourse of many minds.

From *The New York Review of Books* (21 February 2013)

Oliver Sacks was evacuated from London aged six, during the Blitz. His large extended family contained a number of renowned scientists and doctors, and Sacks would grow up to become 'the poet laureate of medicine' (according to the *New York Times*).

He spent almost fifty years working as a neurologist and wrote many books, including *Awakenings* (1973), *The Man Who Mistook His Wife for a Hat* (1985), *Musicophilia* (2007), *Hallucinations* (2012), as well as the memoirs *Uncle Tungsten* (2001) and *On the Move* (2015).

Susan Greenfield (1950–)

In the 1950s, all little boys wore shorts, most typically with a Fair Isle pullover and tie: they were mini-men of the era, albeit showing their pale knees and lacking the hallmark pipe of their happy-family fathers. Meanwhile, we girls were never, ever dressed in anything other than, well, dresses. The notion of wearing trousers of any length would have been alien and heretical, irrespective of the occasion. At my kindergarten the strategy for PE classes was simple: tuck all the swirling material below the waist into your knickers. Luckily they too were voluminous, elasticised at the waist, reaching halfway down the thigh: they even had pockets. And never go without a bow or two in the hair, albeit festooning the ends of plaits, or anchored firmly above either temple: no hairstyle was too short, and in any case it rarely was anything less than chin-length, to be without some kind of satin, nylon or plastic adornment that emphasised even more the rigid distinction of gender. How different now, where some schools are bending over backwards, both in uniform code and general rules, to blur the male–female divide and deliberately introduce a well-intentioned ambiguity in sexual identity.

Memory and identity are closely interwoven. After all,

the fear we have of dementia, where 70 per cent of cases are Alzheimer's disease, is surely due to an apparent erosion of identity not seen with other serious conditions such as cancer or heart disease. What is happening in the brain? Humans occupy more ecological niches than any other species on the planet because of the superlative ability of our brains, compared with those of any other animal, to adapt to the environment. Our brains become highly personalised post-natally by the development of unique configurations of connections between the brain cells that characterise the growth of the human brain after birth, personalising it into a 'mind' that is in constant dialogue with the environment. Just as these carefully curated connections increasingly characterise the individual as they have ever more individual experiences, so in Alzheimer's the connections are gradually dismantled: the journey is reversed and the patient recapitulates childhood, and then journeys on into infancy, to a time of no memory, no past or future. Like small children, they are trapped in an immediate present driven by inputs from the raw senses, where there is no robust or continuing sense of self. Only when you have a sufficient arsenal of connections can you have specific memories. And only then, arguably, can you have an identity, a sense of self.

Perhaps, therefore, it's not surprising that first memories usually coincide with the appearance of *self*-consciousness — usually, for many of us, at around three years or so at the earliest; while others claim that experiences are only recalled from as old as six. It might be helpful here to distinguish between a full-blown episode in one's life – say, going to the sea or a birthday party on a particular day, complete with a modest narrative, an event that had a clear beginning-middle-end – and a fleeting flash. The fleeting flash is a memory, but a far more insubstantial one: it has no start or finish, it's just *there*. Such a generic recollection could be a face, an object, an animal or, as in my case, an item of clothing. I know I couldn't have been as old as six: otherwise I would have rebelled and remembered the inevitable repercussions as a real milestone in my life. No, I must have been only three or so, with the connections between my brain cells still insufficiently networked such as to anchor a strong and clear memory of a one-off episode. Instead, this first memory has no associations and no clear storyline: it is just a coat; or, rather, an outfit.

Hanging hazily in the recesses of my mind is a French sky-blue coat. Interestingly enough, the colour is exact and vivid. Accompanying it – and this is essential to deem the whole get-up an 'outfit' – is a muff. The muff is suspended around my neck and serves as an inadequate and far less practical alternative to gloves, or even the less compliant mittens. It is the worst way to keep your hands warm as it prevents all use of them. I hate it.

And there it is: a memory not anchored in any particular moment or relating to any other associations, but haunting me to this day.

(2017)

Baroness Susan Greenfield is a research scientist, author and broadcaster. She has held research fellowships in the Department of Physiology, Oxford; the Collège de France, Paris; and NYU Medical Center, New York. Her various books include *A Day in the Life of the Brain* (2016). She is the founder and CEO of the biotech company Neuro-Bio, which is developing novel treatments for neurodegenerative disorders, such as Alzheimer's disease.

Sebastian Barry (1955–)

This memory may possess the quality of being true, since I am more of a camera in it than a spectator of myself. Memories in which you can observe yourself moving about are maybe a little suspect. Nevertheless, this memory may be suspect for all that. But it is also complicated. It is of the bars of a cot, but not my own cot. It is a cot in the room of a hospital. I know where this hospital is, a huge old Georgian building on Harcourt Street in Dublin. I am not sure if it is still a hospital these days. I remember tall high windows and gloom and also that signature bareness of childhood recollections, as if because in my extreme youthfulness I don't have names for every object I therefore haven't retained them in memory. It may have been full of nameless medical clutter. I am possibly one and a half years old, or older, I think I must be walking by now. I think I am walking because I presume I must be, for my sister to be able to push me down the front steps of our house, as she has innocently done, causing me to break my nose. I take no stand on this issue. She is only a baby and can do what she wants. Then I have healed up, I presume, and then she pushes me out a window. But at least it is the ground floor, and it merely serves to break my nose again. Let me say immediately I have always loved my sister. This desire to murder your new sibling, this interloper extraordinaire, is understandable and universal.

The outcome was, I began to speak through my nose, in so far as I was speaking, so a clever surgeon was engaged to rectify it. Hence my presence in this cot. Hence the bars. I am staring and staring at the tall old Georgian door, willing my mother to come back to me. I have no idea how long I have been waiting. Minutes or hours might be all the one. I am standing on the soft mattress with great resolve and holding onto the bars and I am staring at the solid-looking, blank, dark space. I am thinking now the door must be open, but so placed that a person entering will only be seen at the last moment in the frame. I am staring, staring. My eyes are so focused the air is fuzzy and blurred like the smoke of a fire. But it is also clear, with the clarity of enormous attention. That is the benefice of memory, that many contradictory things are possible in the same instant. It is the fecundity we are allowed. Maybe it is a true memory. Who can say? There is a funnel, a channel of vision that I make between my eyes and the empty door. It might be true. How brown everything is. In this memory my mother never comes. I am straining and straining, willing her to appear. It might be true. Staring and staring. She never comes, she never comes, and then she does.

(2018)

Sebastian Barry is the only novelist to have twice won the Costa Book of the Year. As well as various plays and collections of poetry, his award-winning novels include *A Long Long Way* (2005), *The Secret Scripture* (2008) and *Days Without End* (2016). He was appointed the Laureate for Irish Fiction in 2018.

Melvyn Bragg (1939–)

When I began to write this it was as if a drill had bored a large hole in the dam of the reservoir of childhood. Out of it gushed, spurted, cascaded an immersion of sensations and impressions which have been stored away for decades. It's another world, another person. Yet it's also whom I was and still am.

I am a very unreliable witness here. Some years ago I wrote a novel, *The Soldier's Return*, which began with a man, based on my father. I remembered the afternoon he had arrived back home after the Second World War. I would be about six. I 'saw him' clearly turning the corner of our yard in the small northern town in which we lived. His kitbag, his smile, my mother leaving the doorstep to meet him, me being swept up and thrown high up into the air by this stranger-father . . . Every detail was precise.

When my mother read it, she said, 'It wasn't like that. It wasn't like that at all.'

She then described how on that day we had gone to the nearby city of Carlisle, to the railway station, because in a phrase which could come out of any epic, 'We got word the men were coming home.'

Carlisle was a city which made engines for the powerful

trains which pull Britain together. I was mad on trains. And I was going to meet my father whose photograph I had most likely kissed every night before taking the candle to bed. Yes. Old times. Gaslight downstairs, wax upstairs.

My mother said we (wives, sisters, daughters, friends), 'got up a special bus' to meet the returning servicemen. It is very likely that I had never travelled a distance of eleven miles in a bus in my life, let alone been to the legendary metropolis of Carlisle.

Yet despite every effort after my mother told me the truth, I could not recall a particle of what must have been the biggest day in my short life.

I can remember other things that happened when I was six – and have been verified! For instance, two of my uncles marched me off to church to answer the call for trebles in the choir and a few weeks later, as the youngest choirboy, I read the first lesson in the service of the Nine Carols and Nine Lessons. I remember being splayed with terror, especially when I hit the phrase, 'And the serpent beguiled her and she did eat.' But I cannot remember the day of my father's return.

So beware.

I do remember a tricycle handed over by a cousin who had grown out of it. I turned it into a Spitfire in no time and bowled down Station Road on the lookout for Messerschmitts. And then there was the bright-red blazer that my mother must have bought for me. What I remember was tearful arguments when I refused to take it off to go to bed. Then there was the stone fight with the Market Hill gang, in which a stone missed my left eye by an eighth of an inch and caused a stream of blood that was extremely impressive. There was the majestic rocking horse in the corner of the first class of the infants' school, which lured me there way earlier than I need have been so I could grab the first ride and stay on just as long as possible . . . And more and more as that foreign, familiar time races through the blood once again. But if I were to choose one thing it would not be an event but a feeling.

I remember and can reinhabit the sensation of unlimited freedom in that little town which in the mid-twentieth century still had all the best and worst characteristics of a large Victorian village.

Bare of cars, streets and alleyways, small ginnels and yards in which three or four houses (one room up, one room down) were huddled around the common WC and the one wash house – so many ways to escape pursuit from other gangs from other streets with whom we seemed to be in constant combat.

I was never more than two shouts from my own house and safety. My mother would go onto the street and say, 'Where is he?' That would be passed to one or at the most two people and she would know the answer. Just as she must have felt reassured, I too by a sort of umbilical understanding also felt constantly reassured, safe.

This wrapping in recognition was intensified by what happened on the streets, where you nodded to or mostly greeted every single person you met, many of whom would enquire about your father and mother.

I know now that there were dangerous people in the

town, that misery and violence were there, but the truth is we children felt collectively watched over and were allowed to be at full liberty.

Despite the fact that the town was on black-out the moment it became dark and wardens came round with shielded torches to check the blinds, I could even in that dark, with friends, roam around like a cat. Down Meeting House Lane, through the winding ancient Crofts, along Birdcage Walk, cutting from Church Street past the slaughterhouse into Water Street . . . Games of Chessy taking over the whole town centre, games of Tiggy. Always running, shouts in the dark, free as could be, while outside our nest of the town the world was smashing itself to pieces in the name, so they said, of a freedom which ran through our young hands like warm sand, unforgettable and immeasurable it now seems.

(2018)

Melvyn Bragg began his broadcasting career at the BBC in 1961. He has written several award-winning novels and works of non-fiction. He has also edited and presented *The South Bank Show* for the last forty years and chairs *In Our Time* on BBC Radio 4. An honorary fellow of the Royal Society and of the British Academy, he was given a peerage in 1998 and made a Companion of Honour in 2018.

Nicholas Humphrey (1943–)

I am in my mother's arms as she rushes down the stairs to the basement. Before we're halfway down, there is a bang followed by a terrible roar. The house shudders and a row of green bottles falls from a shelf onto our heads. We collapse in a heap at the bottom of the stairs. Mother takes my face in her hands and stares at me, eyes wide. She kisses my forehead and there is blood on her mouth. I see there's blood on the floor. Green glass and red blood. And then I don't remember.

I can date this exactly. It was 23 June 1944. There is an online map of the bombs that fell on London in the Second World War, which shows the location, date and type of bomb. This was a V1 flying bomb, a 'doodlebug', launched from northern France. My mother must have heard the distant hum growing to a loud harsh rattle, then the silence as its motor cut off above the intended target and it went into a dive. We were lucky. It flew over us and exploded on Highgate School's playing field, a few hundred yards away. Our house was undamaged, and the cut on my head was only skin-deep. My mother's parents were not quite so lucky. They lived in a big house overlooking the playing field, and the explosion blew in their front door. When we went round to see how they were coping, they explained to my elder brother that a big wind had knocked the door down. My brother said he didn't know bombs made so much wind.

In 2015 a blue plaque, to commemorate my grandfather, the scientist A. V. Hill, was put up on the house. I had to make a speech on the front steps. That's when I thought to research the date. I knew the memory went back to when I was a toddler. But I hadn't realised quite how young I actually was: only fifteen months old. For a first memory, this is unusually early. At fifteen months I could not possibly have remembered the story in the words I've used above. There would have been only the sequence of sensory images and my associated feelings to hold on to. A memory from that stage must have had something very special going for it.

I believe it was the look in my mother's eyes that fixed this for me. Neuroscience has shown that fear-faces have a fast track to the amygdala nucleus in the brain. There they shout: this is important, take note, write this memory! The amygdala channel is active early on, and it can make for rapid and indelible storing of information that has been highlighted by the message in another's eyes. Research with monkeys, for example, has shown that while an infant monkey will reach out to touch a snake on first encounter, if it sees another monkey reacting with fear when it does so, it will pull back and be scared of snakes ever after.

Fear expressed by someone else is especially potent. But the amygdala is open to other emotional expressions also.

Whenever we observe another person reacting strongly – either negatively or positively – to something in our vicinity, this can permanently mark the event for us. Someone else's disgust can turn us off for life. But equally someone else's excitement and pleasure can turn us on.

If my first memory relates to my seeing my mother's terror, my second in fact relates to seeing her being thrilled. However, to begin with, I did not recognise this as a memory at all. All I had to go on for many years was that I held in my head a snatch of apparently meaningless – but happy-making – speech. 'Mainadzear'. I liked to say this to myself. Through my childhood it served me as a kind of acoustic comfort object. Aged eight, at boarding prep school, I would say it at bedtime, kneeling by the bed, while other boys said their prayers. I had no idea what it meant. But it felt good and personal. My own 'Rosebud'.

It was not till I was twenty or so that something clicked in my mind, and the full memory returned. Now, I am in the entrance hall of my grandparents' house – the same house where the door blew in. It's a Sunday, and we are there for the regular Sunday tea. 'Mainadzear', my grandmother is saying it in an important voice. I look to my mother for explanation, and see her eyes opening wide again. But this time it's not fear, it's surprise and excited anticipation. My father too. And then, suddenly, the words resolve, and – to my older self – they now make sense: 'Maynard's here'.

Maynard Keynes, the economist, was my grandmother's brother. If this visit, as I now guess, was near the end of the war, when he was shuttling back and forth to Washington, pleading with the Americans for the financial bailout of Britain, he can rarely have had time to come to tea in Highgate. But just because his visits were rare and his war work so important, when he did turn up it must have felt to the assembled company like an unexpected visit from the King. No wonder if their faces signalled to me, straight to my amygdala: mark this!

Maynard died on 21 April 1946, and the last date on which he might plausibly have had time to visit would have been late in 1945. Then at most I was two and a half years old. I would have been old enough by then to have had the modicums of language. When children are learning to speak they regularly take in and repeat particular words before they understand their referents. But if I marked 'Mainadzear' as something well worth saying, whose meaning time would tell, I must have waited in vain to hear it said again. So, all it could be was a free-floating talisman.

(2018)

The theoretical psychologist **Nicholas Humphrey** is known for his work on the evolution of human intelligence and consciousness. He studied mountain gorillas with Dian Fossey in Rwanda and was the first person to prove the existence of 'blindsight' in monkeys. He is emeritus professor of psychology at the London School of Economics. He is also the only scientist to have edited the literary magazine *Granta*.

Javier Marías (1951–)

A month after being born in Madrid in September 1951, I was taken to America and there – in Wellesley, Massachusetts, to be precise – I spent the next six or seven months of my life. I don't really remember anything from that time, although sometimes I think I do, for this reason: in 1955, when I was just four, my father was employed by Yale University to teach there for the whole academic year, and he again took all the family – on this occasion to New Haven, Connecticut. This second stay in America has inevitably become superimposed upon the first. I can't possibly have any memories of Wellesley, and yet, when I went back there to teach for a term in 1984, I seemed to recognise landscapes, smells and Lake Waban. I was even invited to a party at the same house where my parents, my older brothers and I lived from 1951 to 1952, and it did seem vaguely familiar. This was doubtless an illusion, or perhaps the place I did recall – New Haven – shared certain similarities with the place I couldn't possibly remember – Wellesley. The snow, though, was definitely similar, and thus, for me, one of my first memories was seeing my footprints in the snow, the sound the snow made when my foot sank into it, the amusing sensation of having the ground give way beneath my childish feet.

Changing countries at an early age (even for only a few months) had the strange effect of erasing almost completely what had happened before, as if my life were starting over, or as if the unconscious work of storing away memories had only begun there and then. The first image I have of the United States is of a bright-yellow train travelling through fields, possibly while we were being driven from the airport to New Haven. That cheerful, lively colour provoked a feeling of elation in me, as if it were a sign of good things to come. Yes, that's what I felt, at least I think I did.

I have many other memories of the time I spent there, memories that seem to me the first of my existence, although they're not. There is one, though, that doesn't quite fit with that period, but rather with the months spent in Wellesley, because, in my memory, I was still in my pram, whereas by the time I was four years old in New Haven, I was already confidently walking and running. On leaving a shop, my mother suddenly realised that I'd picked something up, clearly with no intention of paying for it. I wouldn't even have known what paying meant, or what property was. My mother, who, I imagine, was more amused than embarrassed, either took it back or bought it on my behalf. If that memory is real, then my first memory is of me as unwitting shoplifter.

There are only a couple of memories dating, I assume, from before my second trip to America. I have a vague idea that, shortly before our departure, my classmates, boys and girls of three or four, whom I would hardly have known at all, gave me a special send-off. Another clearer memory – clearer because, although it's older, it's a memory of something that happened more than once – is this: as in most metro stations in big cities, the curved walls of the platforms in the Madrid metro were covered in huge advertisements. One blue-toned poster was apparently advertising a popular painkiller called Okal. Obviously, I knew nothing of this at the time. All I saw was the picture of a woman in great pain or grief, with a few tears trickling down her cheeks. Not knowing what the advertisement was about or what a painkiller was, I attributed her expression and her tears to some irrepressible sadness. I often saw this advertisement and, whenever I did, I felt very sorry for the woman, and in my still imperfect, but inventive, Spanish – as inventive as children's language tends to be – I would tug at my mother's sleeve and, deeply affected, say: *'Mía, la asula lloa'* (*'Mira, la azula llora'* – 'Look, the blue lady's crying'). In Spanish, the suffix *'-a'* usually indicates the feminine, but *'azul'*, unlike most adjectives, but like a few other colours, remains the same regardless of the gender of the accompanying noun. There is, therefore, no such word as *'azula'*; it doesn't and cannot exist, because *'azul'* is an invariable adjective. Children, of course, don't obey rules (because they don't know them), and they speak and make themselves understood as best they can, and my two-year-old self was committing an early grammatical transgression. Some might say that I've continued to transgress in my writing ever since (albeit consciously this time).

129

That memory combines two things: the freedom to use language as I wish and the experience of feeling compassion or pity for someone else, because what I distinctly remember is that whenever I tugged at my mother's sleeve and said over and over, '*La asula lloa*', I wanted her to do something about it, to stop the lady crying, or what I perceived as crying. At the time, there was something I still didn't know, something that has caused me more than a few headaches since: namely, that you can't intervene in representations of any sort, not in paintings, novels or films. If, in a painting, a figure is standing with his or her back to us, the figure will remain like that for ever, the face for ever invisible; if Madame Bovary dies at the end of her invented story, so it will be until the end of time for each new reader or re-reader; if, at the beginning of Hitchcock's *Vertigo*, the policeman attempting to help James Stewart plummets into the void, he will plummet eternally, every time you see the film. The only way of intervening in fictions, or in any other form of representation – the only way to stop '*la azula*' crying – is to become the author, the one who decides what happens.

Translated from the Spanish by Margaret Jull Costa (2018)

The novelist **Javier Marías** has published sixteen novels, three collections of short stories and several volumes of essays, as well as translations of various classic English texts into Spanish, notably *Tristram Shandy*.

Michael Morpurgo (1943–)

Philbeach Gardens, off the Warwick Road in west London. Probably 1948. Winter.

Walk down Philbeach Gardens, a long crescent of somewhat dour turn-of-century houses, with rather pretentious porticos, and you will come to St Cuthbert's, a high Victorian church with a narrow spire pointing like a finger up to the sky, reminding me as a child where God was. I grew up in a flat in one of these houses. I was an altar boy in the church but remember little about it. I do recall feeling proud of my surplice – it made me feel good to pull it over my head and feel its whiteness covering me – and I think I remember too the gloom of the place, and the heavy scent of incense, to me, then and now, the smell of God. I went to my first school in the adjoining church hall. We each had our individual island, made of cut-out coloured lino, that we had to sit down on, cross-legged and silent, when the teacher clapped her hands – some teacher's cunning plan for crowd control. But, sadly, any other memories of my nursery education have all but faded.

Opposite the church you will find an incongruous block

of post-war flats, squeezed in between the older houses in the crescent. The house next door to this modern block, to the right as you look at it from the street, was ours. Where the modern block now stands was a bomb site when I was little, and this was our forbidden playground. On the street side there was a high chain-link fence, with a notice on it, telling us to keep out, but we didn't. We could crawl unseen into this crumbling Narnia through a hole in the wall of our basement. Once in there we could climb the crumbling walls, build dens in the cellar, hope to find unexploded bombs, play hide-and-seek and war games, marvel at the butterflies and the birds, catch frogs and toads and slow-worms. It was our secret haven.

No child growing up in those smog-bound grey years could remain unaware for long of the war that everyone had just endured. I was too young to remember my evacuation to Northumberland to avoid the V2 bombing, and our return to London, to understand why that bomb site was there. But bit by bit the realisation of what that war had meant began to dawn on me.

There was the photo of my uncle Pieter on the mantlepiece in his RAF uniform, an uncle I had never known because he had been killed, aged twenty-one, before I was born. He's the only relative of mine who never aged, who will be for us for ever young. My mother cried sometimes when his name was mentioned. My first glimpse of grief. Then there was the old soldier, wearing his medals on his blazer, sitting on the pavement outside the cigarette shop on the corner, with his dog, his cap of pennies beside him. He had one leg.

I know I have had all these memories, but if I am honest I no longer recall them at all clearly. My first memory that is still crystal clear to me has had a profound effect on my life, on what I have written, on who I have come to be, on what I believe.

I always looked forward to Eric's visits, because I admired him, and because he seemed to like us. He dressed very smartly, his shoes shining, his trousers crisply creased. And he smiled and laughed easily – growing up, there was not much laughter in our house.

But his visits always came with a severe warning, from my mother. 'Now remember, Michael, do not stare at him. Last time Eric came, you stared at him, again. I've told you. It's rude to stare, especially at Eric. Jack will be very cross if you stare. Remember that.' Jack was my stepfather. He had an imposing presence and a deep, rasping voice, and could be frightening when he was cross. So every time Eric came I tried very hard not to stare.

On the visit I recall most clearly, we met him in the hallway, to shake hands. I looked steadfastly at his waistcoat, not up at his face. The hand I shook was strange. It felt incomplete, like no other. But I did not look at it, because I knew I would stare at that too. The sitting and talking around the fire was difficult to endure, not because it was boring. Eric was never boring. He told jokes, he played draughts with me. But all the while I had to remember never to look up at his face, because if I did, I knew I would stare. And then Jack would be cross.

I was never much good at resisting temptation. After tea and the draughts were over, and the grown-ups were sitting and smoking and talking among each other, and paying no attention to me, I gave in to my temptation, as I knew I would. I did it gradually, surreptitiously. I liked Eric's waistcoat, especially his gold watch chain which always fascinated me. My eyes followed the chain up to the lapel of his jacket, and they did not stop there. They had a will of their own now. They were looking at his white collar and stripy tie, at his neck and chin, and then at his face. There my eyes stopped, and stared, and would not move.

One side of Eric's face was like other men's faces. The other was not. One eye was deeper in its socket, and one ear was not the same as the other ear. The skin over his cheek was drawn tight and unnaturally smooth, and looked as thin as rice paper, not wrinkled like the rest of his face. The skin was discoloured too, and that whole side of his face hardly moved when he smiled. He saw me looking and smiled at me. He seemed not to mind me staring at all. So I went on looking at him, and as I did so, I was remembering the story of how Eric's face had come to be as it was, of how his hand had become incomplete.

My mother had told me the story, often, in part at least I think, to shame me into not staring at him. The story had had the opposite effect. Sitting in front of me in our sitting room was a live hero. We had three kinds of heroes when I was young: comic-book heroes, like Dan Dare; footballing heroes whose faces we knew mostly from cigarette cards; and war heroes, soldiers, sailors and especially pilots. Eric had been a pilot in the Fleet Air Arm. He used to fly on and off aircraft carriers and shoot down German planes. To me, this was a proper hero, and here he was, in the flesh, better than any comic-book hero, any footballer. Eric was the real thing.

One day, the story goes, on returning from operations to land his damaged plane on a carrier, he had crashed and been badly burnt. For months he had been in hospital in East Grinstead under a wonderful surgeon called Dr McIndoe, who had remade his face and hands. Eric was one of hundreds of patients of this remarkable man, who pioneered so much of the plastic surgery and trauma therapy we have come to expect today. His patients were known fondly as McIndoe's 'guinea pigs'.

When Eric said goodbye to me in the hallway in Philbeach Gardens that day, he looked at me and I looked at him. It was a moment I have never forgotten. I knew what war had done to houses, to my uncle Pieter on the mantlepiece, and to my mother to make her cry, to the old soldier with his dog on the street corner. Now I understood what it did to flesh. And Eric knew I understood, I was sure of it.

So I did not need, later on, to read Wilfred Owen or Siegfried Sassoon, or Edward Thomas, to know the pity and the futility of war. I knew it first from Eric's face.

[Eric Pearse is now in his nineties. I met him again not that long ago. My mother and Jack would be pleased with me. I did not stare. But I did look at him with enormous affection and respect.]

(2018)

Michael Morpurgo's many novels include *War Horse* (1982 – adapted by the National Theatre for the stage and directed by Steven Spielberg on screen), *Why the Whales Came* (1985), *Kensuke's Kingdom* (1999) and *Private Peaceful* (2003). He served as Children's Laureate from 2003 to 2005 and was knighted in 2018.

PART TWO

THE SENSE OF
A BEGINNING

Introduction

The earliest memory of English adventurer Austen Layard was of hugging a lion.

Layard was three years old and in the Jardin des Plantes, Paris. He found himself beside a lioness and her cub. Little Austen 'resolutely' scooped the cub 'into my arms, to the astonishment and alarm of my nurse'. His brother Frederic, 'terrified at the sight of the animal, set up a lusty howl'.* The lioness, presumably, was no less affronted. Layard was – from the outset – a person who seized whatever he desired.

By the age of twenty-eight, he had accrued various accomplishments befitting a gentleman of empire. Having grown up in France (the family moving from Britain on account of the chronic asthma his father had contracted in Ceylon) and then Florence, Layard had been steeped in art history from a tender age; he later lived among the desert tribes of Mesopotamia; he was a formidable horseman; he spoke multiple languages fluently; renowned for his diplomatic wiles and a world expert in ancient Persian and Ottoman inscriptions, he had fast risen in the ranks of the embassy in Constantinople.

* Sir A. Henry Layard G.C.B., D.C.L.: Autobiography and Letters from his Childhood until his appointment as H.M. Ambassador at Madrid, chapter 1: 'Family History and Childhood'.

So when Layard got wind that the Reverend Percy Badger, no less, had found a slab covered in cuneiform inscription* among the mounds of Nimrud, he not only spied an opportunity to put these various skills to use but also another 'lion cub' for the taking.

Layard set about campaigning with his boss – the ambassador, Sir Stratford Canning – to permit him to lead a dig. Layard had envied the French consul general Paul Botta's recent discovery of an Assyrian palace city, in 1843. He was now determined to be the first to uncover whatever other antiquities lay buried beneath the desert dust. Layard was sure that Botta's findings represented at minimum a tenth of the site's potential treasures. He was convinced that the relics hidden there would ultimately rival the Elgin Marbles. They might even include the remains of the lost city of Nineveh, the ancient Neo-Assyrian capital where East once met West. He smelt glory and renown. His name would live on. Layard presented a compelling case to Canning. He promised that the expedition would 'obtain the largest possible number of well-preserved objects of art at the least possible outlay of time and money'.

On 8 November 1845, he set off for Nineveh. Laden with guns, spears, shovels and greyhounds, Layard's raft floated down the Tigris for over seven hours – until it reached the riverbank directly opposite Nimrud (in today's geography, he had arrived on the outskirts of Mosul in Iraq). There Layard stopped for the night, taking shelter among the

* One of the earliest forms of writing, 'cuneiform' is Sumerian script – wedge-shaped marks made with a reed on wax tablets.

Jehesh tribe. He bedded down inside a hovel but couldn't sleep for excitement. His bed overlooked the distant mounds across the water. Soon his mind was awash with 'visions of palaces underground, of gigantic monsters, of sculptured figures, and endless inscriptions'.

Layard commenced his excavation early the next morning with a band of locals, digging into one of the mounds. They immediately uncovered a chamber of marble. Once part of the ancient North-West Palace (as it transpired), the room was covered – floor to wall – in finely wrought inscriptions. After levering himself down into the room, Layard was overjoyed to find also, in its corner, a scattering of beautiful ivory figurines. His collection was underway.

For the next two years, Layard dwelt among the ruins. Every day something else of importance would pitch up. He documented the discoveries, painstakingly drawing every object's dimensions and transcribing endless cuneiform inscriptions. Soon he was struggling to keep pace with the findings, even with hundreds of local men now working to his commands. Often another priceless, beautiful artefact would be raised up too fast into the light – at which point, it would disintegrate before Layard's eyes, filling them with tears.

By the time of his departure in the summer of 1847, Layard had completed 300 drawings of the antiquities. Several hundred tons of sculpture had been transported home to England. Nineveh had not only been discovered but thoroughly plundered. Layard had laid claim to the remains of eight Assyrian palaces, not to mention the Library of Ashurbanipal with its 22,000 cuneiform tablets.

Among them were seven 2,700-year-old clay tablets. Inscribed in Babylonian script atop them was the *Enûma Eliš* (which translates as 'When on high'). Its epic text describes how humankind was created. The story dates from the Bronze Age (approximately the eighteenth to sixteenth centuries BC). As such, it is widely regarded as the most ancient creation myth on record. It is thought that the tract would have been recited at the Akitu festival, which was the Babylonian harvest festival. This ritual would have taken place in spring, the season of fresh starts (hence its buoyant name in English and, in Greek, Άνοιξη, meaning 'opening'). The text begins by declaring its world as a time before the sky or earth even had a name. The Babylonians had carved, with the most delicate striations in wet clay, a narrative for the ages.

Even origin stories must have their beginnings.

I have often said, when working in genre filmmaking, that nobody can entirely reinvent the wheel but they can certainly try to give it a new spin. Today's cinemas are dominated by superhero movies. This past decade, Marvel Studios has most notably been in the vanguard of these 'tentpole' box-office hits. Conceptually, the superhero genre (and the comic-book tradition from which it sprang) is founded upon a timeless narrative construct: 'the origin story'. A Hollywood staple, the demand for this formula – colourful creation myths – has in recent years allowed for countless 'reboots' of familiar characters, giving rise to franchise upon franchise, and titles such as *Batman Begins* and *Avengers Assemble*.

George, my son, developed an interest in superheroes later than some other kids (perhaps because he had been waylaid – from the moment of his first kick – by an obsession with all things football). When, aged eight, he did discover an interest in superhero movies, I decided to encourage the new pursuit and offered to treat him to a few of the best recent examples, so that he might start to build a collection. However, George was very picky about which films he would watch: he only wanted to see the *first* in each series. This was not down to any worries about entering a franchise's narrative mid-stream, although such a concern would have been entirely valid, but more because he was intent on observing how each character *became* that superhero in the first place.

No wonder that Hollywood continues to recast the origin story anew for wave after wave of audiences! George was manifesting a quasi-primal desire to watch the beginnings of things, I observed. Or was there more afoot? Was this in fact about George growing up and seeking out role-model archetypes for this maturation, as one eminent psychologist proposed? Or was it born out of the dwindling of my role, as he reached towards maturity: *my father, the fading hero*?! Neither, I think, of the above. His superego was not yet in full flight, nor were adolescence and puberty quite in sight. If anything bigger was afoot, it was that George just enjoyed the comic-book gloss on that touchstone of 'where did we come from?' (as opposed to the analyst's implied 'where am I going?'). If anything, *this* is the underlying question he sought to answer via a spider's bite or planetary explosion.

This age-old quandary informs our thinking in so many areas, often – as with my son – without us realising. Whether you think we sprang *ex nihilo* from chaos, sloped ashore from Darwin's prebiotic 'warm little pond' or fire-worked out of matter and energy; if you look towards burning bushes or serpents in trees; abide by the Qur'an, Torah or the Bible – you too will have pondered the primordial teaser of where we sprang from.

Around this time, I bought for our family a beautiful book called *The Origin of (almost) Everything*. The compendium, published by the *New Scientist*, is introduced by Professor Stephen Hawking, in whose own first memory we have already shared. Hawking explained that we are 'the product of primordial quantum fluctuations'. Yet as with the *Enûma Eliš*, origin stories demand creation myths – just as we demand to know where we came from (in the same way we grope for answers as to where we will all end up going).

The most compelling explanation of our lifetimes remains that an infinitesimal eruption of matter from energy occurred some 13.7 billion years ago and, suddenly, out of nothing, emerged everything.

It would be wrong to suggest that the Big Bang theory itself exploded eureka-like from a single brain. Scientists built on each other's work to reach cosmic conclusions. Yet Albert Einstein's theories of relativity continue to prevail as one of the greatest achievements of the human mind and certainly transformed our conception of space and time. In a broader sense, it would be fair to trace the foundations for Einstein's mindset – and hence his discoveries – all the way back to the realisation he made as a child (don't take my word for it – take his, later in this section). It left a 'deep and lasting impression' upon him. As little Albert held a compass for the first time, aged four or five, he understood that 'something deeply hidden had to be behind things'.

Like Einstein, in our different ways, we all thirst for answers. So much so that sometimes along the way we forget some of the questions. Today the Big Bang theory is itself being exploded. As theoretical science probes at the event horizon – exploring *superstring*, *quantum triangles* and such – the same questions linger. Could a moment of pure 'singularity' really occur? How could there be effect without any cause? In other, simpler words: how *on earth* could time have commenced in this way?

Questioning what occurred *before* time existed is itself just another temporal construct and, as such, surely a doomed enterprise. The composer and author Constant Lambert had it about right when he prissily proclaimed time to be 'rather vulgarly dramatic; it is the sentimentalist of the dimensions'. Constant by name, constant by nature.

Barack Obama's favourite book as a child was a similar collection of origin stories. His mother had given him the volume, but it was Obama's father, an absent Kenyan, whose own story grew entwined with those related within the well-thumbed pages. To the child's mind, his dad's origins were as exotic and alluring as the wonders described in the book. Soon the boy had come to conflate the sense of his own origination with the tree of life and Promethean fire. His father's physiognomy, as captured in crumbly family albums that smelt of mothballs — eyes behind thick glasses that gazed across time into young Barack's own — took on a magical light. It seems that this narrative — the child's paternity — soon overpowered those other creation myths. The aching absence of his dad, whose own African fatherland was a world away and who even shared the boy's name, informed the future president's reading not only of the volume but also of himself. The background of his parentage, as recounted by his mother, 'swaddled' Obama. It rooted him, he would later recall, 'in the center of a vast and orderly universe'.* Five-year-old Barack bought into the book's origin stories wholesale — not questioning logic or physics, let alone religious dogma. He didn't once query, for instance, how the tortoise of Hindu lore could support the weight of the entire world on its shell. These 'distant mysteries' were as one, 'each story self-contained and as true as the next'. They left young Barack 'contented . . . to be carried off into peaceful dreams'. Unquestionably, though, the most transcendent of these creation myths remained that of his own genesis.

Forty-five or so years later, midway through his tenure as president of the United States, Obama's origin story was bastardised in the mainstream media. His ultimate successor in

* As recounted in his memoir, *Dreams from My Father* (1995).

the White House wheezed onto this bandwagon, challenging the veracity of Obama's Hawaiian birthplace. In a series of contentious tweets and 'birther' statements, Donald Trump manipulated the underlying racial and religious fault lines in his country's consciousness, tapping into the most fundamental insecurities within the American nation-state's sense of its own beginnings. This viral conspiracist routine captured the imaginations of many US citizens. Such is the power of a creation myth.

Like Obama, another totemic world leader, Nelson Mandela, also put great stock in the mythos of a father he never knew; or, rather, *a version of* the dad he never knew. Mandela wrote in his memoir of 'the abiding connection to the Thembu royal house' that his father bestowed upon him at birth, along with a birth name (Rolihlahla) that means 'troublemaker'. Mandela's father, Gadla Henry Mphakanyiswa, was a chief 'by both blood and custom'. According to his son, Gadla was a kingmaker. He was the prime minister of the Thembuland in all but title and a historian who would pass on his knowledge with captivating oratory, despite being illiterate. He had four wives and thirteen children; each family unit had their own *kraal* (or homestead). He fulfilled his role as a chieftain-among-men in time-honoured, patrilineal and proud tradition.

Yet soon after Rolihlahla was born, his father was stripped of the chieftainship by a white magistrate. Gadla had refused to appear before the court at short notice to account for the oxen of one of his 'subjects', citing the reason that he was *Andizi ndisaqula*, or 'girding for battle'. In Mandela's own words, 'this defiance was not a fit of pique, but a matter of principle'. Gadla was deposed by the official as a consequence.

The incident became the defining moment of Nelson Mandela's childhood. It paved the first stepping stone on his own 'long walk to freedom'. The 'matter of principle' inspired him to assume his father's 'proud rebelliousness' and 'stubborn sense of fairness', all already built into the name that Gadla had bestowed upon him.

Yet Mandela was much too young to be aware of these events as they unfolded and so could not possibly have remembered them. By his own admission, the deprivation to his family of all land and herd, and with them revenue – not to mention the termination of the Mandela family chieftainship – predates his earliest memories. His father's gift for oratory and stubborn propensity for justice prevailed regardless. They lived on – to global effect – within his son. Family mythos became memory and changed the course of history.

We constantly like hearing of such beginnings but, in an emotional sense, too many of us don't scrutinise them enough for ourselves. Why ever not? We endlessly look for the finish lines, final countdowns and root for happy endings. Just consider how many of us persist in believing in some form of afterlife. Similarly, during emotional crises, individuals quest after 'closure'. Rarely, however, do we consider the flipsides. We don't even have words for them:

otherwise, logically, 'beforelife' and 'inception' would be equally familiar constructs. Emotionally, it would behove us to scrutinise these matters more.

In these pages alone, Henning Mankell movingly describes how, as the end of his life neared, a primal need to reroute to its beginning overcame him. It provided some peace. For our comings hither are just as intriguing – if not more so – than our goings thither.

It may be true that we like, however tautological, to 'begin at the beginning' and to order 'first things first' (*What's your name? Date of birth? Where are you from? How did you two meet?*) and yet I simply don't agree with Joan Didion, who said apropos of leaving New York, that 'it's easy to see the beginnings of things and harder to see the ends'.

Literary critic Frank Kermode examined this instinctive temporality of ours in 'The End', the opening chapter of his 1966 landmark study, *The Sense of an Ending*. In considering this perennial quest for delineations, Kermode wrote:

> It makes little difference – though it makes some – whether you believe the age of the world to be six thousand years or five million years, whether you think time will have a stop or that the world is eternal; there is still a need to speak humanly of a life's importance in relation to it – a need in the moment of existence to belong, to be related to a beginning and to an end.

Such is our need as humans for time, Frank (of whom I happen to have fond childhood memories) was saying.

He went on to demonstrate why we need a rectilinear, as opposed to cyclical, view of our lifetimes. By exposing the springs and cogs of how we conceive of ourselves, Frank showed in the process that even the minutiae of daily life have their little plots.

Let us take a very simple example, the ticking of a clock. We ask what it says: and we agree that it says *tick-tock*. By this fiction we humanize it, make it talk our language. Of course, it is we who provide the fictional difference between the two sounds; tick is our word for a physical beginning, tock our word for an end.

We live in the spaces that run between such lines. Time present and time past are both contained in time future: and when all are triangulated, we craft ourselves a narrative. Or, measuring this out with Frank's words again, and his elaboration upon *tick* and *tock*:

What enables them to be different is a special kind of middle. We can perceive a duration only when it is organized.

Frank's friend Edward Said, another great critic of the last century, seconded this in his subsequent study *Beginnings: Intention and Method*. Said explained how beginnings are inherently consolatory as they 'compensate us for the tumbling disorder of brute reality that will not settle down'. He expanded on this, declining the methods we instinctively call upon to fashion a sense of self-existence:

> We create sequences, periods, forms, and measurements that suit our perceptual needs. Once we have seen them, these orders are left alone: we assume that they go on ordering to time's end, and there is nothing we can do about it. These mediating orders are in their turn commanded and informed by one or another moderately intelligible force, whether we call it history, time, mind, or, as is the case today, language.

At the outset of his own book entitled *The Sense of an Ending,* an altogether different work published some forty-five years after Kermode's, Julian Barnes – who has traversed memory and time overtly in his fictions – winked at Frank. He tacitly acknowledged up front his novella's debt to its namesake, Frank's critical study. In doing so, he staked a claim upon the title. The homage is wrapped up in an allusion to Frank's tick-tock thesis. After briefly listing a series of vivid *explicit memories,* his narrator protests that he has always struggled to understand time. Not the grander theories about it – quantum mechanics and such – but the daily passage that 'clocks and watches assure us passes regularly: *tick-tock, click-clock . . .*' [my italics].

Both Frank and Barnes are reminding us that time will tell. Its passage – however artificially – fashions our storylines. Because it is only by finding ways of measuring existence, by giving it shape, that we imbue it with any sense.

In many of the extracts that follow here – as well as the brand-new pieces written specially for this book – we are invited to travel through time and enter wondrous *imaginaria*. Along the way, by proxy, we explore anew our very own arrivals.

The train of thought is always the same. It is the engine that Carl Jung fired up when inhabiting his earliest memories, traversing a shining 'unattainable land of dreams'. This realm has another name: Childhood.

Indeed, the naming of names has always provided as good a place as any with which to begin our life stories. Names serve as signifiers of who we are as much as anything else – or, as the Romans neatly posited, *'Nomen omen'*. Choosing a baby's name is a privilege for a parent. It generally works out all right. We grow into them. Jung described this osmosis as 'the grotesque coincidence between a man's name and his peculiarities'.

The translation of Saroo Brierley's original name bears this out. He had not learnt how to pronounce his first name properly before he was separated from his family. He got it wrong. Only once he was reunited with his mother decades later did Saroo learn that his name was originally 'Sheru', which translates as 'lion'. This convergence of name and identity after the event is rich with dramatic irony and was seized upon by the filmmakers as the eponymous title for Brierley's 'biopic' life story. 'Lion' handsomely captures the dogged courage Brierley showed in pursuing his long-lost home. He had only the faintest memories by way of breadcrumbs but, after scouring Google Earth and other online resources, he was able to follow that trail home.

The tale serves as a modern parable. Its mechanisms will be familiar to many. In recent years, homegrown genealogy has boomed from a hobby into big business. Yet while we clamber ever higher into family trees to figure out exactly who we think we are, squirrelling into past lives, what's ever really in a name?

Once upon a time, an ancestor of mine made one fine *den* of a *hole*. He would have been a hardened hermit. Hoary and ornery. Or perhaps even a cave dweller: a pair of lantern eyes flickering amid barnacled gloom.

My father comes from Lancashire, the wellspring of various lines of Hol-dens (I suppose our reclusive progenitor can't have been entirely hermetic his whole life, then). Getting on for fifty years ago, Dad fell down a rabbit hole, headlong into love. He swept the girl along with him and soon they were married. Her maiden name was Warren. Not much has been made within our family of this hole-in-two; yet I, for one, have always enjoyed the ticklish serendipity of its punchline.

Although, as I write this now, in a silent room in an empty house atop a steep hillside on a remote island, the anecdote takes on new resonance. My parents are outgoing and gregarious individuals and yet both have chosen to work in rooms of their own. For a long while now, they have also lived entirely alone (the marriage ending while I was a young child). Their other offspring, my siblings, are also in their different ways far from strangers to solitude.

153

Now, I don't go in for mumbo-jumbo mysticism or holistic readings of life — *and yet,* a family by any other name . . .

In such roundabout ways, a family's own etymology can inspire a mnemonist to become a memoirist. Indeed, authors will frequently begin their life stories with their names. Their task may by definition be retrospective and yet I take exception to Evelyn Waugh's outlandish assertion (in his own memoir *A Little Learning*) that 'only when one has lost all curiosity about the future has one reached the age to write an autobiography'.

The memoirist may be a nostalgist, sure, but his or her insights on the past will be myopic if there is no telescope trained on the horizon. Besides, a memoir is by necessity framed in the present moment of the writer transposing those remembrances into words. For these reasons, Waugh's incurious declaration is not so much mischievous as disingenuous. It immediately deadens his own life story. Hindsight only ever allows us to look backwards, after all, because we are moving forwards. There is a first time for everything.

The following pages celebrate this. Many of the people appearing herein as children grew up to blaze trails and break ground. For example, Sidney Poitier, who became the first African American to win the Academy Award for Best Actor in a Leading Role, in 1963 (it would take almost forty more years until another black actor, Denzel Washington, would be awarded the same accolade). In these pages, Poitier describes how — as a boy in the Caribbean watching cowboy movies — he first realised that he wanted to go to Hollywood (but only because he thought that it was where cows were corralled). That movie theatre's projector shed new light on the future for Poitier. It flickered an alternative reality, one that he went after.

Other greats of modern history or culture have also described seeing the light during their early years. Paul McCartney, for instance, has described seeing Elvis Presley for the first time as 'a spark that lit up the dark room of our adolescence'. And you can't light a fire without a spark: Bruce Springsteen – whose early memories appear here – has waxed biblical about Presley's appearance on *The Ed Sullivan Show*, identifying it as his own personal 'big bang'. It was 'a moment of light, blinding as a universe birthing a billion new suns'. Young Bruce blinked agog as one man, armed only with a guitar and gyrating hips, shook up an entire generation.

Biographers have speculated about what Elvis's own first memories might have been. His childhood was not without tragedy. Presley was, throughout his life, poignantly aware that his twin brother Jesse had not survived their birth. Pronounced stillborn some thirty-five minutes after Elvis's arrival, Jesse was buried in an unmarked grave in Priceville cemetery in their hometown of Tupelo, Mississippi. Many years later, after finding fame, Elvis would enlist various people to try to figure out exactly where in Priceville his brother had been buried. To no avail.

Nor were his early years always easy. At the age of three – just the time that long-term memories usually take root – Elvis travelled cross-country in a Greyhound bus

155

with his mother, Gladys Love. They were on their way to visit his father, Vernon. The disorientation and excitement of the journey, not to mention that they were going to see Daddy, would have been plenty to stimulate the child's amygdala and hippocampus. Upon arrival, the revelation that Vernon was actually waiting for them in the state penitentiary can only have enhanced the emotional impact of the episode.

Often, equally, it's the happier memories that stick. One specific attribute of little Elvis unsurprisingly dominates recollections of those early years: his voice. Gladys, for one, would fondly recall how of a Sunday her son – then only one – would jump down from the pew and totter into the aisle of their church to sing along with the choir, swaying in time all the while. Likewise, singing is all that remains on record from Presley himself about those first years: 'Since I was two years old all I knew was gospel music,' he recalled; and, separately, 'I remember when I was little, people would listen to me singing around the housing project where we lived.'*

Plenty of other kids have grown up singing in fine voice and not become big bangs. Elvis and Gladys were speaking with hindsight. They were endowing those earliest memories with a gloss of destiny.

Other superstar singers' first memories are less prepossessing. Leonard Cohen claimed his, for example, was peeing on a doctor aged three during a medical examination.

* For a more in-depth account of Presley's childhood and memories, see Ray Connolly's biography *Being Elvis: A Lonely Life*.

Yet even Cohen – who was far more into rebirth than reminiscence – could not resist embellishing the incident with an aura of significance. He mischievously baptised it, 'a sparkling moment because I wasn't punished for it, yet it produced a sense of alarm in the atmosphere that I found exciting'.*

For all the self-mythology on display in these pages, sometimes childhood talent really can be burnished by immaculate timing and, via some miraculous alchemy, a kid's future is made golden. This used to be called Providence.

Other iconic figures in this section also reveal, like Elvis Presley, how they found their own callings. We discover with them the disciplines in which they became, for many around the world, the greatest ever. These are *first times* that become *everything*: Astaire finds his feet; Ali throws the first punch; Pelé kicks off; Pavarotti (like The King) pipes up; Bolt sprints for home. The rest is history.

Frank Kermode explored such 'turns', or fulcra, in autobiographies in an essay called 'Palaces of Memory'. Frank isolated these touchstones as 'the point of epiphany or conversion, seen as the moment when the person under description individuates or selves himself, as it were, finds the point from which all can be seen to cohere . . .'

Self-creation myths, we might call them.

Many of the extracts appearing herein are, accordingly, from the incipient pages of memoirs. The opening chapters

---

* Leonard Cohen's first memory appeared in an interview with Kristine McKenna for *LA Weekly* during May, 1988.

of life stories. Authors often bemoan the peril of the blank page. How they must turn nothing into something. When first putting pen to paper, the writer's task is to build a bridge to the reader. It is constructed with imaginings and memories. Edward Said understood the challenge when he wrote:

> Properly considered, a beginning shows us how much language, with its perpetual memories of silence, can do to summon fiction and reality to an equal space in the mind. In this space certain fiction and certain reality come together as identity.

This is the art of memoir. Memory and perspective are melded to recapture experience. When such notes are struck, a voice makes itself heard.

Nowhere is that truer than in *The Prelude* by William Wordsworth. A landmark of imaginative memory that spans fourteen books of verse, its seventeen manuscripts and various editions remain the subject of continual debate and scholarship.

The Prelude itself starts with the poet's earliest recollections. Wordsworth recalls being 'a four-years' child, a naked boy . . .' The verse unfurls as brightly as springtime sunshine, running free with a lyricism redolent of pre-conscious imaginative thought.[*]

---

[*] For an example of such 'pre-conscious imaginative thought', from 1805 edition of Book One: 'A child, I held unconscious intercourse / With the eternal Beauty, drinking in / a pure organic pleasure . . .'

For all its flow, though, the verse is nothing if not self-aware. Just as he will eventually end the poem with a religious harking back to its own beginning, Wordsworth fast makes acknowledgement in Book One of the inherent limitations of origin stories:

> Who knows the individual hour in which
> His habits were first sown even as a seed?
> Who that shall point as with a wand, and say
> 'This portion of the river of my mind
> Came from yon fountain?'*

Yet such obstacles did not prevent him from sustaining an epic voyage around his inner and outer worlds. Suffused with the sublime, his masterpiece – published posthumously – shall rightfully have the last word on beginnings and the spiritual joys to be discovered in their exploration.

> I am so loth to quit
> Those recollected hours that have the charm
> Of visionary things, and lovely forms
> And sweet sensations, that throw back our life
> And almost make our infancy itself
> A visible scene on which the sun is shining . . .†

---

* From the 1799 edition of *The Prelude*.
† From Book One of the 1805 edition.

Booker T. Washington (1856–1915)

From the time that I can remember anything, almost every day of my life has been occupied in some kind of labour; though I think I would now be a more useful man if I had had time for sports. During the period that I spent in slavery I was not large enough to be of much service, still I was occupied most of the time in cleaning the yards, carrying water to the men in the fields, or going to the mill, to which I used to take the corn, once a week, to be ground. The mill was about three miles from the plantation. This work I always dreaded. The heavy bag of corn would be thrown across the back of the horse, and the corn divided about evenly on each side; but in some way, almost without exception, on these trips, the corn would so shift as to become unbalanced and would fall off the horse, and often I would fall with it. As I was not strong enough to reload the corn upon the horse, I would have to wait, sometimes for many hours, till a chance passer-by came along who would help me out of my trouble. The hours while waiting for someone were usually spent in crying. The time consumed in this way made me late in reaching the mill, and by the time I got my corn ground and reached home it would be far into the night. The road was a lonely one, and often led through dense forests. I was always frightened. The woods were said to be full of soldiers who had deserted from the army, and I had been told that the first thing a deserter did to a Negro boy when he found him alone was to cut off his ears. Besides, when I was late in getting home I knew I would always get a severe scolding or flogging.

I had no schooling whatever while I was a slave, though I remember on several occasions I went as far as the school-house door with one of my young mistresses to carry her books. The picture of several dozen boys and girls in a schoolroom engaged in study made a deep impression upon me, and I had the feeling that to get into a schoolhouse and study in this way would be about the same as getting into paradise . . .

[After the coming of freedom], the question of having some kind of a school opened for the coloured children in the village began to be discussed by members of the race. As it would be the first school for Negro children that had ever opened in that part of Virginia, it was, of course, to be a great event, and the discussion excited the widest interest . . .

When, however, I found myself at the school for the first time, I also found myself confronted with two other difficulties. In the first place, I found that all of the other children wore hats or caps on their heads, and I had neither hat nor cap. In fact, I do not remember that up to the time of going to school I had ever worn any kind of covering upon my head, nor do I recall that either I or anybody else had even thought anything about the need of covering for my head. But, of course, when I saw how all the other boys were dressed, I began to feel quite uncomfortable. As usual, I put the case before my mother, and she explained to me that she had no money with which to buy a 'store hat,' which was a rather new institution at that time among the members of my race and was considered quite the thing for young and old to own, but that she would find a way to help me out of the difficulty. She accordingly got two pieces of 'homespun' (jeans) and sewed them together, and I was soon the proud possessor of my first cap.

The lesson that my mother taught me in this has always remained with me, and I have tried as best I could to teach it to others. I have always felt proud, whenever I think of the incident, that my mother had strength of character enough not to be led into the temptation of seeming to be that which she was not – of trying to impress my school-mates and others with the fact that she was able to buy me a 'store hat' when she was not. I have always felt proud that she refused to go into debt for that which she did not have money to pay for. Since that time I have owned many kinds of caps and hats, but never one of which I have felt so proud as of the cap made of the two pieces of cloth sewed together by my mother. I have noted the fact, but without satisfaction, I need not add, that several of the boys who began their careers with 'store hats' and who were my schoolmates and used to join in the sport that was made of me because I had only a 'homespun' cap, have ended their careers in the penitentiary, while others are not able now to buy any kind of hat.

My second difficulty was with regard to my name, or rather *a* name. From the time when I could remember anything, I had been called simply 'Booker.' Before going to school it had never occurred to me that it was needful or appropriate to have an additional name. When I heard the school-roll called, I noticed that all of the children had at least two names, and some of them indulged in what seemed to me the extravagance of having three. I was in deep perplexity, because I knew the teacher would demand of me at least two names, and I had only one. By the time the occasion came for the enrolling of my name, an idea occurred to me which I thought would make me equal to the situation; and so, when the teacher asked me what my full name was, I calmly told him 'Booker Washington,' as if I had taken the name all my life; and by that name I have since been known. Later in my life I found that my mother had given me the names of 'Booker Taliaferro' soon after I was born, but in some way that part of my name seemed to disappear and for a long while was forgotten, but as soon as I found out about it I revived it, and made my full name 'Booker Taliaferro Washington.' I think there are not many men in our country who have had the privilege of naming themselves in the way I have.

More than once I have tried to picture myself in the position of a boy or man with an honoured and distinguished ancestry which I could trace back through a period of hundreds of years, and who had not only inherited a name, but fortune and a proud family homestead; and yet I have sometimes had the feeling that if I had inherited these, and had been a member of a more popular race, I should have been inclined to yield to the temptation of depending upon my ancestry and my colour to do that for me which I should do for myself. Years ago I resolved that because I had no ancestry myself I would leave a record of which my children would be proud, and which might encourage them to still higher effort.

From *Up from Slavery* (1901)

Booker T. Washington was born in Virginia, the son of an African American slave called Jane. After emancipation, she moved her family to West Virginia.

Washington would emerge as the dominant leader of the African American community for his generation. He was the author of fourteen books, an educator, advising presidents and founding the National Negro Business League. Washington's work was not without controversy but laid the foundations for future generations of civil rights leaders in America.

Emmeline Pankhurst (1858–1928)

The impressions of childhood often have more to do with character and future conduct than heredity or education. I have not personally suffered from the deprivation, the bitterness and sorrow which bring so many men and women to a realisation of social injustice. My childhood was protected by love and a comfortable home. Yet, while still a very young child, I began instinctively to feel that there was something lacking, even in my own home, some false conception of family relations, some incomplete ideal.

The vague feeling of mine began to shape itself into conviction about the time my brothers and I were sent to school. The education of the English boy, then as now, was considered a much more serious matter than the education of the English boy's sister. My parents, especially my father, discussed the question of my brothers' education as a matter of real importance. My education and that of my sister were scarcely discussed at all. Of course we went to a carefully selected girls' school, but beyond the facts that the head mistress was a gentlewoman and that all the pupils were girls of my own class, nobody seemed concerned. A girl's education at that time seemed to have for its prime object the art of 'making home attractive' – presumably to migratory male relatives. It used to puzzle me to understand why I was under such a particular obligation to make home attractive to my brothers. We were on excellent terms of friendship, but it was never suggested to them as a duty that they make home attractive to me. Why not? Nobody seemed to know.

The answer to these puzzling questions came to me unexpectedly one night when I lay in my little bed waiting for sleep to overtake me. It was a custom of my father and mother to make the round of our bedrooms every night before going themselves to bed. When they entered my room that night I was still awake, but for some reason I chose to feign slumber. My father bent over me, shielding the candle flame with his big hand. I cannot know exactly what thought was in his mind as he gazed down at me, but I heard him say, somewhat sadly, 'What a pity she wasn't born a lad.'

My first hot impulse was to sit up in bed and protest that I didn't want to be a boy, but I lay still and heard my parents' footsteps pass on toward the next child's bed. I thought about my father's remark for many days afterward, but I think I never decided that I regretted my sex. However, it was made quite clear that men considered themselves superior to women, and that women apparently acquiesced in that belief.

From *My Own Story* (1914)

After attending her first suffrage meeting at fourteen, **Emmeline Pankhurst** returned home a confirmed suffragette. She would go on to lead the suffragette movement, dying only weeks before equal voting rights were granted to women in Britain during July 1928.

Eleanor Roosevelt (1884–1962)

Very early I became conscious of the fact that there were people around me who suffered in one way or another. I was five or six when my father took me to help serve Thanksgiving dinner in one of the newsboys' clubhouses which my grandfather, Theodore Roosevelt, had started. He was also a trustee of the Children's Aid Society for many years. My father explained that many of these ragged little boys had no homes and lived in little wooden shanties in empty lots, or slept in vestibules of houses or public buildings or any place where they could be moderately warm, yet they were independent and earned their own livings.

Every Christmas I was taken by my grandmother to help dress the Christmas tree for the babies' ward in the Post-Graduate Hospital. She was particularly interested in this charity.

Auntie Grace took us to the Orthopaedic Hospital which my grandfather Roosevelt had been instrumental in helping Dr. Newton Schaefer to start and in which the family was deeply interested. There I saw innumerable little children in casts and splints. Some of them lay patiently for months in strange and curious positions. I was particularly interested

168

in them because I had a curvature myself and wore for some time a steel brace which was vastly uncomfortable and prevented my bending over.

Though he was so little with us, my father dominated all this period of my life. Subconsciously I must always have been waiting for his visits. They were irregular, and he rarely sent word before he arrived, but never was I in the house, even in my room two long flights of stairs above the entrance door, that I did not hear his voice the minute he entered the front door. Walking downstairs was far too slow. I slid down the bannisters and usually catapulted into his arms before his hat was hung up.

My father never missed an opportunity for giving us presents, so Christmas was a great day and I still remember one memorable Christmas when I had two stockings, for my grandmother had filled one and my father, who was in New York, brought one on Christmas morning.

One more sorrow came to my father the winter that my mother died. My little brother Ellie never seemed to thrive after my mother's death. Both he and the baby, Josh, got scarlet fever, and I was returned to my cousin Susie and, of course, quarantined.

The baby got well without any complications, but Ellie developed diphtheria and died. My father came to take me out occasionally, but the anxiety over the little boys was too great for him to give me a good deal of his time.

On August 14, 1894, just before I was ten years old, word came that my father had died. My aunts told me, but I simply refused to believe it, and while I wept long and went to bed still weeping I finally went to sleep and began the next day living in my dream-world as usual.

My grandmother decided that we children should not go to the funeral, and so I had no tangible thing to make death real to me. From that time on I knew in my mind that my father was dead, and yet I lived with him more closely, probably, than I had when he was alive.

From *This Is My Story* (1937)

Eleanor Roosevelt was born Anna Eleanor Roosevelt, to influential Manhattan socialite parents.

In later life, Roosevelt's human rights work championed the rights of women in the workplace, African and Asian Americans' civil rights, and those of Second World War refugees. She was the first chair of the UN Commission on Human Rights and oversaw the drafting of the Universal Declaration of Human Rights. This followed her years in the White House with husband Franklin D. Roosevelt (her father's fifth cousin). She remains the longest-serving First Lady in US history (1933–45).

Zora Neale Hurston (1891–1960)

Grown people know that they do not always know the why of things, and even if they think they know, they do not know where and how they got the proof. Hence the irritation they show when children keep on demanding to know if a thing is so and how the grown folks got the proof of it. It is so troublesome because it is disturbing to the pigeonhole way of life. It is upsetting because until the elders are pushed for an answer, they have never looked to see if it was so, nor how they came by what passes for proof to their acceptances of certain things as true. So, if telling their questioning young to run off and play does not suffice for an answer, a good slapping of the child's bottom is held to be proof positive for anything from spelling Constantinople to why the sea is salt. It was told to the old folks and that had been enough for them, or to put it in Negro idiom, nobody didn't tell 'em but they heard. So there must be something wrong with a child that questions the gods of the pigeonholes.

I was always asking and making myself a crow in a pigeon's nest. It was hard on my family and surroundings, and they in turn were hard on me. I did not know then, as I know now, that people are prone to build a statue of the kind of person that it pleases them to be. And few people want to be forced to ask themselves, 'What if there is no more like my statue?' The thing to do is to grab the broom of anger and drive off the beast of fear.

I was full of curiosity like many other children, and like them I was as unconscious of the sanctity of statuary as a flock of pigeons around a palace. I got few answers from other people, but I kept right on asking, because I couldn't do anything else with my feelings.

Naturally, I felt like other children in that death, destruction and other agonies were never meant to touch me. Things like that happened to other people, and no wonder. They were not like me and mine. Naturally, the world and the firmaments careened to one side a little so as not to inconvenience me. In fact, the universe went further than that – it was happy to break a few rules just to show me preferences.

For instance, for a long time I gloated over the happy secret that when I played outdoors in the moonlight the moon followed me, whichever way I ran. The moon was so happy when I came out to play, that it ran shining and shouting after me like a pretty puppy dog. The other children didn't count.

But, I was rudely shaken out of this when I confided my happy secret to Carrie Roberts, my chum. It was cruel. She not only scorned my claim, she said that the moon was paying me no mind at all. The moon, my own happy private-playing moon, was out in its play yard to race and play with her.

We disputed the matter with hot jealousy, and nothing would do but we must run a race to prove which one the moon was loving. First, we both ran a race side by side, but that proved nothing because we both contended that the moon was going that way on account of us. I just knew that the moon was there to be with me, but Carrie kept on saying that it was herself that the moon preferred. So then it came to me that we ought to run in opposite directions so that Carrie could come to her senses and realize the moon was mine. So we both stood with our backs to our gate, counted three and tore out in opposite directions.

'Look! Look, Carrie!' I cried exultantly. 'You see the moon is following me!'

'Aw, youse a tale-teller! You know it's chasing me.'

So Carrie and I parted company, mad as we could be with each other. When the other children found out what the quarrel was about, they laughed it off. They told me the moon always followed them. The unfaithfulness of the moon hurt me deeply. My moon followed Carrie Roberts. My moon followed Matilda Clarke and Julia Moseley, and Oscar and Teedy Miller. But after a while, I ceased to ache over the moon's many loves. I found comfort in the fact that though I was not the moon's exclusive friend, I was still among those who showed the moon which way to go. That was my earliest conscious hint that the world didn't tilt under my footfalls, nor careen over one-sided just to make me glad.

But no matter whether my probings made me happier or sadder, I kept on probing to know. For instance, I had a stifled longing. I used to climb to the top of one of the huge chinaberry trees which guarded our front gate, and look out over the world. The most interesting thing that I saw was the horizon. Every way I turned, it was there, and the same distance away. Our house then was in the center of the world. It grew upon me that I ought to walk out to the horizon and see what the end of the world was like. The daring of the thing held me back a while but the thing became so urgent that I showed it to my friend, Carrie Roberts, and asked her to go with me. She agreed. We sat up in the trees and disputed about what the end of the world would be like when we got there – whether it was sort of tucked under like the hem of a dress, or just was a sharp drop off into nothingness. So we planned to slip off from our folks bright and soon next morning and go see.

I could hardly sleep that night from the excitement of the thing. I had been yearning for so many months to find out about the end of things. I had no doubts about the beginnings. They were somewhere in the five acres that was home to me. Most likely in Mama's room. Now, I was going to see the end, and then I would be satisfied.

As soon as breakfast was over, I sneaked off to the meeting place in the scrub palmettoes, a short way from our house and waited. Carrie didn't come right away. I was on my way to her house by a round-about way when I met her. She was coming to tell me that she couldn't go. It looked so far that maybe we wouldn't get back by sundown, and then we would both get a whipping. When we got big enough to wear long dresses, we could go and stay as long as we wanted to. Nobody couldn't whip us then. No matter how hard I begged, she wouldn't go. The thing was too bold and brazen to her thinking. We had a fight, then. I had to hit Carrie to keep my heart from stifling me. Then I was sorry I had struck my friend, and went on home and hid under the house with my heartbreak. But I did not give up the idea of my journey. I was merely lonesome for someone brave enough to undertake it with me. I wanted it to be Carrie. She was a lot of fun, and always did what I told her. Well, most of the time, she did. This time it was too much for even her loyalty to surmount. She even tried to talk me out of my trip. I couldn't give up. It meant too much to me. I decided to put it off until I had something to ride on, then I could go by myself.

So for weeks I saw myself sitting astride of a fine horse. My shoes had sky-blue bottoms to them, and I was riding off to look at the belly-band of the world.

It was summer time, and the mockingbirds sang all night long in the orange trees. Alligators trumpeted from their stronghold in Lake Belle. So fall passed and then it was Christmas time.

Papa did something different a few days before Christmas. He sort of shoved back from the table after dinner and asked us all what we wanted Santa Claus to bring us. My big brothers wanted a baseball outfit. Ben and Joel wanted air rifles. My sister wanted patent leather pumps and a belt. Then it was my turn. Suddenly a beautiful vision came before me. Two things could work together. My Christmas present could take me to the end of the world.

'I want a fine black riding horse with white leather saddle and bridles,' I told Papa happily.

'You, what?' Papa gasped. 'What was dat you said?'

'I said, I want a black saddle horse with . . .'

'A saddle horse!' Papa exploded. 'It's a sin and a shame! Lemme tell you something right now, my young lady; you aint' white.* Riding horse! Always trying to wear de big hat! I don't know how you got in this family nohow. You ain't like none of de rest of my young 'uns.'

'If I can't have no riding horse, I don't want nothing at all,' I said stubbornly with my mouth, but inside I was sucking sorrow. My longed-for journey looked impossible.

'I'll riding-horse you, Madam!' Papa shouted and jumped to his feet. But being down at the end of the table big enough for all ten members of the family together, I was near the kitchen door, and I beat Papa to it by a safe margin. He chased me as far as the side gate and turned back. So I did not get my horse to ride off to the edge of the world. I got a doll for Christmas.

Since Papa would not buy me a saddle horse, I made me one up. No one around me knew how often I rode my prancing horse, nor the things I saw in far places. Jake, my puppy, always went along and we made great admiration together over the things we saw and ate. We both agreed that it was nice to be always eating things.

From *Dust Tracks on a Road* (1942)

---

* Hurston's note: 'That is a Negro saying that means: "Don't be too ambitious. You are a Negro and they are not meant to have but so much."'

Zora Neale Hurston was born in Florida, one of eight children. Her father was a Baptist preacher. She worked as a maid before studying literature and anthropology at Howard, Barnard and Columbia universities. Hurston then played a key role in the Harlem renaissance of the 1920s and 1930s, writing novels such as *Their Eyes Were Watching God* (1937) and *Moses: Man of the Mountain* (1939). In later years, however, she dropped away from the literary scene and worked again as a domestic servant, before dying in poverty back in Florida.

Woody Guthrie (1912–1967)

Ours was just another one of those little towns, I guess, about a thousand or so people, where everybody knows everybody else; and on your way to the post office, you'd nod and speak to so many friends that your neck would be rubbed raw when you went to get your mail if there was any. It took you just about an hour to get up through town, say hello, talk over the late news, family gossip, sickness, weather, crops and lousy politics. Everybody had something to say about something, or somebody, and you usually knew almost word for word what it was going to be about before you heard them say it, as we had well-known and highly expert talkers on all subjects in and out of this world.

Old Windy Tom usually shot off at his mouth about the weather. He not only could tell you the exact break in the exact cloud, but just when and where it would rain, blow, sleet or snow; and for yesterday, today, and tomorrow, by recalling to your mind the very least and finest details of the weather for these very days last year, two years, or forty years ago. When Windy Tom got to blowing it covered more square blocks than any one single cyclone. But he was our most hard-working weather man – Okemah's Prophet – and we would of fought to back him up.

I was what you'd call just a home-town kid and carved my initials on most everything that would stand still and let me. W. G. Okemah Boy. Born 1912. That was the year, I think, when Woodrow Wilson was named to be the president and my papa and mama got all worked up about good and bad politics and named me Woodrow Wilson too. I don't remember this any too clear.

I wasn't much more than two years old when we built our seven-room house over in the good part of Okemah. This was our new house, and Mama was awful glad and proud of it. I remember a bright yellow outside – a blurred haze of a dark inside – some vines looking in through windows.

Sometimes, I seem to remember trying to follow my big sister off to school. I'd gather up all of the loose books I could find around the house and start out through the gate and down the sidewalk, going to get myself a schoolhouse education, but Mama would run out and catch me and drag me back in the house kicking and bawling. When Mama would hide the books I'd walk back to the front porch for my stage, and the grass, flowers, and pickets along our fence would be my crowd of people; and I made up my first song right there:

> Listen to the music,
> Music, music;
> Listen to the music,
> Music band.

From *Bound for Glory* (1943)

Woody Guthrie was born in Oklahoma and left home as a teenager, to make his way by odd jobs and singing. He recorded his influential *Dust Bowl Ballads* in New York during the 1930s. Always prolific – and famed for his guitar's slogan, 'This machine kills fascists' – Guthrie's best-known song remains 'This Land Is Your Land'.

Albert Einstein (1879–1955)

However brief and limited one's working life may be, and however predominant may be the ways of error, the exposition of that which is worthy of communication does nonetheless not come easy – today's person of 67 is by no means the same as was the one of 50, of 30, or of 20. Every reminiscence is colored by today's being what it is, and therefore by a deceptive point of view. This consideration could very well deter. Nevertheless much can be lifted out of one's own experience which is not open to another consciousness . . .

For me it is not dubious that our thinking goes on for the most part without use of signs (words) and beyond that to a considerable degree unconsciously. For how, otherwise, should it happen that sometimes we 'wonder' quite spontaneously about some experience? This 'wondering' seems to occur when an experience comes into conflict with a world of concepts which is already sufficiently fixed in us. Whenever such a conflict is experienced hard and intensively it reacts back upon our thought world in a decisive way. The development of this thought world is in a certain sense a continuous flight from 'wonder'.

181

A wonder of such nature I experienced as a child of 4 or 5 years, when my father showed me a compass. That this needle behaved in such a determined way did not at all fit into the nature of events, which could find a place in the unconscious world of concepts (effect connected with direct 'touch'). I can still remember – or at least believe I can remember – that this experience made a deep and lasting impression upon me. Something deeply hidden had to be behind things.

From *Autobiographical Notes* (1949)

Albert Einstein is generally considered to be the most influential physicist of the twentieth century, particularly due to his theory of relativity. He won the Nobel Prize in Physics in 1921 for his explanation of the photoelectric effect.

C. S. Lewis (1898–1963)

. . . This absence of beauty, now that I come to think of it, is characteristic of our childhood. No picture on the walls of my father's house ever attracted – and indeed none deserved – our attention. We never saw a beautiful building nor imagined that a building could be beautiful. My earliest aesthetic experiences, if indeed they were aesthetic, were not of that kind; they were already incurably romantic, not formal. Once in those very early days my brother brought into the nursery the lid of a biscuit tin which he had covered with moss and garnished with twigs and flowers so as to make it a toy garden or a toy forest. That was the first beauty I ever knew. What the real garden had failed to do, the toy garden did. It made me aware of nature – not, indeed, as a storehouse of forms and colours but as something cool, dewy, fresh, exuberant. I do not think the impression was very important at the moment, but it soon became important in memory. As long as I live my imagination of Paradise will retain something of my brother's toy garden. And every day there were what we called 'the Green Hills'; that is, the low line of the Castlereagh Hills which we saw from the nursery windows. They were not very far off but they were, to children, quite unattainable. They taught me longing — *Sehnsucht*; made me for good or ill, and before I was six years old, a votary of the Blue Flower . . .

It will be clear that at this time — at the age of six, seven, and eight — I was living almost entirely in my imagination; or at least that the imaginative experience of those years now seems to me more important than anything else. Thus I pass over a holiday in Normandy (of which, nevertheless, I retain very clear memories) as a thing of no account; if it could be cut out of my past I should still be almost exactly the man I am. But imagination is a vague word and I must make some distinctions. It may mean the world of reverie, day-dream, wish-fulfilling fantasy. Of that I knew more than enough. I often pictured myself cutting a fine figure. But I must insist that this was a totally different activity from the invention of Animal-Land. Animal-Land was not (in that sense) a fantasy at all. I was not one of the characters it contained. I was its creator, not a candidate for admission to it. Invention is essentially different from reverie; if some fail to recognise the difference that is because they have not themselves experienced both. Anyone who has will understand me. In my day-dreams I was training myself to be a fool; in mapping and chronicling Animal-Land I was training myself to be a novelist. Note well, a novelist; not a poet. My invented world was full (for me) of interest, bustle, humour, and character; but there was no poetry, even no romance, in it. It was astonishingly prosaic. Thus if we use the word imagination in a third sense, and the highest sense of all, this invented world was not imaginative. But certain other experiences were, and I will now try to record them. The thing has been much better done by Traherne and Wordsworth, but every man must tell his own tale.

The first is itself the memory of a memory. As I stood beside a flowering currant bush on a summer day there suddenly arose in me without warning, and as if from a depth not of years but of centuries, the memory of that earlier morning at the Old House when my brother had brought his toy garden into the nursery. It is difficult to find words strong enough for the sensation which came over me; Milton's 'enormous bliss' of Eden (giving the full, ancient meaning to 'enormous') come somewhere near it. It was a sensation, of course, of desire; but desire for what? not, certainly, for a biscuit-tin filled with moss, not even (though that came into it) for my own past. *Ἰοὐλίαν ποθῶ** – and before I knew what I desired, the desire itself was gone, the whole glimpse withdrawn, the world turned commonplace again, or only stirred by a longing for the longing that had just ceased. It had taken only a moment of time; and in a certain sense everything else that had ever happened to me was insignificant in comparison . . .

[The quality described] is that of an unsatisfied desire which is itself more desirable than any other satisfaction. I call it Joy, which is here a technical term and must be sharply distinguished both from Happiness and from Pleasure. Joy

---

* Oh, I desire too much.

(in one sense) has indeed one characteristic, and one only, in common with them; the fact that anyone who has experienced it will want it again.

From *Surprised by Joy* (1955)

C. S. Lewis grew up in Belfast. A lover of animals and stories about them (especially Beatrix Potter's tales), at the age of four Lewis adopted his pet dog's name when the animal was killed by a car: for the rest of his life, he was known to friends and family as 'Jack'.

His memoir *Surprised by Joy* was published a year before he met his beloved wife Joy Davidman. Lewis would react to her death in his book *A Grief Observed* (1961), which he initially published under a pseudonym.

Today, he is best remembered for his series of fantasy novels, *The Chronicles of Narnia*.

Fred Astaire (1899–1987)

Being born in a Midwestern city has its advantages. Omaha was just right for a home town. Although it was a city, population a little over 100,000 as I remember, it had the flavour, the neighbourliness, and that small-town feeling without actually being one.

We lived in a wooden frame house on North Nineteen Street, about twenty minutes' walk to the business district and not much faster by buggy. My father used to take me to town on Sunday afternoons, riding beside him in the two-seater to visit his friends at Saks' Cigar Store. Father was in the brewery business. He was a lively man with a sense of humour and an Austrian accent. A favourite quip of his was 'There are two kinds of Austrians – musicians and rascals – I, of course, am a musician!'

Another thing I remember about Omaha is the rumbling of locomotives in the distance as engines switched freight cars in the evening when we sat on the front porch and also after I went to bed. That and the railroad whistles in the night, going someplace. I used to imagine that I was riding

187

on a train. Aside from these few impressions I have almost no memories of my earliest youth.

Of course, I played with other boys and had the usual childhood adventures. I recall, too, having scarlet fever, with a quarantine sign on the front door.

My sister played with paper dolls (she played with them for a surprisingly long time). Adele had a yen for paper dolls, somewhat the same as I had for railroads. She told me recently that she remembers trying to get me to play paper dolls with her and that I would have none of it. This I was pleased to hear.

Like most girls of her age, Adele went to dancing school. She was a little more than a year older than I and attended Chambers' Dancing Academy on West Farnum Street. I did not.

I remember the school only because at various times I went with my father or mother to deliver or pick up my sister. I saw little girls hopping, whirling, learning how to dance. Perhaps I should have been inspired by this, but the truth is I cannot remember that I had any reaction at all. Dancing was merely something that my sister did, something that all little girls did. I let it go at that and the hell with it.

They said Adele was good. She was featured in school recitals and was a local prodigy. Looking back at the family scrapbook now, I can see that she was a charmer at the age of six, but I can't say I was aware of it then.

The story goes that one time when I had gone with my mother to fetch Adele, I put on a pair of ballet slippers. I found them in a corner while I was dawdling around the place, killing time, waiting for Adele to finish her lesson. I had seen other children walk on their toes, so I put on the slippers and walked on my toes. It was as simple as that.

I don't recall that this created any particular excitement. In fact, I am not certain that I recall the incident. It may be one of those childhood tales so often told that you begin to think you remember it yourself. At any rate, it seems to be true that I walked on my toes, aged four, showing off, probably, but certainly not inspired by any ambitions to dance.

From *Steps in Time* (1959)

Fred Astaire – born Frederick Austerlitz – is widely recognised as the most influential dancer in the history of stage or screen musicals. Subsequent dancers ranging from Rudolf Nureyev to Michael Jackson openly acknowledged Astaire's influence. Dancing in public from a very young age with his sister Adele, his career would eventually span seventy-six years. He performed in more than ten Broadway and West End stage musicals and over thirty feature films.

Gavin Maxwell (1914–1969)

At the age of six or seven, I would go off quite alone with my butterfly-net and killing bottle, alone among the bog myrtle and heather under the windy summer sky and I would swipe and miss and cry because I'd missed, and I learned what it was to be alone. Having learned it, I wanted no other day-long company than my own, excepting my brother Aymer's, and this remained true for years.

For my age I suppose I knew a lot about butterflies and moths. I knew and had collected all the species that were common at Elrig, and from the picture-books in which I would get lost in reverie I knew what all the other British butterflies looked like, even to the magic Camberwell Beauty – somehow equated in my mind with my only sight of the Crown Jewels at the Tower of London, an unbelievable splendour flowering from crimson velvet. Far into my adult life I retained a curious, quite precise feeling of exhilaration and wonder at seeing for the first time in the flesh some bird or beast that before I had known only from pictures, as if one were meeting for the first time some notoriety long worshipped from afar. I can remember one of these occasions with an extraordinary subjective vividness, besides experiencing the scene as a tableau viewed from outside as though I were a spectator of some-body else's action. A little boy of about five or six, dressed in a black-and-white kilt, a grey flannel shirt, a white cotton sun-hat. He is carrying a butterfly-net and killing bottle, and he stands in a marshy hollow filled with bog myrtle and rushes. Suddenly a very large butterfly whizzes past at very high speed, but not so fast that the boy cannot recognise it as something he has never seen, but whose coloured por-traits he has pored over in illustrated butterfly books. The butterfly passes but does not disappear, it goes on racing round, always out of range of the swiping net. The boy falls to his knees – prickles of myrtle stems among the soft sphagnum moss – and starts praying aloud. 'Please God let me catch the Dark Green Fritillary.' And God answered my prayer, strengthening an absolute belief that could not be called into question.

I can see them all in their glory; the splendid burnish on the wings of a Small Copper as he fans them gently, poised on the round blue cushion of a scabious flower; the satin sheen, so delicately bordered with seed pearls, of a Common Blue, or folded upward to show the wings' underside, the pearls arranged as an even layer on a surface of white kid; the peach and pale velvet of a Painted Lady; the aggressive tiger colouring of the Tortoise-shells on the sun-cracked sills of the long attic; the hard, burning shimmer of the little hunting wasps, each as bright as a cut jewel. I saw them all in their glory with the undimmed and finely focused eye of a six-year-old, and though their descendants are resplendent still they can never be quite so bright as those seeming heralds of the millennium.

From *The House of Elrig* (1965)

Gavin Maxwell, a naturalist and writer, was brought up in the small village of Elrig, in south-west Scotland. His most celebrated book remains *Ring of Bright Water* (1960), in which he described how he brought a smooth-coated otter back to Scotland from Iraq. This sub-species of otter had not been previously identified by the London Zoological Society, upon closer inspection. As a result, it is today still known as 'Maxwell's Otter'.

Martin Luther King, Jr (1929–1968)

It is quite easy for me to lean more toward optimism than pessimism about human nature mainly because of my childhood experiences.

In my own life and in the life of a person who is seeking to be strong, you combine in your character antitheses strongly marked. You are both militant and moderate; you are both idealistic and realistic. And I think that my strong determination for justice comes from the very strong, dynamic personality of my father, and I would hope that the gentle aspect comes from a mother who is very gentle and sweet.

Two incidents happened in my late childhood and early adolescence that had a tremendous effect on my development. The first was the death of my grandmother. She was very dear to each of us, but especially to me. I sometimes think I was her favourite grandchild. I was particularly hurt by her death mainly because of the extreme love I had for her. She assisted greatly in raising all of us. It was after this incident that for the first time I talked at any length on the doctrine of immortality. My parents attempted to explain it to me, and I was assured that somehow my grandmother still lived.

I guess this is why today I am such a strong believer in personal immortality.

The second incident happened when I was about six years of age. From the age of three I had a white playmate who was about my age. We always felt free to play our childhood games together. He did not live in our community, but he was usually around every day; his father owned a store across the street from our home. At the age of six we both entered school – separate schools, of course. I remember how our friendship began to break as soon as we entered school; this was not my desire but his. The climax came when he told me one day that his father had demanded that he would play with me no more. I never will forget what a great shock this was to me. I immediately asked my parents about the motive behind such a statement.

We were at the dinner table when the situation was discussed, and here for the first time I was made aware of the existence of a race problem. I had never been conscious of it before. As my parents discussed some of the tragedies that had resulted from this problem and some of the insults they themselves had confronted on account of it, I was greatly shocked, and from that moment on I was determined to hate every white person. As I grew older and older this feeling continued to grow.

My parents would always tell me that I should not hate the white man, but that it was my duty as a Christian to love him. The question arose in my mind: How could I love a race of people who hated me and who had been responsible for breaking me up with one of my best childhood friends? This was a great question in my mind for a number of years.

I always had a resentment toward the system of segregation and felt that it was a grave injustice. I remember a trip to a downtown shoe store with Father when I was still small. We had sat down in the first empty seats at the front of the store. A young white clerk came up and murmured politely:

'I'll be happy to wait on you if you'll just move to those seats in the rear.'

Dad immediately retorted, 'There's nothing wrong with these seats. We're quite comfortable here.'

'Sorry,' said the clerk, 'but you'll have to move.'

'We'll either buy shoes sitting here,' my father retorted, 'or we won't buy shoes at all.'

Whereupon he took me by the hand and walked out of the store. This was the first time I had seen Dad so furious. That experience revealed to me at a very early age that my father had not adjusted to the system, and he played a great part in shaping my conscience. I still remember walking down the street beside him as he muttered, 'I don't care how long I have to live with this system, I will never accept it.'

And he never has. I remember riding with him another day when he accidentally drove past a stop sign. A policeman pulled up to the car and said:

'All right, boy, pull over and let me see your license.'

My father instantly retorted: 'Let me make it clear to you that you aren't talking to a boy. If you persist in referring to me as boy, I will be forced to act as if I don't hear a word you are saying.'

The policeman was so shocked in hearing a Negro talk to him so forthrightly that he didn't quite know how to respond. He nervously wrote the ticket and left the scene as quickly as possible.

There was a pretty strict system of segregation in Atlanta. For a long, long time I could not go swimming, until there was a Negro YMCA. A Negro child in Atlanta could not go to any public park. I could not go to the so-called white schools. In many of the stores downtown, I couldn't go to a lunch counter to buy a hamburger or a cup of coffee. I could not attend any of the theaters. There were one or two Negro theaters, but they didn't get any of the main pictures. If they did get them, they got them two or three years later.

When I was about eight years old, I was in one of the downtown stores of Atlanta and all of a sudden someone slapped me, and the only thing I heard was somebody saying, 'You are that nigger that stepped on my foot.' And it turned out to be a white lady. Of course I didn't retaliate at any point; I wouldn't dare retaliate when a white person was involved. I think some of it was part of my native structure – that is, that I have never been one to hit back. I finally told my mother what had happened, and she was very upset about it. But the lady who slapped me had gone, and my mother and I left the store almost immediately.

I remember another experience I used to have in Atlanta. I went to high school on the other side of town – to the

Booker T. Washington High School. I had to get the bus in what was known as the Fourth Ward and ride over to the West Side. In those days, rigid patterns of segregation existed on the buses, so that Negroes had to sit in the backs of buses. Whites were seated in the front, and often if whites didn't get on the buses, those seats were still reserved for whites only, so Negroes had to stand over empty seats. I would end up having to go to the back of the bus with my body, but every time I got on that bus I left my mind up on the front seat. And I said to myself, 'One of these days, I'm going to put my body up there where my mind is.'

From *The Autobiography of Martin Luther King, Jr*, edited by Clayborne Carson (published posthumously in 1998, so listed here by the date of Dr King's death)

During the less than thirteen years of **Dr Martin Luther King, Jr**'s leadership of the American civil rights move-ment – from December 1955 until April 1968 – African Americans achieved more genuine progress towards racial equality in America than during the previous 350 years.

Dr King's 'I Have a Dream' speech remains one of the most revered orations in the English language. He was awarded the Nobel Peace Prize in 1964. Aged thirty-five, he was then its youngest ever recipient.

Pablo Neruda (1904–1973)

I'll start out by saying this about the days and the years of my childhood: the rain was the one unforgettable presence for me then. The great southern rain, coming down like a waterfall from the Pole, from the skies of Cape Horn to the frontier. On this frontier, my country's Wild West, I first opened my eyes to life, the land, poetry, and the rain . . .

My parents had come from Parral, where I was born. There, in central Chile, vineyards thrive and wine is plentiful. My mother, Doña Rosa Basoalto, died before I could have a memory of her, before I knew it was she my eyes gazed upon. I was born on July 12, 1904, and a month later, in August, wasted away by tuberculosis, my mother was gone.

. . . There was a picture of my mother. She was a lady dressed in black, slender, with a faraway look. I have been told that she wrote poems, but I have never seen them, only the lovely portrait.

My father had married again; his second wife was Doña Trinidad Candia Marverde, my stepmother. I find it hard to believe that this is what I must call the guardian angel of my childhood. She was devoted and loving, and had a countrywoman's sense of humour and a diligent, inexhaustible kindness.

As soon as my father came in, she would turn into a quiet shadow, as did all the women there in those days.

I saw mazurkas and quadrilles danced in that living room.

At home we had a trunk filled with fascinating things. A marvellous parrot preened on a calendar at the bottom of the chest. One day, while my mother was going through that sacred ark, I reached for the parrot and fell in, head first. As I got older, I used to open the trunk on the sly. There were some lovely fragile fans in it.

I recall something else in that trunk. The first love story that intrigued me passionately. It consisted of hundreds of postcards sent by someone who signed himself Enrique or Alberto, I don't remember which, all addressed to María Thielman. These cards were marvellous. They were photographs of the great actresses of the day, embossed with little chips of glass and sometimes with real hair pasted on the heads. There were also castles, cities, and foreign landscapes. For years I found pleasure only in the pictures. But, as I grew older, I read those love notes written in a flawless hand. I always imagined the suitor as a man with a derby, a cane, and a diamond stickpin. His messages, sent from all corners of the globe, were filled with reckless passion expressed in dazzling phrases, with love that threw caution to the winds. I, too, began to fall in love with María Thielman. I imagined her as a haughty actress diademed, covered with pearls. But how did these letters come to be in my mother's trunk? I never found out . . .

I have often been asked when I wrote my first poem, when poetry was born in me.

I'll try to remember. Once, far back in my childhood, when I had barely learned to read, I felt an intense emotion and set down a few words, half rhymed but strange to me, different from everyday language. Overcome by a deep anxiety, something I had not experienced before, a kind of anguish and sadness, I wrote them neatly on a piece of paper. It was a poem to my mother, that is, to the one I knew, the angelic stepmother whose gentle shadow watched over my childhood. I had no way at all of judging my first composition, which I took to my parents. They were in the dining room, immersed in one of those hushed conversations that, more than a river, separate the world of children and the world of grownups. Still trembling after this first visit from the muse, I held out to them the paper with the lines of verse. My father took it absentmindedly, read it absentmindedly, and returned it to me absentmindedly, saying: 'Where did you copy this from?' Then he went on talking to my mother in a lowered voice about his important and remote affairs.

That, I seem to remember, was how my first poem was born, and that was how I had my first sample of irresponsible literary criticism.

From *Memoirs* (1974), translated by Hardie St. Martin

Pablo Neruda was awarded the Nobel Prize in Literature in 1971. Gabriel García Márquez called him 'the greatest poet of the twentieth century in any language'.

Neruda served as Chilean ambassador to France, representing Salvador Allende's regime in Paris. Shortly after the coup that ousted Allende in 1973, Neruda died in circumstances that have since been acknowledged as unnatural and suspicious.

Muhammad Ali (1942–2016)

The story that my boxing career began because my bike was stolen is a true one, as far as it goes. But that was only a part of it. I was twelve years old, and me and Johnny Willis, my closest buddy, had been out riding on our bikes until the rain got too heavy. We were looking for something else to do when Johnny suddenly remembered seeing an ad for a black business exhibition at Columbia Auditorium on 4th and York. The auditorium is a big recreational center, with a boxing gym and a bowling alley. Every year the black people in the city hold a big bazaar, the Louisville Home Show, at the Columbia Gym.

At first I didn't want to go to the Home Show very much, but when we read the leaflet we saw that there would be free popcorn, free hot dogs and free candy. Besides, my father had bought me a new bike for Christmas, a Schwinn with red lights and chrome trim, a spotlight in the front, whitewall tires and chrome spokes and rims, and I wanted to show it off.

At the show we focused in on the food, and we hung around eating until seven o'clock, when everybody was leaving.

The rain was still coming down heavy as we left, so it took a while for us to notice that my bicycle was gone. Angry and frightened of what my father would do, we ran up and down the streets, asking about the bike. Someone told us to go downstairs to the Columbia Gym. 'There's a policeman, Joe Elsby Martin, down there in the recreation center. Go and see him.'

I ran downstairs, crying, but the sights and sounds and the smell of the boxing gym excited me so much that I almost forgot about the bike.

There were about ten boxers in the gym, some hitting the speed bag, some in the ring, sparring, some jumping rope. I stood there, smelling the sweat and rubbing alcohol, and a feeling of awe came over me. One slim boy shadowboxing in the ring was throwing punches almost too fast for my eyes to follow.

'You'll have to give me a report,' Martin said calmly, and wrote down what I had told him. Then, as I was about to go, he tapped me on the shoulder. 'By the way, we got boxing every night, Monday through Friday, from six to eight. Here's an application in case you want to join the gym.'

I was about 112 pounds, skinny, and I'd never had on a pair of boxing gloves. I folded up the paper and stuck it in my pocket, thinking it was a poor thing to take home instead of a bike. That night my father bawled me out for being so careless. And for once I was in total agreement with him. I told him I was sorry, and I meant it.

That Saturday I was home looking at a TV show called *Tomorrow's Champions*, an amateur boxing show, and there was the face of Joe Martin, working in the corner with one of his boys.

I nudged my mother. 'Bird, that's the man I told about the bicycle. He wants me to come and box. Where's that application?'

She had taken the paper out of my pocket when she washed my clothes, but now she went and got it. 'You want to be a boxer?' She was serious.

'I want to be a boxer,' I said.

'How you going to get down there? It's a long way off. Your bike is gone. There's no carfare for that.'

'Oh, I'll borrow someone else's bike,' I said. 'And I don't have nothin' else to do.'

I remember my father looked uncertain. Then someone outside opened the door and yelled, 'Johnny Willis's out here waiting for Cassius.'

That decided it. 'Well, boxing is better than running around with Willis and that gang,' my father said. 'Anything will beat that. Let him go.'

When I got to the gym, I was so eager I jumped into the ring with some older boxer and began throwing wild punches. In a minute my nose started bleeding. My mouth was hurt. My head was dizzy. Finally someone pulled me out of the ring.

At that moment I was thinking I would be better off in the streets, but a slim welterweight came up and put his arms around my shoulders, saying, 'You'll be all right. Just don't box these older fellows first. Box the fellows who are new like you. Get someone to teach you how to do it.'

But there was hardly anybody to teach me anything. Martin knew a little. He could show me how to place my feet and how to throw a right cross, but he knew very little else. I was fighting like a girl, throwing wild, loopy punches. But something was driving me and I kept fighting and I kept training. And although I still roamed the streets with the gang, I kept coming back to the gym.

From *The Greatest: My Own Story* (1975), written with Richard Durham

Muhammad Ali announced that he no longer wished to be known by his slave name of Cassius Clay soon after becoming heavyweight champion of the world in 1964, following his victory over Sonny Liston, a major upset. Ali would later be stripped of his title, after his arrest for refusing to fight in the Vietnam War.

He went on to be crowned champion an unprecedented three times, winning landmark bouts such as 'The Thrilla in Manila' and 'The Rumble in the Jungle'. Ali proclaimed himself 'The Greatest'. Few have disagreed with the assessment.

Luciano Pavarotti (1935–2007)

Mother likes telling people that when I was born and lying screaming beside her, the doctor said, *'Mamma mia, che acuti!'* ('What high notes!') Mothers everywhere have anecdotes to pull out when life makes the prophecies in the stories true, especially Italian mothers. Now mother says that I got the voice from my father, and from her, the heart and romance in my music.

My father's name is Fernando. He was a baker. I never thought of ourselves as rich or poor. We always had enough. We never had an automobile and we didn't have a radio until long after other people had them. My father's little motor-bike was the family transportation. I never thought about what we didn't have; I am still that way. All around me I see people making themselves unhappy by such thoughts.

I didn't think about the future either. What child does? I just lived every day as it came, the days were beautiful.

My biggest memory of my childhood is my playing all the time. No child ever played as long and hard as I did . . .

I was only about five or six when I discovered I had a voice. It was a fine alto voice but nothing sensational. Even though my voice was only average, I used to love to sing. My father had a very fine tenor voice – he still does – and thought of attempting a career himself. He decided against it, mainly because he didn't feel his nerves were strong enough for the professional life. Even today when he sings a solo for the church, he is a nervous wreck a week ahead of time.

Vocal music was the most important thing in the world to my father. He would bring home records of all the great tenors of the day – Gigli, Martinelli, Schipa, Caruso – and would play them over and over. Hearing those great voices all the time, it was inevitable that I would try to sing like that too. It was almost as though I was forced to become a tenor.

I used to go into my room and close the door and, at the top of my lungs, sing 'La donna è mobile' – in a child's voice, of course. Of the sixteen families in the building, fourteen of them would yell at me to shut up.

That's funny because when I was very small – about five – I had a toy mandolin. I would take it into the courtyard behind our building where there was a fountain. I would carry a little child's chair and set it up by the fountain and serenade all the apartments. The neighbours used to love these concerts – maybe I didn't scream so much – and would toss candies and nuts to me. Does this mean that I became a professional at five?

When I tried singing opera a few years later, they all went crazy and wanted to kill me. Not all. One man, I remember, told me I would be a singer. He knew, he said, because I had the right breathing. Everyone in Italy is an expert on singing – everyone – my barber, my father, my grandfather.

They all have opinions about how to sing, what voices sound right, which are being incorrectly produced, and on and on. One neighbour, at least, heard in my child's voice the potential of a singer.

In those early days, however, serious thoughts of singing were very far away.

From *My Own Story* (1981), written with William Wright

Luciano Pavarotti was born in Modena in northern Italy. He made his debut at the Metropolitan Opera House in New York in 1968. Pavarotti went on to become one of the greatest tenors of all time.

Alongside José Carreras and Plácido Domingo, he appeared in a series of high-profile concerts during the 1990s. Billed as the 'Three Tenors', the trio first performed on the eve of the 1990 World Cup final, held in his native Italy. Four years later, to mark the 1994 World Cup in the USA, they took to the stage again in Los Angeles. Around 1.3 billion viewers tuned in.

The Dalai Lama (1935–)

My earliest memories are very ordinary. Some people put great emphasis on a person's first recollections, but I do not. Amongst mine I remember, for example, observing a group of children fighting and running to join with the weaker side. I also remember the first time I saw a camel. These are quite common in parts of Mongolia and occasionally they were brought over the border. It looked huge and majestic and very frightening. I also recall discovering one day that I had worms – a common affliction in the East.

One thing that I remember enjoying particularly as a very young boy was going into the hen coop to collect the eggs with my mother and then staying behind. I liked to sit in the hens' nest and make clucking noises. Another favourite occupation of mine as an infant was to pack things in a bag as if I was about to go on a long journey. 'I'm going to Lhasa, I'm going to Lhasa,' I would say. This, coupled with my insistence that I be allowed to sit at the head of the table, was later said to be an indication that I must have known that I was destined for greater things. I also had a number of dreams as a small child that were open to a similar interpretation, but I cannot say categorically that I knew of my future all along. Later on, my mother told me several stories which could be taken as signs of high birth. For example, I never allowed anyone but her to handle my bowl. Nor did I ever show fear of strangers . . .

When I was not quite three years old, a search party that had been sent out by the Government to find the new incarnation of the Dalai Lama arrived at Kumbum monastery. It had been led there by a number of signs. One of these concerned the embalmed body of my predecessor, Thupten Gyatso, the Thirteenth Dalai Lama, who had died aged fifty-seven in 1933. During its period of sitting in state, the head was discovered to have turned from facing south to north-east. Shortly after that the Regent, himself a senior lama, had a vision. Looking into the waters of the sacred lake, Lhamoi Lhatso, in southern Tibet, he clearly saw the Tibetan letters *Ah*, *Ka* and *Ma* float into view. These were followed by the image of a three-storeyed monastery with a turquoise and gold roof and a path running from it to a hill. Finally, he saw a small house with strangely shaped guttering. He was so sure that the letter *Ah* referred to Amdo, the north-eastern province, so it was there that the search party was sent.

By the time they reached Kumbum, the members of the search party felt that they were on the right track. It seemed likely that if the letter *Ah* referred to Amdo, then *Ka* must indicate the monastery at Kumbum – which was indeed three-storeyed and turquoise-roofed. They now needed to locate a hill and a house with a peculiar guttering. So they began to search the neighbouring villages. When they saw the gnarled branches of juniper wood on the roof of my parents' house, they were certain that the new Dalai Lama would not be far away. Nevertheless, rather than reveal the purpose of their visit, the group asked only to stay the night. The leader of the party, Kewtsang Rinpoché, then pretended to be a servant and spent much of the evening observing and playing with the youngest child in the house.

The child recognised him and called out 'Sera lama, Sera lama'. Sera was Kewtsang Rinpoché's monastery. Next day they left – only to return a few days later as a formal deputation. This time they brought with them a number of things that had belonged to my predecessor, together with several similar items that did not. In every case, the infant correctly identified those belonging to the Thirteenth Dalai Lama saying, 'It's mine. It's mine.' This more or less convinced the search party that they had found the new incarnation. However, there was another candidate to be seen before a final decision could be reached. But it was not long before the boy from Taktser was acknowledged to be the new Dalai Lama. I was that child.

Needless to say, I do not remember very much of these events. I was too small. My only real recollection is of a man with piercing eyes. These turned out to belong to a man named Kenrap Tenzin, who became my Master of the Robes and later taught me to write.

As soon as the search party had concluded that the child from Taktser was the true incarnation of the Dalai Lama, word was sent back to Lhasa informing the Regent. It would be several weeks before official confirmation was received.

Until then, I was to remain at home. In the meantime, Ma Bufeng, the local Governor, began to make trouble. But eventually I was taken by my parents to Kumbum monastery, where I was installed in a ceremony that took place at dawn. I remember this fact particularly as I was surprised to be woken and dressed before the sun had risen. I also remember being seated on a throne.

From *Freedom in Exile* (1990)

His Holiness the 14th Dalai Lama, Tenzin Gyatso, describes himself as a simple Buddhist monk. He is the spiritual leader of Tibet. In 1989 he was awarded the Nobel Peace Prize for his non-violent struggle for the liberation of Tibet.

Rosa Parks (1913–2005)

One of my earliest memories of childhood is hearing my family talk about the remarkable time that a white man treated me like a regular little girl, not a little black girl. It was right after World War I, around 1919. I was five or six years old. Moses Hudson, the owner of the plantation next to our land in Pine Level, Alabama, came out from the city of Montgomery to visit and stopped by the house. Moses Hudson had his son-in-law with him, a soldier from the North. They stopped in to visit my family. We southerners called all northerners Yankees in those days. The Yankee soldier patted me on the head and said I was such a cute little girl. Later that evening my family talked about how the Yankee soldier had treated me like I was just another little girl, not a little black girl. In those days in the South white people didn't treat little black children the same way as little white children. And old Mose Hudson was very uncomfortable about the way the Yankee soldier treated me. Grandfather said he saw old Mose Hudson's face turn red as a coal of fire. Grandfather laughed and laughed.

From *My Story* (1992), written with Jim Haskins

Rosa Parks refused to give up her bus seat to a white person on 1 December 1955. Her action inspired the African American community to boycott Montgomery buses for over a year and led to her becoming an icon of resistance to racial segregation. The United States Congress ordained her 'the first lady of civil rights' in 1999 and, upon her death in 2005, Parks became the first woman ever to lie in honour in the Capitol Rotunda in Washington DC.

Johnny Cash (1932–2003)

The first song I remember singing was 'I Am Bound for the Promised Land.' I was in the back of a flatbed truck on the road to Dyess, Arkansas, from the first house I remember living in: the place next to the tracks out in the woods near Kingsland, Arkansas, where my family had ended up after a succession of moves dictated by the rigors of the Depression. That was a real bare-bones kind of place, three rooms in a row, the classic shotgun shack. It shook like the dickens every time a train went by. It wasn't as bad as the house I'd been born in, though. I don't remember living in that one, but I saw it once when I went to visit my grandfather. It was a last resort. It didn't have windows; in winter my mother hung blankets or whatever she could find. With what little we had, my parents did a lot.

The new house toward which the flatbed truck was taking us was something else, a brand new deal of the New Deal. Late in 1934, Daddy had heard about a new program run by the Federal Emergency Relief Administration in which farmers like him who had been ruined by the Depression were to be resettled on land the government had bought. As he explained it in later years, 'We heard that we could

215

buy twenty acres of land with no money down, and a house and a barn, and they would give us a mule and a cow and furnish groceries through the first year until the crops came in.' That's exactly what the deal was, and more: in forty-six different places in the agricultural United States, these 'colonies' were being created on a cooperative basis. In the settlement toward which we were headed, we and all the other families would have a stake in the general store, the cannery, the cotton gin, and other facilities; we were all responsible for them and we all shared in their profits, if any. The cotton we produced would go into the communal crop to be sold higher up the line for better prices than small individual crops could be. So as I've said in the past, I grew up under socialism – kind of. Maybe a better word would be communalism.

Our new community was named after the administrator of the FERA program for Arkansas, W. R. Dyess. All in all, it covered about 16,000 acres of Delta bottomland in Mississippi County. It was laid out like the spokes of a wagon wheel. Our place was Number 266, out on Road Three, about two and a half miles from the center.

I remember coming to that house so clearly. It took us two days to travel the 250 miles from Kingsland, first on gravel roads and then on dirt roads turned to mud by a hard, bitterly cold rain. We had to stop overnight by the roadside in the truck the government had sent for us, and we kids slept in the back with just a tarpaulin between us and the rain, listening to Moma cry and sing.

Sometimes Moma would cry and sometimes she'd sing,

and sometimes it was hard to tell which was which. As my sister Louise put it later, that was one of the nights when you couldn't tell. It all sounded the same.

When we finally got to Dyess, the truck couldn't get up the dirt road to our house, so Daddy had to carry me on his back the last hundred yards through the thick black Arkansas mud – gumbo, we called it. And that's where I was when I saw the Promised Land: a brand new house with two big bedrooms, a living room, a dining room, a kitchen, a front porch and a back porch, an outside toilet, a barn, a chicken house, *and* a smokehouse. To me, luxuries untold. There was no running water, of course, and no electricity; none of us even dreamed of miracles like that.

The house and the outbuildings were simple and basic, but sound, and identical to all the homesites in the colony. All of them were built to the same plan by the same thirty-man construction crew, who'd complete one site every two days, then move on to the next. I vividly remember the sight of their empty paint buckets, five of them, sitting in the middle of the living room floor, the only objects in the house: green for the trim, white for everything else. We settled in as best we could that first night. I don't remember how we stayed warm.

The next day, Daddy put on a pair of hip waders and went out to take stock of our land. It was jungle – I mean real jungle. Cottonwood and elm and ash and hickory as well as scrub oak and cypress, the trees and vines and bushes tangled up so thick in places that you couldn't get through, some of it under water, some of it pure gumbo – but Daddy could see its potential. 'We've got some good land,' he said simply when he came back, with an air of hope and thanks we could all feel. That was a significant remark.

From *Cash* (1997), written with Patrick Carr

Johnny Cash was simply christened 'J. R.' by his farming family in Kingsland, Arkansas.

After discharge from the US Air Force, he signed to Sun Records in 1955 and recorded 'I Walk the Line'. Its success led Cash to become the best-known country music performer in the world. He was nicknamed the 'Man in Black' after his 1971 hit of the same name.

Paula Fox (1923–2017)

The Reverend Elwood Amos Corning, the Congregational minister who took care of me in my infancy and earliest years and whom I called Uncle Elwood, always saw to it that I didn't look down and out. Twice a year, in the spring and fall, he bought a few things for me to wear, spending what he could from the yearly salary paid to him by his church. Other clothes came my way donated by the mothers in his congregation whose own children had outgrown them. They were mended, washed, and ironed before they were handed on.

In early April, before my fifth birthday, my father mailed Uncle Elwood two five-dollar bills and a written note. I can see him reading the note as he holds it and the bills in one hand, while with the index finger of the other he presses the bridge of his eyeglasses against his nose because he has broken the sidepiece. This particularity of memory can be partly attributed to the rarity of my father's notes – not to mention enclosures of money – or else to the new dress that part of the ten dollars paid for. Or so I imagine.

Th next morning Uncle Elwood drove me in his old Packard from the Victorian house on the hill in Balmville, New York, where we lived, to Newburgh, a valley town

219

half an hour distant and a dozen miles north of the Storm King promontory, which sinks into the Hudson River like an elephant's brow.

We parked on Water Street in front of a barbershop where I was taken at intervals to have my hair cut. One morning after we had left the shop, and because I was lost in reverie, staring down at the sidewalk but not seeing it, I reached up to take Uncle Elwood's hand and walked nearly a block before I realized I was holding the hand of a stranger. I let go and turned around and saw that everyone who was on the street was waiting to see how far I would go and what I would do when I looked up. Watching were both barbers from their shop doorway, Uncle Elwood with his hands clasped in front of him, three or four people on their way somewhere, and the stranger whose hand I had been holding. They were all smiling in anticipation of my surprise. For a moment the street was transformed into a familiar room in a beloved house. Still, I was faintly alarmed and ran back to Uncle Elwood.

Our destination that day was Schoonmaker's department store, next to the barbershop. When we emerged back on the sidewalk, he was carrying a box that contained a white dotted-swiss dress. It had a Peter Pan collar and fell straight to its hem from a smocked yoke.

Uncle Elwood had written a poem for me to recite at the Easter service in the church where he preached. Now I would have something new to wear, something in which I could stand before the congregation and speak his words. I loved him, and I loved the dotted-swiss dress.

220

Years later, when I read through the few letters and notes my father had written to Uncle Elwood, and which he had saved, I realized how Daddy had played the coquette in his apologies for his remissness in supporting me. His excuses were made with a kind of fraudulent heartiness, as though he were boasting, not confessing. His handwriting, though, was beautiful, an orderly flight of birds across the yellowing pages . . .

One early afternoon — I had not yet learned to read — I was sitting on a step below the landing, an open book on my lap, inventing a story to fit the illustrations. It was raining. From the little table on which it sat in a dark corner at the foot of the staircase, I heard the telephone ringing. Uncle Elwood came from his study to answer it. 'Mr. Fox?' I heard him ask in a surprised voice.

I flew up the stairs to my room, closed the door, and got under the bedclothes. Soon Uncle Elwood knocked on the door, saying the call had been from my father, Paul, who was in Newburgh, about to take a cab to Balmville. 'Won't you open your door?' he asked me.

The word *father* was outlandish. It held an ominous note. I was transfixed by it. It was as though I had emerged from a dark wood into the sudden glare of headlights.

Uncle Elwood persuaded me at last to come out of my room. He looked back to make sure I was following him down the stairs. After the alarm set off in me when I heard 'Mr. Fox,' I felt flat and dull. In the living room I stared listlessly at a new *National Geographic* lying on the

221

oak library table next to an issue of the *Newburgh News*, open to the page where the minister's weekly column appeared. On top of the big radio with a pinched face formed by various dials, on which we listened to *Amos and Andy*, there was a bronze grouping, a lion holding its paw, lifted an inch or so above the head of a mouse. I had gazed at it often, wondering if the lion was about to pat the mouse or kill it.

I had not longed for my father. I couldn't think how he had known where to find me.

I wandered into the hall, pausing before a large painting I had seen a thousand times, a landscape of the Hudson Valley. Dreaming my way into it, I walked among the hills, halted at a waterfall that hung from the lip of a cliff; in the glen below it there was an Indian village, feathery columns of smoke rising straight up from tepees. The painting was bathed in an autumnal light as yellow as butter, the river composed of tiny regular waves that resembled newly combed blue-gray hair, gleaming as though oiled.

I heard loud steps on the porch. My father suddenly burst through the doors carrying a big cardboard box. He didn't see me in the shadowed hall as he looked around for a place to set down the box.

In those first few seconds, I took in everything about him; his physical awkwardness, his height — he loomed like a flagpole in the dim light — his fair curly hair all tumbled about his head, and his attire, odd to me, consisting of a wool jacket different in fabric and pattern from his trousers. He caught sight of me, dropped the box to the floor, its unsealed flaps parting to reveal a number of books, and exclaimed, 'There you are!' as if I'd been missing for such a long time that he'd almost given up searching for me. Then at last! – I'd turned up in this old house.

Not much he said during the afternoon he spent with me had the troubling force of those words, and their joking acknowledgement that much time had elapsed since my birth.

I felt compelled to smile, though I didn't know why.

I bent toward the books. I guessed by their bright colors that they were meant for me. Eventually Uncle Elwood read them all aloud: *Robin Hood, King Arthur and the Knights of the Round Table, Tom Sawyer, Water Babies, Aesop's Fables, A Child's Garden of Verses, The Jungle Book* and *Treasure Island*.

At some happy moment, I lost all caution. When my father got down on all fours, I rode him like a pony.

It was twilight when he left. The rain had stopped. As he turned back on the bottom porch step to hold up his arm in a salute that seemed to take in the world, and before he stepped into the taxi he'd ordered to return for him, the sun emerged from a thick cloud cover and cast its reddish glow over his face as though he'd ordered that, too.

The next morning, I woke at first daylight and ran down the staircase to the living room in my nightclothes, knowing against my wish to find him there – that I wouldn't.

From *Borrowed Finery* (1999)

Paula Fox was the author of many children's books – for which she won both the Newbery and Hans Christian Andersen awards – as well as six novels for adults, including *Desperate Characters* (1970), which Jonathan Franzen has called 'one of the greatest novels ever written by an American'.

Chinua Achebe (1930–2013)

One of the earliest memories I can summon from the realm of childhood was a homecoming that was extraordinary even for such recollections. I was returning to my ancestral home for the first time. The paradox of returning for the first time need not detain us now because there are more engaging things at hand. I was five years old and riding in a motor vehicle also for the first time. I had looked forward very much to this experience, but it was not working out right. Sitting in the back of the truck and facing what seemed the wrong way, I could not see where we were going, only where we were coming from. The dust and the smell and the speed and the roadside trees rushing forward as we rushed back finally overcame me with fear and dizziness. I was glad when it all finally came to a halt at my home and my town.

The reason for my frightening journey was that my father, after thirty years in missionary work, founding a new church here and tending a fledgling one there, had earned his rest and a pension of thirty shillings a month and was taking his family to his ancestral home, to a house he scraped to build in the final years of his evangelism. It was a grand house with an iron roof and whitewashed earth walls, a far cry from the thatch-roofed mission house we had just left.

Of all our family, only my father had ever lived in Ogidi, to which he now brought us, and he had not lived there since he first began teaching for the Anglican Mission in 1904; it was now 1935. My mother, who had served beside him since their marriage five years into his career, had grown up in her own town, twenty-odd miles away.

Soon after our return to Ogidi, my father preached a homecoming sermon at St Philip's Anglican Church, which he had helped to found at the turn of the century. I don't remember the sermon but I do remember one of its consequences. My father had presumably told the congregation something about missionary journeys that had begun in 1904, and they were so taken with the antiquity of it all that they nicknamed him, there and then, Mister Nineteen-Four, which did not sound to me like an unambiguous encomium. But worse was to come to my siblings and me at school as Nineteen-Four's children. I am not sure why I found the sobriquet as disagreeable as I did. In any event, it helped me to fix in my mind the idea that Ogidi people were not very nice and that school was an unfriendly place. My homecoming did not begin too well.

From *Home and Exile* (2000)

Chinua Achebe (born Albert Chinụalụmọgụ Achebe) was a Nigerian novelist, poet and critic. His first novel, *Things Fall Apart* (1958), is the most widely read book in modern African literature. He won the Man Booker International Prize in 2007.

Sidney Poitier (1927–)

I've told the story before, but I think it bears repeating here: the story of [my mother's] concern at the time of my birth, and her going to the soothsayer. She was rightly concerned because I was a very premature baby, born unexpectedly while my parents were traveling to Miami to sell a hundred boxes of tomatoes at the Produce Exchange. When I arrived weighing in at less than three pounds, the question was, Is there enough there to take hold? My father, who had lost several children already to disease and stillbirth, was somewhat stoical about the situation. He went to a local undertaker in the 'colored' section of Miami to prepare for my burial, coming home with a shoebox that could serve as a miniature casket.

My mother, however, felt that I could be saved. One afternoon she left the house where they were staying to visit the local palm-reader and diviner of tea leaves. After some intense gazing back and forth, and much silence, the sooth-sayer closed her eyes and took my mother's hand. There was more silence, an uncomfortably long silence, and then the soothsayer's face began to twitch. Her eyes rolled back and forth behind their lids. Strange sounds began to gurgle up from her throat. Then all at once her eyes flew open again and she said, 'Don't worry about your son. He will survive and he will not be a sickly child. He will grow up to be . . . he will travel to most of the corners of the earth. He will walk with kings. He will be rich and famous. Your name will be carried all over the world. You must not worry about that child.'

So for fifty cents, my mother found the support she needed for backing a long shot. She came home and ordered my father to remove the shoebox of a casket from the house — there would be no need for it. And so it followed, for reasons that my mother and I believed were better left unquestioned, that I pulled through.

I wasn't a spoiled child. As soon as I was big enough to lift a bucket, I carried water for my mother. I went into the woods to gather bramble to make our cooking fire. Even as a toddler I had my jobs, my purpose, and I knew that I had to contribute to the thin margin of our survival. But I was a child bathed in love and attention.

My mother wasn't my only guardian angel. One day my sister Teddy said to me, 'What are you going to do? What would you like to do when you grow up?' And I remember — at that time I was about twelve — I told my sister that I would like to go to Hollywood and become a cowboy.

I had just seen my first movie — it was a cowboy movie, of course — and I thought it was the most amazing thing. I had no idea that Hollywood meant the movie business. I thought Hollywood was where they raised cows, and where they used horses to keep the cows corralled, and where the cowboys were the good guys, and they were always fighting the bad guys, who were trying to either steal the cows or do something to the people who owned the cows, and I wanted to do *that* kind of work.

Teddy laughed, but the laughter wasn't *at* me; she laughed *with* me. She was somebody who really loved me a lot, like my mom. She was more than ten years older, and she laughed. I'm sure she must have thought it was so wonderful that I was having this terrific dream, but she didn't correct me, she didn't say, 'That's such a way-out fantasy.' She didn't say, 'Who do you think you are? Man, you better get your feet on the ground. Boy, you got a long way to go.' No, she obviously had dreams too.

About ten years later the family was able to gather in a theatre in Nassau to see the first picture I ever made, something called *No Way Out*. This was in 1950, and it was the first time my parents had ever seen a movie. It must have been something like a fantasy for them, a dream. I'm not entirely sure how much they grasped of the concept.

My mother was sitting there, a woman who really didn't know anything about movies. My father was sitting there, a guy who really didn't know anything about movies. The movie played, and they were absolutely enthralled with what they saw, letting go with 'That's my kid!' and all that. But near the end of the movie Richard Widmark pistol-whips me in the basement of some house. He's hitting me with this pistol, the butt of this pistol. He's beating the crap out of me with this pistol, and my mother jumps up in the theatre and yells, 'Hit him back, Sidney! Hit him back!

You never did nothing to him!' In front of everybody. My brothers and sisters are squirming and laughing, saying, 'Mama, sit down, sit down.' But she's not joking. She's for real, completely in the moment. 'Hit him back, Sidney! Hit him back!'

From *The Measure of a Man* (2000)

Sidney Poitier was born in Miami but raised in the Bahamas. He was nominated for an Academy Award for his role in *The Defiant Ones* in 1958 before becoming the first African American actor to win for a leading role in 1963, for *Lilies of the Field*. His other landmark films include *In the Heat of the Night* (1967) and *Guess Who's Coming to Dinner* (1967). Poitier was knighted as a citizen of the Bahamas in 1974 and awarded an Honorary Oscar at the Academy Awards in 2002.

Orhan Pamuk (1952–)

From a very young age, I suspected there was more to my world than I could see: somewhere in the streets of Istanbul, in a house resembling ours, there lived another Orhan so much like me that he could pass for my twin, even my double. I can't remember where I got this idea or how it came to me. It must have emerged from a web of rumours, misunderstandings, illusions and fears. But in one of my earliest memories, it is already clear how I've come to feel about my ghostly other.

When I was five I was sent to live for a short time in another house. It was at the end of one of their many stormy separations that my parents arranged to meet in Paris, and it was decided that my older brother and I should remain in Istanbul, in separate places. My brother remained in the heart of the family with our grandmother in the Pamuk Apartments, in Nişantaşi. But I would be sent to stay with my aunt in Cihangir. Hanging on the wall in this house, where I was treated with the utmost kindness, was a picture of a small child. Every once in a while, my aunt or uncle would point at him and say with a smile, 'Look! That's you.'

The sweet, doe-eyed boy inside the small white frame did

look a bit like me, it's true. He was even wearing the cap I sometimes wore. I knew I was not that boy in the picture (a kitsch representation of a 'cute child' that someone had brought back from Europe). And yet I kept asking myself – is this the Orhan who lives in that other house?

Of course now I, too, was living in another house. It was as if I'd had to move here before I could meet my twin, but as I wanted only to return to my real home, I took no pleasure in the idea of making his acquaintance. Each time my aunt and uncle teased me about being the boy in the picture I felt my mind unravelling: my ideas about myself, my house, my picture and the picture I resembled, the boy who looked like me, and the other house would slide about in a confusion that made me long all the more to be at home again, surrounded by my family.

Soon my wish came true. But the ghost of the other Orhan in another house somewhere in Istanbul never left me. Throughout my childhood and well into adolescence, he haunted my thoughts. On winter evenings, walking through the streets of the city, I would gaze into other people's houses through the pale orange light of home and dream of happy, peaceful families living comfortable lives. Then I would shudder, thinking that the other Orhan might be living in one of these houses. As I grew older, the ghost became a fantasy and the fantasy a recurrent nightmare. In some dreams I would greet this Orhan – always in another house – with shrieks of horror; in others the two of us would stare each other down in eerie, merciless silence. Afterwards, as I wafted in and out of sleep, I would cling

233

ever more fiercely to my pillow, my house, my street, my place in the world. Whenever I was unhappy, I imagined going to the other house, the other life, the place where the other Orhan lived, and in spite of everything, I'd half convince myself that I was he and took pleasure in imagining how happy he was, such pleasure that, for a time, I felt no need to seek out the other house in that imagined part of the city . . .

I was born in the middle of the night on 7 June 1952, in a small private hospital in Moda. Its corridors, I'm told, were peaceful that night, and so was the world. Aside from the Strombolini Volcano's having suddenly begun to spew flames and ash two days earlier, relatively little seems to have been happening on our planet. The newspapers were full of small news – a few stories about the Turkish troops fighting in Korea, a few rumours spread by the Americans stoking fears that the Northern Koreans might be preparing to use biological weapons. In the hours before I was born, my mother had been avidly following a local story: two days earlier, the caretakers and 'heroic' residents of the Konya Student Centre had seen a man in a terrifying mask trying to enter a house in Langa through the bathroom window; they'd chased him through the streets to a lumber yard, where, after cursing the police, the hardened criminal had committed suicide; a dry-goods seller identified the corpse as a gangster who the year before had entered his shop in broad daylight and had robbed him at gunpoint. When she was reading the latest on this drama, my mother was alone

234

in her room, or so she told me with a mixture of regret and annoyance many years later. After taking her into hospital, my father had grown restless and when my mother's labour failed to progress, he'd gone out to meet with friends. The only person with her in the delivery room was my aunt, who'd managed to climb over the hospital's garden wall in the middle of the night. When my mother first set eyes on me, she found me thinner and more fragile than my brother had been.

I feel compelled to add 'or so I've been told'. In Turkish we have a special tense that allows us to distinguish hearsay from what we've seen with our own eyes; when we are relating dreams, fairy tales, or past events we could not have witnessed, we use this tense. It is a useful distinction to make as we 'remember' our earliest life experiences, our cradles, our baby carriages, our first steps, as reported by our parents, stories to which we listen with the same rapt attention we might pay some brilliant tale that happened to concern some other person. It's a sensation as sweet as seeing ourselves in our dreams, but we pay a heavy price for it. Once imprinted in our minds, other people's reports of what we've done end up mattering more than what we ourselves remember. And just as we learn about our lives from others, so, too, do we let others shape our understanding of the city in which we live.

At times when I accept as my own the stories I've heard about the city and myself, I'm tempted to say, 'Once upon a time I used to paint. I hear I was born in Istanbul, and I understand that I was a somewhat curious child. Then, when

235

I was twenty-two, I seem to have begun writing novels without knowing why.' I'd have liked to write my entire story this way – as if my life were something that happened to someone else, as if it were a dream in which I felt my voice fading and my will succumbing to enchantment. Beautiful though it is, I find the language of epic unconvincing, for I cannot accept that the myths we tell about our first lives prepare us for the brighter, more authentic second lives that are meant to begin when we awake.

From *Istanbul: Memories and the City* (2005)

Orhan Pamuk's novels include *The White Castle* (1985), *My Name is Red* (1998), *Snow* (2002 – winner of the Prix Médicis Étranger) and *The Museum of Innocence* (2008). In 2005, he was charged by the Turkish government with 'insulting Turkishness' after acknowledging the Armenian genocide of 1915–17. Pamuk was awarded the Nobel Prize in Literature the following year.

John McGahern (1934–2006)

The soil in Leitrim is poor, in places no more than an inch deep. Underneath is daub, a blue-grey modelling clay, or channel, a compacted gravel. Neither can absorb the heavy rainfall. Rich crops of rushes and wiry grasses keep the thin clay from being washed away.

The fields between the lakes are small, separated by thick hedges of whitethorn, ash, blackthorn, alder, sally, rowan, wild cherry, green oak, sycamore, and the lanes that link them under the Iron Mountains are narrow, often with high banks. The hedges are the glory of these small fields, especially when the hawthorn foams into streams of blossom each May and June. The sally is the first tree to green and the first to wither, and the rowan berries are an astonishing orange in the light from the lakes every September. These hedges are full of mice and insects and small birds, and sparrowhawks can be seen hunting all through the day. In their branches the wild woodbine and dog rose give off a deep fragrance in summer evenings, and on their banks grow the foxglove, the wild strawberry, primrose and fern and vetch among the crawling briars. The beaten pass the otter takes between the lakes can be traced along these

237

banks and hedges, and in quiet places on the edge of the lakes are the little lawns speckled with fish bones and blue crayfish shells where the otter feeds and trains her young. Here and there surprising islands of rich green limestone are to be found. Among the rushes and wiry grasses also grow the wild orchid and the windflower. The very poorness of the soil saved these fields when old hedges and great trees were being levelled throughout Europe for factory farming, and, amazingly, amid unrelenting change, these fields have hardly changed at all since I ran and played and worked in them as a boy.

A maze of lanes link the houses that are scattered sparsely about these fields, and the lanes wander into one another like streams until they reach some main road. These narrow lanes are still in use. In places, the hedges that grow on the high banks along the lanes are so wild that the trees join and tangle above them to form a roof, and in the full leaf of summer it is like walking through a green tunnel pierced by vivid pinpoints of light.

I came back to live among these lanes thirty years ago. My wife and I were beginning our life together, and we thought we could make a bare living on these small fields and I would write. It was a time when we could have settled almost anywhere, and if she had not liked the place and the people we would have moved elsewhere. I, too, liked the place, but I was from these fields and my preference was less important.

A different view of these lanes and fields is stated by my father: 'My eldest son has bought a snipe run in behind the

Ivy Leaf Ballroom,' he wrote. In some ways, his description is accurate. The farm is small, a low hill between two lakes, and the soil is poor. My father would have seen it as a step down from the world of civil servants, teachers, doctors, nurses, policemen, tillage inspectors to which he belonged. Also, it was too close to where my mother's relatives lived and where I had grown up with my mother. The very name of the Ivy Leaf Ballroom would have earned his disapproval.

A local man, Patsy Conboy, built it with money he made in America. He first called it Fenaghville – it was the forerunner of the Cloudlands and the Roselands – and later it became, more appropriately, the Ivy Leaf. All through the 1950s and into the 1960s he hired famous dance bands. In spite of being denounced from several pulpits, the ballroom prospered and Patsy Conboy became a local hero, dispensing much employment. People came by bus, by lorry, hackney car, horse trap, on bicycle and on foot to dance the night away. Couples met amid the spangled lights on the dusty dance floor and invited one another out to view the moon and take the beneficial air: 'There wasn't a haycock safe for a mile around in the month of July.' All the money Patsy Conboy made on the dancehall was lost in two less rooted ventures: a motorcycle track that turned into a quagmire as soon as it was used and an outdoor, unheated swimming pool amid the hundreds of small lakes and the uncertain weather. They were not rooted in the permanent need that made the ballroom such a success.

Patsy was more than able to hold his ground against the

pulpits. When he was losing money digging the unheated swimming pool out of daub and channel, men turned up for work with letters from their priests stating that they had large families to support and should be employed. Patsy was unmoved: 'My advice to you, Buster, is to dump the priest and put a cap on that oil well of yours. They have been capping such oil wells for years in America. Families are smaller and everybody is better off.'

He was living close by when we bought the snipe run. The Ivy Leaf was then a ruin, its curved iron roof rusted, its walls unpainted, and Patsy had gone blind. Nothing about Patsy or his ballroom or the snipe zigzagging above the rushes would have commended themselves to my father. We settled there and were happy. My relationship with these lanes and fields extended back to the very beginning of my life.

When I was three years old I used to walk a lane like these lanes to Lisacarn School with my mother. We lived with her and our grandmother, our father's mother, in a small bungalow a mile outside the town of Ballinamore. Our father lived in the barracks twenty miles away in Cootehall, where he was a sergeant. We spent the long school holidays with him in the barracks, and he came and went to the bungalow in his blue Baby Ford on annual holidays and the two days he had off in every month. Behind the bungalow was a steep rushy hill, and beside it a blacksmith's forge. The bungalow which we rented must have been built for the blacksmith and was a little way up from the main road that ran to Swanlinbar and Enniskillen and the North. The short pass from the road was covered with clinkers from the forge. They crunched like grated teeth beneath the traffic of hoofs and wheels that came and went throughout the day. Hidden in trees and bushes on the other side of the main road was the lane that led to Lisacarn where my mother taught with Master Foran. Lisacarn had only a single room and the teachers faced one another when they taught their classes, the long benches arranged so that their pupils sat back to back, a clear space between the two sets of benches on the boarded floor. On the windowsill glowed the blue Mercator globe, and wild flowers were scattered in jamjars on the sills and all about the room. Unusual for the time, Master Foran, whose wife was also a teacher, owned a car, a big Model-T Ford, and in wet weather my mother and I waited under trees on the corner of the lane to be carried to the school. In good weather we always walked. There was a drinking pool for horses along the way, gates to houses, and the banks were covered with all kinds of wild flowers and vetches and wild strawberries. My mother named these flowers for me as we walked, and sometimes we stopped and picked them for the jamjars. I must have been extraordinarily happy walking that lane to school. There are many such lanes all around where I live, and in certain rare moments over the years while walking in these lanes I have come into an extraordinary sense of security, a deep peace, in which I feel that I can live for ever. I suspect it is no more than the actual lane and the lost lane becoming one for a moment in an intensity of feeling, but without the usual attendants

241

of pain and loss. These moments disappear as suddenly and as inexplicably as they come, and long before they can be recognized and placed.

From *Memoir* (2005)

John McGahern published his first novel, *The Barracks* (1963) while still working as a schoolteacher in Dublin. When his second novel, *The Dark* (1965), was banned for its uncompromising attitudes towards sex, he was dismissed from his teaching position. Later novels included *The Leavetaking* (1974), *The Pornographer* (1979) and *Amongst Women* (1990).

On his death, the *Guardian*'s obituary described McGahern as 'the most important Irish novelist since Samuel Beckett'.

Pelé (1940–)

However long we may live, we never forget the time when we were young. Memory is like a film which we alone can watch. For me, childhood is the best part of that film: time and again my thoughts return to my experiences, the innocence and mischief of that time, and the dreams and nightmares too . . .

It was in São Lourenço in 1944 that something happened that would change all our lives – mine especially. My father received an invitation from the football club in Bauru, north-west of São Paulo, to play there but also, crucially, to take on a job as a local government functionary. He went on to Bauru to find out more about the city and the proposal. He liked it, and my mother was delighted at the prospect of the non-football job, which would bring the family some security and improve our financial circumstances. We would finally, she hoped, be able to escape the suffocation of near-destitution. Things look different to children, though – we knew nothing, life just carried on as normal. Zoca, Maria Lúcia and I were still very young.

My father managed to convince my mother. We sent on ahead what little luggage we had. The people from Bauru sent us our tickets, and off we went. I found the train journey completely exhilarating: in many ways it is my first real memory – at the age of four the happiness that train journey gave me is engraved on my mind. I spent almost the whole journey glued to the window, transfixed by the constantly changing view. The train went slowly but that was fine by me: all the more time to take in the scenery. It was the first time I was really aware of what my country looked like; or at least, that part of it. In those days the nearest we had to air-conditioning was to open the big windows on either side of the carriage, and on one long corner I was so curious to see the front of the train and the plume of the engine that I leaned out too far and would have fallen had it not been for my father. He yanked me back to safety, under a gaze from my mother that reproached me for my irresponsibility. My time on this earth could have ended right there. But God was keeping an eye on me . . . Sitting between them for the remainder of the journey I didn't take any more risks . . .

[In Bauru] we started to spend more and more time dreaming about football and when we could next get to play. We had no kit, of course – not even a ball, and we had to make do with stuffing paper or rags into a sock or stocking, shaping it as best we could into a sphere and then tying it with string. Every now and then we would come across a new sock or bit of clothing – sometimes, it must be said, from an unattended clothes-line – and the ball would get a little bit bigger, and we'd tie it again. Eventually it came to resemble something close to a proper football.

Which is more than could be said for the pitch – my first

matches were held in the prestigious Rubens Arruda Street stadium: 'goalposts' of old shoes at either end, one where the street finished in a cul-de-sac and the other where it crossed with Sete de Setembro Street (named after Brazil's Independence Day); the touchlines more or less where the houses began on either side. But for me at the time it was like the Maracanã, and the place where I began to develop my skills. As well as the chance to spend time with friends and test myself against them, this was when I first learned the joy of controlling the ball, making it go the way I wanted it to, at the speed I wanted it to – not always easy with a ball made of socks. Playing football soon became more than just a pastime, it became an obsession.

From *Pelé: The Autobiography* (2006), written with Orlando Duarte and Alex Bellos, translated by Daniel Hahn

Born Edson Arantes do Nascimento in Minas Gerais, **Pelé** made his international debut for Brazil aged sixteen. He won his first World Cup winner's medal after scoring twice in the 1958 final against Sweden. He won another winner's medal at the 1970 World Cup. By the time of the latter, he had already scored 1,000 goals in professional football.

Pelé was awarded Player of the Century by FIFA in 1999, alongside Diego Maradona. The same year, he was elected Athlete of the Century by the International Olympic Committee.

Maya Angelou (1928–2014)

I was born in St. Louis, Missouri, but from the age of three I grew up in Stamps, Arkansas, with my paternal grandmother, Annie Henderson, and my father's brother, Uncle Willie, and my only sibling, my brother Bailey.

At thirteen I joined my mother in San Francisco. Later I studied in New York City. Throughout the years I have lived in Paris, Cairo, West Africa, and all over the United States.

Those are facts, but facts, to a child, are merely words to memorize, 'My name is Johnny Thomas. My address is 220 Center Street.' All facts, which have little to do with the child's truth.

My real growing up world, in Stamps, was a continual struggle against a condition of surrender. Surrender first to the grown-up human beings who I saw every day, all black and all very, very large. Then submission to the idea that black people were inferior to white people, who I saw rarely.

Without knowing why exactly, I did not believe that I was inferior to anyone except maybe my brother. I knew I was smart, but I also knew that Bailey was smarter, maybe because he reminded me often and even suggested that maybe he was the smartest person in the world. He came to that decision when he was nine years old.

The South, in general, and Stamps, Arkansas, in particular had had hundreds of years' experience in demoting even large adult blacks to psychological dwarfs. Poor white children had the license to address lauded and older blacks by their first names or by any names they could create.

Thomas Wolfe warned in the title of America's great novel that 'you can't go home again.' I enjoyed the book but I never agreed with the title. I believe that one can never leave home. I believe that one carries the shadows, the dreams, the fears and dragons of home under one's skin, at the extreme corners of one's eyes and possibly in the gristle of the earlobe.

Home is that youthful region where a child is the only real living inhabitant. Parents, siblings, and neighbors are mysterious apparitions who come, go, and do strange unfathomable things in and around the child, the region's only enfranchised citizen.

Geography, as such, has little meaning to the child observer. If one grows up in the Southwest, the desert and open skies are natural. New York, with the elevators and subway rumble and millions of people, and Southeast Florida, with its palm trees and sun and beaches, are to the children of those regions the way the outer world is, has been, and will always be. Since the child cannot control that environment, she has to find her own place, a region where only she lives and no one else can enter.

I am convinced that most people do not grow up. We find

parking spaces and honor our credit cards. We marry and dare to have children and call that growing up. I think what we do is mostly grow old. We carry accumulation of years in our bodies and on our faces, but generally our real selves, the children inside, are still innocent and shy as magnolias.

We may act sophisticated and worldly but I believe we feel safest when we go inside ourselves and find home, a place where we belong and maybe the only place we really do.

From *Letter to My Daughter* (2008)

The writings of author and activist **Dr Maya Angelou** first came to global prominence with her memoir *I Know Why the Caged Bird Sings* in 1969. She wrote six more volumes of autobiography, as well as essays and many volumes of poetry. Dr Angelou was given the Presidential Medal of Freedom by President Obama and received over fifty honorary degrees from universities all over the world during her lifetime.

Usain Bolt (1986–)

It won't come as a surprise to learn that the way I lived when I was young had everything to do with how I came to be an Olympic legend. There was adventure everywhere, even in my own house, and from the minute I could walk I was tearing about the home, because I was the most hyperactive kid ever. Not that anyone would have imagined that happening when I was born because, man, I came out *big* – nine and a half pounds big. I was such a weight that Pops later told me one of the nurses in the hospital had even made a joke about my bulk when I'd arrived.

'My, that child looks like he's been walking around the earth for a long time already,' she said, holding me up in the air.

If physical size had been the first gift from Him upstairs, then the second was my unstoppable energy. From the minute I arrived, I was fast. I did not stop moving, and after I was able to crawl around as a toddler I just wanted to explore. No sofa was safe, no cupboard was out of reach and the best furniture at home became a climbing frame for me to play on. I wouldn't sit still; I couldn't stand in one place for longer than a second. I was always up to something, climbing on everything, and I had way too much enthusiasm for my folks to handle. At one point, probably after I'd banged my head or crashed into a door for the hundredth time, they took me to the doctors to find out what was wrong with me.

'The boy won't stop moving,' cussed Pops. 'He's got too much energy! There must be something wrong with him.'

The doc told them that my condition was hyperactivity and there was nothing that could be done; I would grow out of it, he said. But I guess it must have been tough on them at the time, tiring even, and nobody could figure out where I'd got that crazy power from. My mom wasn't an athlete when she was younger, nor was Pops. Sure, they used to run in school, but not to the standard I would later reach, and the only time I ever saw either one of them sprint was when Mom once chased a fowl down the street after it ran into our kitchen. It had grabbed a fish that was about to be thrown into a pot of dinner. *Woah!* It was like watching the American 200 and 400 Olympic gold medallist Michael Johnson tearing down the track. Mom chased that bird until it dropped the fish and ran into the woods, fearing for its feathers. I always joked that I'd got my physique from Dad (he's over six foot tall and stick thin like me), but Mom had given me all the talent I needed.

The pace of life in Trelawny suited Mom and Pops. They were both country people and had no need to live anywhere busy like Kingston, but they worked *hard*. They weren't ones for putting their foot* up, not for one second. Take Pops, he was the manager at a local coffee company. A lot of beans were produced in the Windsor area, which was several miles south of Coxeath, and it was his job to make sure they got into all the big Jamaican factories. He was always up early, travelling around the country from one parish to the next. Most nights he came home late. Sometimes, when I was little, if I went to bed before six or seven in the evening, I wouldn't see him for days because he was always working, working, working. Whenever he came back to the house at night I was fast asleep.

Mommy had that same tough work ethic. She was a dress-maker, and the house was always full of materials, pins and thread. Everyone in the village came to our door whenever they needed their clothes repairing, and if she wasn't feeding me, or pulling me down from the curtains, Mom was always stitching and threading cotton, or fixing buttons. Later, when I got a bit older, I was made to help her and I was soon able to hem, sew and pin materials together. Now I know what to do if ever I rip a shirt†, though I'll still ask her to mend it because Mom has always been a fixer. If she knew how something worked, like an iron, then she could usually repair it whenever the appliance broke. I think it's one of the reasons why I became so carefree as a kid. Mom was always ready to sort out anything I'd busted around the house.

---

* Bolt footnotes this: In patois or English creole we use the word 'foot' to describe any part of the leg – the thigh, the feet, the calves; to put your foot up is to put your feet up. Other phrases are 'bad', which often means good, and 'silk' which means stylish.

† Bolt: Come on man, get serious – I buy a new one. Don't be so ridiculous.

I never went hungry living in Coxeath, because it was a farming community and we lived off whatever grew in the area, which was a lot. There were yams, bananas, coca, coconut, berries, cane, jelly trees, mangoes, oranges, guava. Everything grew in and around the backyard, so Mom never had to go to a supermarket for fruit and vegetables. There was always something in season, and I could eat whenever I wanted. Bananas would be hanging from the trees, so I just reached up and tore them down. It didn't matter if I didn't have any money in my pocket; if my stomach rumbled I would find a tree and pick fruits. Without realising, I was working to a diet so healthy that my body was being packed with strength and goodness.

And then the training started.

Coxeath's wild bush was like a natural playground. I only had to step out of my front door to find something physical to do. There was always somewhere to play, always somewhere to run and always something to climb. The woods delivered an exercise programme suitable for any wannabe sprinter, with clearings to play in and assault courses made from broken coconut trees. Forget sitting around all day playing computer games like some kids do now; I loved to be outside, chasing around, exploring and running barefoot as fast as I could.

Those forests might have looked wild and crazy to an outsider, but it was a safe place to grow up. There was no crime, and nothing dangerous lurked among the sugar cane. True, there was a local snake called the Jamaican Yellow Boa, and even though it was a harmless intruder, people always freaked out if one slithered into the house. I once heard of some dude attacking one with a machete before throwing the dead body into the street. To make sure the snake was 100 per cent gone, he then flattened it with the wheels of his car and set the corpse on fire. That was pest control, Trelawny-style.

I ran everywhere, and all I wanted to do was chase around and play sports. As I got a bit older, maybe around the age of five or six, I fell in love with cricket and I'd play whenever I was allowed out in the street. Any chance I could get, I'd be batting or bowling with my friends. Mostly we used tennis balls for our games, but if we ever hit a big six into the trees or the nearby cow pen, I'd make a replacement out of rubber bands or some old string. We would then spend hours bowling and spinning our homemade balls through the air. When it came to making wickets I was even more creative – I'd get into the trunk of a banana tree and tear out a big piece of wood. Then I would carve three stumps into the bark and shape the bottom until it was flat. That way it stood up on the ground. If we were desperate, we would even play with a pile of stones or a cut-up box instead of a proper wicket.

It wasn't all fun, though. There were chores to do for the family, even as a kid and, oh man, did I have to work sometimes! Pops was worried that I wouldn't pick up the same work ethic that he had when he was little, so once I'd got old enough he would always tell me to do the easier jobs around the house, like the sweeping. Most of the time I was cool with it, but if ever I ran off, he would start complaining.

'Oh, the boy is lazy,' said Dad, time after time. 'He should do some more work around the place.'

As I got older and stronger I was made to do more physical work around the house, and that I hated. We had no pipe water back then, so it became my job to carry buckets from the nearby stream to the family yard, where our supply was stored in four drums. Every week, if Pops was at home, I was ordered to fill them up and that was bad news because each drum held 12 buckets, which meant 48 trips to the river and back. It was tough work, as those buckets were heavy, and I would do anything to get out of carrying them.

Eventually, I figured that I couldn't be doing 48 trips to fill the drums, it took too long, so instead I would hold two at a time and struggle home with double the weight, despite the extra, painful effort. In my mind I was cutting corners, but carrying two buckets at a time developed me physically: I could feel my arms, back and legs getting bigger with every week. The chores soon built up my muscles, and without ever going to the gym or using weights, I was taking my first steps towards developing some serious muscle. Get this: my laziness was actually making me *stronger*. Combined with the walking, climbing and running, my dad's housework was helping me to become a bigger, more powerful person.

The funny thing was that Mom never forced me to do anything I didn't want to do, especially if Pops wasn't around. If I really grumbled hard I could cry off from bucket duty and he would never find out. The lectures would only start if ever he came home early from work to catch me slacking off. That's when he would complain. He moaned that Mom loved me too much, and I suppose that was true, but I was her only child, so our bond was extra special.

Sometimes Dad was too strict, though. He didn't like me to leave the house, and if he was home and I was playing he would always force me to stay in sight, usually in the yard. But whenever Pops went to work, Mom allowed me to roam free. Still, I wasn't dumb. Wherever I was, I always listened out for Dad's motorcycle, which would splutter noisily as the wheels came down the hill and into the village. As soon as I heard his engine, I'd drop whatever I was doing and sprint to the house as hard as I could, often getting back before Pops got suspicious.

Sometimes I would sneak away to play at a friend's house which was on a patch of land away from Dad's usual journey home. Listening out for his old bike became more difficult then, but I had a trick up my sleeve. When I snuck out of the house I would always take Brownie, the family dog, with me. The moment Pop's bike came rumbling home, Brownie's ears would prick up long before anyone else could hear a noise. As soon as that dog made to leave, I knew it was my cue to run. In a way, he was giving me a taste of what life would be like in the future:

Listen for the gun . . .
Bang!
Pop the blocks! Run! Run!
My first trainer was a dog. *Ridiculous.*

From *Faster Than Lightning* (2013)

Usain Bolt is the fastest man the world has ever seen. An eight-time Olympic gold medallist, Bolt won the 100 metres, 200 metres and 4 × 100 metres relay at three consecutive Olympic Games before retiring in 2017.

Saroo Brierley (1981–)

When I was growing up in Hobart, I had a map of India on my bedroom wall. My mother – my adoptive mother, Mum – had put it there to help me feel at home when I arrived from that country at the age of six to live with them, in 1987. She had to teach me what the map represented – I was completely uneducated and don't think I even knew what a map was, let alone the shape of India.

Mum had decorated the house with Indian objects – there were some Hindu statues, brass ornaments and bells, and lots of little elephant figurines. I didn't know then that these weren't normal objects to have in an Australian house. She had also put some Indian fabric in my room, across the dresser, and a carved wooden puppet in a brightly coloured outfit. All these things were sort of familiar, even if I hadn't seen anything exactly like them before. Another adoptive parent might have made the decision that I was young enough to start my life in Australia with a clean slate and could be brought up without much reference to where I'd come from. But my skin colour would always have given away my origins, and anyway, she and my father chose to adopt a child from India for a reason.

The map's hundreds of place names swam before me in my childhood. Long before I could read them, I knew that the immense V of the Indian subcontinent was a place teeming with cities and towns, with deserts and mountains, rivers and forests – the Ganges, the Himalayas, tigers, gods! – and it came to fascinate me. I would stare up at the map, lost in the thought that somewhere among all those names was the place I had come from, the place of my birth. I knew it was called 'Ginestlay', but whether that was the name of a city, or a town, or a village, or maybe even a street – and where to start looking for it on that map – I had no idea.

I didn't know for certain how old I was, either. Although official documents showed my birthday as 22 May, 1981, the year had been estimated by Indian authorities and the date was the day I had arrived at the orphanage from which I had been offered up for adoption. An uneducated, confused boy, I hadn't been able to explain much about who I was or where I'd come from.

At first, Mum and Dad didn't know how I'd become lost. All they knew – all anyone knew – was that I'd been picked off the streets of Calcutta, as it was still known then, and after attempts to find my family had failed I had been put in the orphanage. Happily for all of us, I was adopted by the Brierleys. So to start with, Mum and Dad would point to Calcutta on my map and tell me that's where I came from – but in fact the first time I ever heard the name of that city was when they said it. It wasn't until about a year after I arrived, once I'd made some headway with English, that I was able to explain I didn't come from Calcutta at all – a train had taken me there from a train station near 'Ginestlay', which might have been something like 'Bramapour', 'Berampur'. . . I wasn't sure. All I knew was that it was a long way from Calcutta and no one had been able to help me find it.

Of course, when I first arrived, the emphasis was on the future, not the past. I was being introduced to a new life in a very different world from the one I'd been born into, and my new mum and dad were putting a lot of effort into facing the challenges that brought. Mum didn't worry too much about my learning English immediately as she knew it would come through day-to-day use. Rather than trying to rush me into it, she thought it was far more important at the outset to comfort and care for me, and gain my trust. You don't need words for that. She also knew an Indian couple in the neighbourhood, Saleen and Jacob, and we would visit them regularly to eat Indian food together. They would speak with me in my own language, Hindi, asking simple questions and translating instructions and things Mum and Dad wanted me to know about how we'd live our life together. Coming from a very basic background, I didn't speak much Hindi either, but being understood by someone was a huge help in becoming comfortable about my new surrounds. Anything my new parents weren't able to communicate through gestures and smiles we knew Saleen and Jacob could help us with, so we never got stuck.

As children do, I picked up my new language quite quickly. But at first I spoke very little about my past in India. My parents didn't want to push me to talk about it until I was ready, and apparently I didn't show many signs that I gave it much thought. Mum remembers a time when I was seven, when out of the blue I got very distressed and cried out, 'Me begot!' Later, she found out I was upset that I had forgotten the way to school near my Indian home, where I used to walk to watch the students. We agreed then that it probably didn't matter anymore. But deep down, it did matter to me. My memories were all I had of my past, and privately I thought about them over and over, trying to ensure I didn't 'beget'.

In fact, the past was never far from my mind. At night, memories would flash by and I'd have trouble calming myself so I could sleep. Daytime was generally better, with lots of activity to distract me, but my mind was always busy. As a consequence of this and my determination not to forget, I have always recalled my childhood experiences in India clearly, as an almost complete picture – my family, my home and the traumatic events surrounding my separation from them have remained fresh in my mind, sometimes in great detail. Some of these memories were good, and some of them bad – but I couldn't have one without the other, and I couldn't let them go.

From *A Long Way Home* (2013), written with Larry Buttrose

Saroo Brierley was born Sheru Khan in Ganesh Talai, India, but became accidentally separated from his family at the age of five. After somehow surviving on the streets of Kolkata for several months, he was adopted by Sue and John Brierley and went to live in Hobart, Tasmania. Using his vivid childhood memories as landmarks, Brierley digitally retraced his steps in adulthood and, twenty-five years after his departure, was reunited with his biological mother. His memoir was adapted into the 2016 film *Lion*.

Mo Farah (1983–)

Almost everyone in Djibouti lives in the capital. As soon as you get there, you can see why. It's this huge, frenetic place, with traffic and noise everywhere. Men pushing wagons through the streets selling fresh loaves of bread and honking their bicycle horns. There are goats and camels everywhere. In the distance you can hear the *athan*, the call to prayer sung by the muezzin: 'Allah Akbar! God is great!'

Our grandparents lived in a stone house on the out-skirts. Each part of the city is named using a number scale: Quarante-Deux-Trois (40-2-3), Quarante-Deux-Quatre (40-2-4), and so on – a legacy of French colonialism, which continued until 1977. When I was a kid, our house seemed huge. I remember arriving at the house and thinking that Grandma and Grandad lived in a mansion. When I returned to Djibouti many years later, I revisited my old home. I couldn't believe it when I found the right address. I was like, 'Seriously, we lived here?!' The house seemed so much smaller than I'd remembered it.

In Djibouti we had access to all kinds of things that we didn't have in Gebilay. There was a local cinema, basically a dark room with a TV at one end wired up to an old-school

VHS recorder. Whenever Hassan and me had a few coins, we'd be straight off to the 'cinema' with our friends to watch a movie. Sometimes the cinema owner would show one of those old black-and-white Westerns with cowboys and Indians. Other times it was a Disney cartoon or a Hollywood action movie – whatever they happened to have on tape at the time. We didn't care. Most of the time we didn't understand what was being said by the actors anyway (there was no dubbing, and we couldn't read or write in English). We just liked watching the films, seeing all those exotic locations, people doing crazy things. Sometimes I'd get bored and make animal noises over the film. We were just kids having fun.

Dad occasionally visited, flying back to Djibouti from London for a week here or a few days there. I was probably too young to appreciate the difficulties of travelling back to Djibouti from London at the same time as working and studying, not to mention the cost. Looking back, I can understand the reasons why my dad wasn't able to visit more often. But that didn't make it any easier to accept as a young boy. We never had that normal father-son relationship. For me, there was my grandma and my mum, and my brothers, and that was it.

A few people in our neighbourhood had TVs, and we watched programmes whenever we could. My favourite was *Esteban, le Fils du Soleil*, which translates as 'Esteban, Son of the Sun'. It was a French cartoon series from the early 1980s about a Spanish kid called Esteban who goes on this great adventure to the Americas to find a lost city of gold.

(In English, it's known as *The Mysterious Cities of Gold*.) His friends accompany him on his epic quest, including an Incan girl called Zia, and Tao, the last survivor of an ancient civilization. But although Esteban is on the hunt for the cities of gold, that isn't his real mission. Actually, he's searching for his dad. Esteban also wears this cool medallion around his neck that allows him to control the sun. As a kid, I thought this show was the best thing ever on TV. Every day at 6.30 p.m. on the dot, I'd find a TV to watch it. I never missed an episode. I was totally addicted.

But following the adventure of Esteban and his crew was a bit of a challenge for a kid living in Djibouti. The city suffered almost daily power cuts, and more than once I'd sit down to watch the latest episode and then – phhtt! – the power would cut out. The TV screen went blank. No way was that going to stop me. I simply had to know what happened next, so I'd sprint out of the house, racing across the streets and running towards the light of a friend's house several streets away, where I knew the power would still be working. In a matter of minutes I'd get to my friend's house, catch my breath and tune in to *Esteban*. A few minutes later, same thing. Power cut. I'd dart off again in search of the next house where I could watch the programme. Sometimes I'd have to rush between three or four houses across the city just to catch a single episode of *Esteban*. But it was worth it. I was totally mad about that cartoon show.

Looking back on it, I guess it was pretty good training for a career in distance running.

From *Twin Ambitions* (2013), written with T. J. Andrews

Sir Mo Farah, CBE, is Britain's greatest ever distance runner. The most successful British track athlete in modern Olympic Games history, he was the 2012 and 2016 Olympic gold medallist in both the 5000m and 10,000m races.

He was born in Mogadishu, Somalia, but moved at the age of eight to join his father in Britain, leaving his twin brother Hassan behind in Africa. The twin brothers would not be reunited for another twelve years.

Henning Mankell (1948–2015)

In the emotional chaos that enveloped me after my torti-collis had metamorphosed into cancer, I noticed that my memory often transported me back to my childhood.

But it wasn't long before I realised that my memory was trying to help me to understand, to create a starting point that would enable me to cope with the potentially fatal catastrophe with which I had been stricken.

I quite simply had to start somewhere. I had to make a choice. And I was becoming increasingly convinced that the beginning lay somewhere in my early life.

I eventually chose a cold winter's day in 1957.

When I open my eyes that morning I am unaware that the day is going to reveal a big secret.

Quite early I am on my way to school through the dark-ness. I am nine years old. It so happens that my best friend Bosse is ill. I always pick him up from his house, which is only a few minutes' walk from the district courthouse where I live. His brother Göran answers the door and says that Bosse has a sore throat and will be staying at home. I will have to go the rest of the way to school on my own that morning.

Sveg is quite a small town. None of the streets are very long. Although fifty-seven years have passed since that winter's day I can still remember everything in great detail. The few lights suspended on cables across the street are swaying gently in the gusty breeze. The shade on the light outside the ironmonger's has cracked — it wasn't like that yesterday. Evidently it had happened during the night.

It must have been snowing while I was asleep. Somebody has already cleared away the snow outside the furniture shop — that must have been Inga-Britt's dad. He owns the furniture shop. Inga-Britt is another classmate of mine, but she's a girl and we never go to school together. But she can run very fast. Nobody can ever keep up with her.

I can even remember what I had dreamt about that night. I'm standing on an ice floe on the River Ljusnan, which flows past the building where I live. The spring thaw has begun and the floe is floating southwards. Standing on one's own on an ice floe ought to be scary as it is very dangerous. Only a few months ago a boy just a few years older than I am drowned when an unexpected and treacherous hole in the ice opened up in a lake just outside Sveg. He was dragged down and his body has never been found, despite the best efforts of the fire brigade. His teacher drew a cross on his desk at school. It is still there. Everybody in his class is frightened of holes in the ice and accidents and ghosts. Everybody is scared of that unknown thing called Death. The cross on his desk is a source of terror.

But in my dream the ice floe is safe. I know I'm not going to fall into the water.

I cross the road just past the furniture shop and stop out-side the community centre. There are two display panels outside. The cinema changes its programme twice a week, and the films are delivered in brown cardboard boxes from the goods depot at the local railway station. They come either from Orsa to the south or from Östersund. And they are still brought from the station by horse and cart. Engman, who is the caretaker at the community centre, lifts the boxes from the cart. I tried once, but failed miserably: they were too heavy for a nine-year-old. The cardboard boxes contained a bad cowboy film that I eventually watched. It was one of those B-movies where people talk and talk, with a brief gunfight at the end. Practically nothing else happens. And the colours are so peculiar. The people often have pink faces and the sky is more green than blue.

I see from the posters that Engman will be showing *The Hard Man*, which doesn't sound all that attractive, and a Swedish film starring Nils Poppe. The only advantage of the latter is that it is a U certificate and children are allowed in. That means I won't have to crawl in through the basement window that Bosse and I have a secret key for, so that we can always get in that way when the films are adults only.

As I stand there that freezing-cold morning fifty-seven years ago I experience one of those vital moments that will affect the rest of my life. I recall the situation in minute detail, as if the images have been branded into my memory. I am suddenly possessed by unexpected insight. It is as if somebody has given me a good shaking. The words come into my head of their own accord.

'I am myself and no one else. I am me.'

At that moment I find my identity. Until then my thoughts had been childish, as they were meant to be. Now the situation was entirely different. Identity is necessary in order to develop awareness. I am myself and nobody else. I cannot be exchanged for anybody else. Life has suddenly become a serious matter.

I don't know how long I stood there in the freezing-cold darkness, possessed by this new and bewildering understanding. All I remember is that I arrived late for school. Miss Prestjan, my teacher, was already playing the harmonium when I opened the outside door. I hung up my jacket and waited. It was strictly forbidden to go clomping into the classroom once morning prayers and hymns had begun.

It came to an end at last, there was a clattering of desks, and I knocked on the door and went in. As I was hardly ever late Miss Prestjan simply gave me a searching look and nodded. If she had suspected laziness, she would have said something.

'Bosse is ill,' I said. 'He has a sore throat and a temperature. He won't be coming to school today.'

Then I sat down at my desk. I looked around. Nobody had the slightest idea about the secret I was carrying with me. The secret I would keep for the next fifty-seven years.

From *Quicksand* (2014), translated by Laurie Thompson with Marlaine Delargy

Henning Mankell was a writer and activist. He divided his time between his native Sweden and Africa, mostly Mozambique. He wrote over forty novels in his lifetime and is best remembered internationally as the creator of Wallander. He also wrote extensively about his cancer, dying almost two years subsequent to its diagnosis.

There is a museum in Mankell's honour in his hometown, Sveg.

Bruce Springsteen (1949–)

We were pretty poor, though I never thought about it. We were clothed, fed and bedded. I had white and black friends worse off. My parents had jobs, my mother as a legal secretary and my father at Ford. One kerosene stove in the living room was all we had to heat the whole place. Upstairs, where my family slept, you woke on winter mornings with your breath visible. One of my earliest childhood memories is the smell of kerosene and my grandfather standing there filling the spout in the rear of the stove. All of our cooking was done on a coal stove in the kitchen; as a child I'd shoot my water gun at its hot iron surface and watch the steam rise. We'd haul the ashes out the back door to the 'ash heap.' Daily I'd return from playing in that pile of dust pale from gray coal ash. We had a small box refrigerator and one of the first televisions in town. In an earlier life, before I was born, my grandad had been the proprietor of Springsteen Brothers Electric Shop. So when TV hit, it arrived at our house first. My mother told me neighbors from up and down the block would stop by to see the new miracle, to watch Milton Berle, Kate Smith and *Your Hit Parade*. To see wrestlers like Bruno Sammartino face off against Haystacks Calhoun. By the time I was six I knew every word to the Kate Smith anthem, 'When the Moon Comes Over the Mountain.'

In this house, due to order of birth and circumstance, I was lord, king and the messiah all rolled into one. Because I was the first grandchild, my grandmother latched on to me to replace my dead aunt Virginia. Nothing was out of bounds. It was a terrible freedom for a young boy and I embraced it with everything I had. I stayed up until three a.m. and slept until three p.m. at five and six years old. I watched TV until it went off and I was left staring alone at the test pattern. I ate what and when I wanted. My parents and I became distant relatives and my mother, in her confusion and desire to keep the peace, ceded me to my grandmother's total dominion. A timid little tyrant, I soon felt like the rules were for the rest of the world, at least until my dad came home. He would lord sullenly over the kitchen, a monarch dethroned by his own firstborn son at his mother's insistence. Our ruin of a house and my own eccentricities and power at such a young age shamed and embarrassed me. I could see the rest of the world was running on a different clock and I was teased for my habits pretty thoroughly by my neighborhood pals. I loved my entitlement, but I knew it wasn't right.

When I became of school age and had to conform to a time schedule, it sent me into an inner rage that lasted most of my school years. My mother knew we were all way over-due for a reckoning and, to her credit, tried to reclaim me. She moved us out of my grandmother's house to a small, half-shotgun-style house at 39½ Institute Street. No hot water, four tiny rooms, four blocks away from my grandparents. There she tried to set some normal boundaries. It was too late. Those four blocks might as well have been a million miles. I was roaring with anger and loss and every chance I got, I returned to stay with my grandparents. It was my true home and they felt like my real parents. I could and would not leave.

The house by now was functional only in one room, the living room. The rest of the house, abandoned and draped off, was falling down, with one wintry and windblown bathroom, the only place to relieve yourself, and no functioning bath. My grandparents fell into a state of poor hygiene and care that would shock and repel me now. I remember my grandmother's soiled undergarments, just washed, hanging on the backyard line, frightening and embarrassing me, symbols of the inappropriate intimacies, physical and emotional, that made my grandparents' home so confusing and compelling. But I loved them and that house. My grandma slept on a worn spring couch with me tucked in at her side while my grandfather had a small cot across the room. This was it. This was what it had come to, my childhood limitlessness. This was where I needed to be to feel at home, safe, loved.

The grinding hypnotic power of this ruined place and these people would never leave me. I visit it in my dreams today, returning over and over, wanting to go back. It was a place where I felt an ultimate security, full license and a horrible unforgettable boundary-less love. It ruined me and it made me. Ruined, in that for the rest of my life I would struggle to create boundaries for myself that would allow me a life of some normalcy in my relationships. It made me in the sense that it would set me off on a lifelong pursuit of a 'singular' place of my own, giving me a raw hunger that drove me, hell-bent, in my music. It was a desperate, life-long effort to rebuild, on embers of memory and longing, my temple of safety.

From *Born to Run* (2016)

Bruce Springsteen – nicknamed 'The Boss' – grew up in Freehold, New Jersey. He bought his first guitar in 1964, for $18.

His albums, many with the E Street Band, include: *Born to Run* (1975), *Darkness on the Edge of Town* (1978), *Born in the U.S.A.* (1984), *The Ghost of Tom Joad* (1995) and *The Rising* (2002). Springsteen has sold more than 140 million records worldwide, won twenty Grammy Awards, two Golden Globes and an Academy Award. He was awarded the Presidential Medal of Freedom in 2016.

John Banville (1945–)

When does the past become the past? How much time must elapse before what merely happened begins to give off the mysterious, numinous glow that is the mark of true past-ness? After all, the resplendent vision we carry with us in memory was once merely the present, dull and workaday and wholly unremarkable, except in those moments when one has just fallen in love, say, or won the lottery, or has been delivered bad news by the doctor. What is the magic that is worked upon experience, when it is consigned to the laboratory of the past, there to be shaped and burnished to a finished radiance? These questions, which are all only one question, have fascinated me since when, as a child, I first came to the tremendous discovery that creation consisted not just of me and my appurtenances – mother, hunger, a preference for dryness over wetness – but of me on one side and on the other of *the world*: the world of other people, other phenomena, other things.

Let us say, the present is where we live, while the past is where we dream. Yet if it is a dream, it is substantial, and sustaining. The past buoys us up, a tethered and ever-expanding hot-air balloon.

And yet, I ask again, what is it? What transmutation must the present go through in order to become the past? Time's alchemy works in a bright abyss . . .

'Genius,' Baudelaire observes, 'is none other than childhood formulated with precision.' I believe that the great French *decadent*, who was writing here about the equally decadent English essayist Thomas De Quincey, author of *Confessions of an English Opium-Eater*, intended the word 'genius' to be understood in this context as the 'daimon', which the ancient Greeks believed is in every man: his character, indeed his essence. If Baudelaire is correct, then in a sense childhood never ends, but exists in us not merely as a memory or complex of memories, but as an essential part of what we intrinsically are. Every artist knows the truth of this since, for the artist, childhood and the childhood conception of things, is a deep source of what used to be called inspiration, if for no other reason than that it was as children that we first apprehended the world as *mystery*. The process of growing up is, sadly, a process of turning the mysterious into the mundane. We cease to be amazed by things – the sky, the turning of the seasons, love, other people – only because we have grown accustomed to them.

Imagine a being from an immensely distant planet wholly dissimilar to ours, who is sent here to make a comprehensive survey of Earth and its inhabitants and report back to his government, which is contemplating the possibility of a long-range hostile takeover. He makes a quick scout round – he has fabulously fast powers of observation and absorption – and is putting the finishing touches to his report, when it begins to rain: water, falling from the sky! Or someone sneezes – what sudden seizure is this? – or yawns: what does it mean, this silent scream, and why are people roundabout not amazed and appalled by the spectacle? Our alien realises on the spot that his report will have to be torn up and begun again, for this place is far, far more strange than at first he took it to be.

The child, like that alien fact-gatherer, exists in a state of constantly recurring astonishment – at every other moment he encounters something new and extraordinary – but eventually his consciousness becomes blurred. A time comes when, as we sadly say, he has seen it all. But none of us has seen it all: everything is always new, and every time is the first time. We do not grow up; all we do is grow dull.

So the septuagenarian who sits here in damp spring weather writing this quasi-memoir is also that child who, replete with sausage, rasher and Kylemore cake, set off on that long-ago December day aboard the number 10 bus bound for the city centre, or An Lár, as the legend on the front of the bus had it. I look back and see a seven-year-old stranger who yet *is me*. But how can that possibly be, that I am that child, and that that child is me? This question preoccupied the philosopher Wittgenstein, who set it alongside other such conundrums – Is a rose red in the dark? If a lion could speak would we understand him? – that he tried and failed, fascinatingly failed, to solve.

Can the old man be the same being as the child he once was? I have a small white jagged scar in the space between my eyebrows, the legacy of a mishap when I was four or five. One day I was running across the Faythe, the rather oddly named square – in fact it is wedge-shaped – in Wexford where I was born, and crashed into a sharp-edged wooden post that was supporting a newly planted sapling. A couple of years ago I went back to the Faythe to have a look at the old place, and was astounded to find a grove of mature trees flourishing there. I was baffled, for they looked to me as if they had been standing for centuries. 'Ah, no,' my sister gently told me, 'they're only about as old as yourself.' Aghast, I touched a finger to the scar on my brow, thinking: *I was here, alive, when these trees were planted!*

Is the child the father of the man, as Wordsworth claims? If so, is it not a grotesque thought to entertain in old age that one was begat by the child one started out as?

And when does the past become the past?

From *Time Pieces: A Dublin Memoir* (2016)

John Banville won the Man Booker Prize in 2005 for *The Sea*. His many other novels include *The Book of Evidence* (1989), *Eclipse* (2000) and *The Infinities* (2009). He has also published a series of detective novels set in Dublin, under the pseudonym Benjamin Black.

Ursula K. Le Guin (1929–2018)

This poem was written for my poetry group: eight women who meet once a month to read our work to one another and discuss it critically. Each month, one of us offers an assignment, a suggestion of a poetic form to use or a subject to write about. We don't have to do it, but mostly we try to, having found it useful in eliciting poems we didn't know we had in us till we had to write them. This assignment was to write on our earliest or a very early memory.

As the poem says, I wasn't hopeful about finding an earliest memory. I can't distinguish memories that may be from infancy from later ones, because I lived my entire childhood in the same house, with the same people, no travel except to the Napa Valley in June and back to Berkeley in August, no life traumas, few major events of which I was aware. Certain early moments stand out vividly: Intoxicating rocking-horse races in the big dark room with my older brother Karl – but when? – Forbidden to go into that room (daylit this time) because two of my brothers are in it with The Scarlet Fever – but when? – Standing on the garden path in the sunlight, a moment of intense awareness – but was I two, or four, or six? No way to know. This childhood of now almost incredible stability was perhaps blessed by the freedom from having to remember.

So my early years are to me like the memories one might have of an unspectacular, beloved landscape – deep in the soul, not much detail, powerful in its breadth and wholeness.

But I remember my animals in detail. They were stuffed. We briefly had a puppy, but he bit people. Stuffed animals do have the virtue of not biting people or other stuffed animals. They stay where you put them, do what you want them to do and say what you say they say. The value of this docility to children is great: it gives them control over a little, orderly corner of the immense, incomprehensible world. Held in a child's arms, a stuffed rabbit grows warm with the child's warmth – clear evidence that, if you love your rabbit, as I loved Jocken, your rabbit loves you back.

Jocken was my companion from (as far as I knew) birth (probably age three or four). He was about ten inches long, and quite soft, so that he cuddled well. His ears were just long enough to look rabbity. He was magic, because he was the First Animal. Also because his fur lay one way on his left side and the other way on his right side, so that on one side or the other it always lay against the direction of a stroking hand. This was not true of any other animal, and proved that he was magic. When he lost one eye it only made him, like Odin, more so.

As my animal kingdom grew over the years, Babar the Elephant became King, but Jocken was always the Wizard of the realm.

He was with me till I went off to college. There was a

terrible plague of moths in the house one year, and many animals perished, Jocken among them. He had spent all his magic, or given it to me.

(2017)

Early Memory: Jocken

First things lie deep, here in the starting place,
unseparate, composted into ground.
I come here without much hope to find
anything but the once bright images
gone dull with over-use: the jewelled dress;
the yellowish gravel of the garden path;
a redwood wall; quiet water in the bath
reflecting walls and window upside down,
so I was frightened, but the fear is gone.
Only a sense of how intense things were,
how near and piercing, and how dear
the round, still eye, the short, dun, silken fur.

(2012)

Ursula K. Le Guin published twenty-one novels (including, notably, the 'Hainish' and 'Earthsea' books), eleven volumes of short stories, five collections of essays, twelve books for children, six volumes of poetry and four of translation.

In 2014 she was awarded the National Book Foundation Medal for Distinguished Contribution to American Letters and was voted into the American Academy of Arts and Letters in 2017.

Ursula wrote this introduction to her poem 'Jocken' for this anthology, just weeks prior to passing away in January 2018.

Tessa Hadley (1956–)

The beginning of making up stories was surely in the games I played when I was a child. I can't remember a time when I didn't make up imaginary games. Before I could write and before I could read there were dolls and stuffed toys with their own inner lives and characters. These had to be respected and attended to, placated if they were difficult. My toy lion, for instance, was easily offended. He was huffy and awkward and not very bright; his stiff legs wouldn't fold, so he couldn't lie down and couldn't be comforted.

I had two close girl friends in primary school. When we met up at one another's houses at weekends, we puzzled luxuriantly over how to best use our time. Imaginary Games? Or catch up with the admin for our secret society (SSIC), or play with our chemistry sets? We didn't have much interest in chemistry really, we just liked collecting the kit, saving up to buy test tubes and flasks and tiny pots of sodium thiosulphate or potassium permanganate by mail order from a dingy catalogue. And we liked turning blue solutions brown, or making them fizz up. But usually we chose Imaginary Games – that's actually what we called them; and then I would try to invent something, sitting waiting for inspiration with a dressing gown or a blanket draped over my head to cut out distractions. That was my particular role, as the games' instigator.

I don't think I really needed the blanket. I was showing off, like a grown-up writer going on about their sharpened pencils or the kind of notebook they prefer. It was part of a performance, demonstrating the effort of crossing over that threshold and leaving daily reality behind, entering the realm of possibility and romance. I can remember the sensation vividly, trying to enter the blackness and emptiness. Of course I can remember it, because it's what I still do when I'm writing, without the blanket. Like screwing up your eyes, to shut out what's around you – only you're screwing up your whole mind, trying to drop down inside the dark. Then to open your inner eye on something – on some scene or situation whose elements you recognise but which hasn't quite ever occurred to you before with that plausibility, that bright-coloured wholeness and rightness. It's inside you, but your idea seems to have its own life now, independent of you. Those people are actually moving and speaking and feeling: they're not you, but you can watch them.

Not that the Imaginary Game we played was always something brand new. As often as not we'd pick up one of our long-running favourites, as easily extendable as soap operas: governesses and naughty children; the death of Mary Queen of Scots; pirates, with bunk beds for upper and lower decks. One story about eighteenth-century low-life was inspired by a television series I'd been allowed to stay up for at my nana's. In another favourite we were three adult women living on an island, with three daughters – no explanations for the missing men. There was a lot of rowing backwards and forwards from the mainland, and we drew maps of the layout of their houses and the shape of the island; and we always played this one in the school playground, not at home. Certain games belonged ritually in certain places. There was a fear-game for the big dark playground shed with the waste bins in it, where we were allowed to play when it rained. There was a *Man From U.N.C.L.E.* game I played with my brother, but only when our parents couldn't find a babysitter and we were taken along to someone's house for a party, put to sleep in strange beds.

I can remember being a princess in my aunt's house once: my extravagant aunt used to buy Badedas bubble bath, which seemed the height of luxury to me. The princess was walking around in her palace, and I was sustaining that other dimension of possibility in an effort of willed hallucination, seeing the dream and not seeing it, even while I was also moving round inside the real place I knew. The seduction of those games was so powerful – so sensuously thrilling. No wonder we couldn't wait to return to them, picking up the roles we dropped behind us if we were called downstairs for a meal or back into lessons. What we acted out in stories seemed more vivid and more serious than anything in our actual daily lives as children: they had life and death and danger in them – and courage and honour and passionate attachment. Some of them of course, as time went on, had sex in them too – although it was only ever referred to obliquely. There was one very charged game of gypsy caravans, in the bunk beds again; we had a rather vague idea of what was supposed to happen, but were suffused with excitement, felt on the brink of new possibilities.

Books, once I discovered them, fed into the Imaginary Games and fertilised them: the governess game owed something obviously to *Jane Eyre,* which was given to children to read in those days. And *Swallows and Amazons* had a great influence: although I don't think we ever actually pretended to be the Swallows, acting out Arthur Ransome's stories. That would have felt like a transgression, risked bleeding into the precious essence of the originals. It's interesting that so many of our Imaginary Games were set in the past – or at least in our idea of what the past was like. I always had a sense when I was a child that the past was a better place. It was extraordinary to me that there had once been a real time when people wore those clothes and used those things; and I felt a passionate distaste for the present which I can't quite explain now. I suppose that my idea of the past was the dream of an ideal. Part of growing up was adjusting the dream to take in the historical reality I learned about.

When I actually began trying to write stories down on paper, how lifeless and unsatisfactory they seemed at first. Dull words, inert protagonists – compared to the fleshed out and breathing reality of the games. It took another lifetime of new effort to begin to learn to make the words on the page combine in their chemistry to conjure the dream of life I could still find inside: if I trusted myself, if I screwed up my mind and closed my eyes and dropped down into the dark of my imagination.

(2018)

Tessa Hadley has written seven novels, including *Accidents in the Home* (2002), *The London Train* (2011), *The Past* (2015) and *Late in the Day* (2019), and three collections of short stories. She publishes short stories regularly in the *New Yorker*, reviews for the *London Review of Books* and is professor of creative writing at Bath Spa University. In 2016, she was awarded a Windham-Campbell Literature Prize for her fiction, the judges describing Hadley as 'one of English's finest contemporary writers'.

David Eagleman (1971–)

When I was eight years old, my brother and I left the house to find Saturday occupation. On the way out the door, our father warned us not to go near the house under construction. We assured him we wouldn't.

We went straight to the house under construction. Poking around, we found a ladder and ascended to the roof. From there, one could enjoy an arresting view of the mountains of Albuquerque, New Mexico. My brother wandered off to explore other regions, and I went to stand on the edge.

Because of my age, I didn't understand what tar paper was. I didn't know that it was stiff, and I didn't realize that it extended beyond the boundaries of the roof. So when I thought I was stepping to the roof's edge, I was actually stepping on tar paper. My body instantly realized its mistake.

As I fell, I considered grabbing for the roof's edge, but I quickly recognized I was too late for that. Soon I found myself in a spread-eagle position, looking down, down, down to the red brick floor below. As I fell toward what was likely to be my death, I was calmly thinking how similar my fall was to Alice's fall down the rabbit hole in *Alice in Wonderland*. I experienced no fear and no panic. Just a crystal clear thought about a moment from a children's book.

It will not surprise the reader that I lived; but it did surprise my parents and the emergency-room physicians. I had fallen twelve feet and made a pinpoint landing on my nose. I lost blood and cartilage and consciousness.

But what stayed with me was not the pain, but instead a fascination with what had happened.

Some years later, in high-school physics, I computed a paper-and-pencil calculation and realized the fall had only taken 0.6 of a second. I was shocked. How had it seemed so long?

When I grew up, I became a neuroscientist. The experience of the fall's mysteriously long duration never left me. I collected stories from drivers who had been in car accidents, policemen who had been in firefights, firemen who had been inside collapsing buildings. They commonly reported the sensation that time had seemed to proceed more slowly than normal. They had taken in more information about their surroundings. They had scrutinized the car hood crumpling, the suspect reaching into his jacket to draw a weapon, the tipping glass of water in the toppling building – all in very short time windows that seemed lengthy.

Such reports made it seem possible that the brain had a capacity to operate at a higher 'frame rate', essentially the same way a slow-motion camera works.

I wanted to understand this phenomenon better, so I

scoured the literature. But it turned out that no one had ever put the question of slow-motion perception to the test. Why not? Because it would require placing volunteer subjects in life-threatening situations. Not a clear path to tenure for an academic.

But short of an experiment, I realized it was difficult to know whether to take the reports (including my own) seriously. After all, perhaps memory is laid down more richly during such episodes, and when retrospectively reading out the event (*what just happened?*), one has more memory than normal and interprets it as having taken a longer time.

So I decided to design a test.

First, I needed something scary. I packed up stopwatches and pads of paper, and took the members of my laboratory to Astroworld, the local amusement park. We set out to find the most frightening rollercoaster and other terrifying amusements. We had a great time – but at the end of the day, we could find nothing frightening enough to give us the impression that time had moved in slow motion.

We needed something scarier.

Weeks later, and three hundred miles away, we found it: the Suspended Catch Air Device. You go up a very tall tower – 150 feet tall – and then you fall. Backwards. In free fall. You're caught in a suspended net below, going 70 miles per hour when you hit the net.

With some testing, we realized this would be scary enough. I took the plunge myself three times. Each time was equally as terrifying as the last.

But how would we do the experiment?

We engineered an electronic wristband device that we called the perceptual chronometer. It flashes information at the user in such a way that we can measure the speed of vision – and if vision sped up like a slow-motion camera, taking in more frames per second, then we'd be able to quantify that. If, on the other hand, participants were not actually *seeing* in slow motion, but instead just laying down more memory, they would be no faster at reading the display.

We obtained twenty-three participants. First, we measured what each person could see under normal, relaxed circumstances. Next, we harnessed each to a platform that was then winched fifteen stories above the ground. The perceptual chronometer was strapped to the participant's forearm like a wristwatch, and they were then released. They experienced free fall for three seconds before landing (safely) in a net. During the fall, they attempted to read the digits. If higher temporal resolution were experienced during the free fall, the alternation rate should appear slowed, allowing for the accurate reporting of numbers that would otherwise be unreadable.

After the fall, we asked participants to retrospectively reproduce the duration of their fall using a stopwatch. Here, consistent with the verbal reports, their duration estimates of their own fall were about 30 per cent longer than their estimates of the fall of others.

But the surprise came with the chronometer results. Participants were not able to read the numbers in free fall any better than when they were standing calmly on the ground. This was not because they closed their eyes or didn't pay attention (we monitored for that) but because they could not, after all, see time in slow motion. Despite my subjective experience of falling from the roof, I had not, after all, seen in 'bullet time' like Neo in *The Matrix*.

So why did the experience *seem* to last so long? Why do participants report a longer duration, even though they were experiencing things no faster than normal? The answer comes down to a walnut-size area of the brain called the amygdala. In an emergency situation, this area kicks into high gear, commandeering the resources of the rest of the brain and forcing everything to attend to the situation at hand. When the amygdala gets involved, memories are laid down on a secondary memory system. Upon replay, your brain interprets the higher density of data as a longer duration. In this way, duration and memory are linked.

And this is also why time seems to speed up for all of us as we age: as our brains develop better models of the world, little carries much surprise. The memories to be read out are thin, impoverished. In contrast, in your childhood everything is novel – and so the richness of your memories gives the impression of increased duration. When you look back at the end of a childhood summer, it seems to have lasted for a long time; when looking back on an adult summer, it seems to have disappeared rapidly.

So while I don't recommend emergency situations, it sure does make you operate like a child again.

(2018)

David Eagleman is a neuroscientist and author. He heads the Center for Science and Law and serves as an adjunct professor at Stanford University. He is the writer and presenter of the international television series, *The Brain with David Eagleman*, and the author of the companion book, *The Brain: The Story of You* (2015).

Beyond his 100-plus academic publications, Eagleman's other books include *Incognito: The Secret Lives of the Brain* (2011), which explores the neuroscience 'under the hood' of the conscious mind, as well as a novel, *Sum: Forty Tales from the Afterlives* (2009).

PART THREE

RIGHTS OF PASSAGE

Introduction

Tell me the story . . .

So the greatest foundation myth of them all, Homer's *Odyssey*, starts. Its *proem* – the prologue with which all such classical epics commence – is addressed to Calliope, the Muse, herself daughter of Mnemosyne, goddess of Memory. The entreaty comes from Telemachus, who is desperate for news of his father Odysseus.

Begin it, goddess, at whichever point you will . . .

The point of entry will be divine. As such, like all great art, it takes on the ring of inevitability.

To understand why *The Odyssey* continues to fascinate readers three thousand years since its conception, we must set it within the story traditions it distinguishes. Notably, one that was 'invented after memory and before history'*: the *'epic'*. More than any other type of narrative, an *'epic'* renders the

---

* The words of Adam Nicolson, in *The Mighty Dead*.

present continuous with our distant past. It makes the greatest bygone stories resonate in the here and now.

This exchange across time, in turn, reflects the very composition of *The Odyssey*. It has been passed down to us via oral storytelling, sung by heart. Long-ago voices echo through every modern translation. Each note rings as true today as it ever did.

As well as an epic, the *Odyssey* text can also (however inadequately) be defined as a *nostos* narrative, or a homecoming tale – also hugely popular in Ancient Greek literature. The word itself, *nostos*, had powerful connotations. This is shown by its derivative adjective, '*nostimos*', which meant – in Sophocles' book – '*essential, valuable, perfect, the best part of anything*'.* Over time, *nostos* conjoined with another word from the Ancient Greek lexicon, *algos,* which conjured a sense of painful longing for something lost. Together, they formed 'a painful longing for home' – or *nostalgia*.

Odysseus' decade-long quest is to vanquish nostalgia and return to Ithaca. The voyage home follows another ten-year ordeal – the Trojan War – and encompasses many fantastical trials, all designed to hinder his passage. Along the way, he defeats those forces working against him – be it the Lotus-eaters, whose local plants drowse a person into forgetting their 'homecoming', or the Sirens, with their rapturous rhapsodies. These and many other antagonists are overcome thanks to Odysseus' trademark ingenuity.

Even once home, though, the tests and trials

---

* From the *Greek Lexicon of the Roman and Byzantine Periods* by Sophocles.

continue – both for and from Odysseus. He must reorientate himself in a lost world. As Adam Nicolson ironically put it: 'now he is at home, he is more at sea than ever'. Athene dims his eyes and shrivels our hero into an old, broken man. The king must traverse his island as a beleaguered beggar. There are, however, a few features that distinguish him as Odysseus. For not even the gods can erase the marks of childhood.

As he makes his way through the palace gates, our shabby vagrant crosses paths with a mangy mutt. Nestled in a dung heap, the old stray was long ago abandoned, Odysseus is told, and now must live with the vermin. The creature no longer has the strength even to move. Yet, as Odysseus approaches, his ears prick up and his scrawny tail wags. The dog has sniffed out the pauper's true identity. The recognition – or *anagnorisis*, in classical terms – is mutual. In his youth, Odysseus had trained Argus, then himself a puppy, into the fastest, strongest of hunting dogs. Now, though, Odysseus is unable to reveal his true identity to his faithful friend. He must endure yet another trial and walk on – ignoring his old dog. He wipes a solitary tear from his eye and, at that exact moment, some twenty years after being parted from his master, Argus breathes his last.

Later, having infiltrated his old palace and spoken in disguise with his queen, Odysseus finds himself being washed by his elderly nurse, Eurycleia. She immediately recognises a scar on his thigh, received during a boar hunt in his youth. The sight of the scar revolves the narrative backwards. We rewind to his earliest childhood, even learning how

Odysseus came to be named as a baby. Fond old Eurycleia's suspicions have been confirmed. The king is at last home.

The critical scenes of reconciliation with his son Telemachus and, moreover, wife Penelope soon follow, representing the climax of *The Odyssey*. Yet its final moment of recognition still awaits. In its twenty-fourth and last book, Odysseus walks into the orchard of his childhood home. This final reunion not only reroutes the story back to its beginnings – a son in search of his father – it also celebrates the potency of childhood memories.

Odysseus is in two minds whether to test his father Laertes but, in keeping with the rest of his long journey, eventually chooses to quiz him. He pretends to be a foreign prince who hosted Odysseus some five years previously. Laertes is desperate to hear news of his son and bids the stranger to tell him more. As Odysseus continues, prolonging the charade, however, Laertes falls to his knees and begins to pour dust over his head. Taking pity on the grieving old man, Odysseus relents from his wiles for once and reveals himself.

However, the story does not end there. Like father, like son: Laertes demands proof that this man really is his child. Odysseus shows him the scar and describes how he came to have it. Yet it is only once he then relates how, as a little boy, the pair would hold hands and wander through the very same orchard together – Laertes pointing out the different vines and trees, explaining when each ripened – that the father accepts his prodigal son. On hearing this shared memory recollected, Laertes' heart melts. They embrace. Odysseus has finally, truly arrived home in his fatherland.

Homer's *Odyssey* ripples through journeys into Greece today – just as the waves that lap at Hellenic shores are themselves memory traces of Atlantic surges. Various Greek islands host thousands of travellers who have been forced to make twenty-first-century odysseys. Refugee and migrant voices reverberate through this final section. Their displaced memories combine to form a diaspora of tales, all on the move across time and history.

In her fecund, hypnotic description of Chile included here, Isabel Allende loses herself. It is excerpted from her memoir *Paula*: a book that took form as a bedside address to her daughter, who lay comatose in a Spanish hospital.

In the book – as with Prospero and daughter Miranda in *The Tempest* or some of *The Odyssey*'s own filial creation myths – an identity is conjured, as if from thin air, for a child. As Allende describes their family's provenance to silent Paula, heredity is shaped into a story. Imagination and memory become coeval.

My life is created as I narrate, and my memory grows stronger with writing . . . when you wake up we will have months, maybe years, to piece together the broken fragments of your past; better yet, we can invent memories that fit your fantasies.

Societies have come to put a premium upon life stories. As noted, the growth of psychoanalysis since Freud has taught us how to dramatise our memories. The psychologist

Dan McAdams has extensively made the case for life stories informing cognition: 'In the subjective and embellished telling of the past, the past is constructed – history is made.' Aspirational forces drive selective consolidation in an individual's memory. Sometimes this process can be writ large for whole cultures. Museums, for example, enact such a function. We learn something about where we came from. Memory banks or time capsules in essence, they can also provide refuge from a bleak-looking future: a dose of *genesis* allows the visitor to escape their sense of *apocalypse*.

Notions such as these are sometimes angled as '*collective memory*'. Just as the exhilaration of a grand gathering, be it a sporting triumph or an arena concert, can lead to the most uplifting times-of-our-lives, so when people come together in protest – from the suffragettes to #MeToo or #BlackLivesMatter – social movements arise and change begins. Like-mindedness can be good for us. It can lift us up. Equally, such communal energies, if channelled destructively into mob rule, can destroy.

The 'collective memory' of the group is no less provisional than the individual's. Like your or my memory, it is easily manipulated – knowingly or not. Often the *intentionality* of a government or media will exert itself onto a country's sense of self. For example, in a presidential campaign or political crisis, pundits will discuss the need for the candidate or leader to 'control the narrative'. Soon enough, rather like the patient led towards recovering false memories, a populace becomes swept up. Individuation gets entwined in group dynamics – be it the promise of 'shared identity', 'common cause' or 'homeland'. Wisdom becomes received, not perceived. A people wallows in *nostalgia*.

English Heritage declares online that its priority is 'to create inspiring visitor experiences that bring the story of England to life'. This seems fair enough. However, by cherry-picking certain narratives of statehood at the expense of others – as this mission statement implies – a culture risks resentment and unrest. Compounding this, we are taught as children that much of history is remembrance. Again, right on – humanity must collectively never forget certain past (mis)deeds. We remember 'at the going down of the sun and in the morning', 'lest we forget, lest we forget'.* Yet do we take these cultural notions of memory too far sometimes?

In his polemic *In Praise of Forgetting*, David Rieff constructs a manifesto for omissions, writing: 'the conviction that memory is a species of morality now stands as one of the more unassailable pieties of our age.'

People like to forget themselves, after all, and as a species we simply *need* to forget things on a semantic neurological level, in order to remember other, more crucial items. As already noted, a child's longer-term memories only begin to stick once the brain gains the capacity to prioritise experiences as worthy of retention. Besides, we can't possibly remember everything as individuals, nor would we wish to: 'that way, madness lies'. This is borne out by the legendary psychological case of Solomon Shereshevsky – a

* These lines are from the two poems most often quoted as war memorials: 'For the Fallen' by Laurence Binyon and 'Recessional' by Rudyard Kipling.

Russian who in the 1930s claimed to remember absolutely everything, soon gaining notoriety as 'The Man Who Could Not Forget'.*

The point is also illustrated vividly by Jorge Luis Borges' short story 'Funes the Memorious', in which a man is plagued by remembering absolutely everything. Soon Funes' life breaks down. Unable to distinguish between the proliferation of details, he fails to derive any meaning from daily life. In a colloquial sense, he can't see the wood for the trees. The moral of Borges' story, in his own words, is that 'to think is to forget a difference'.

Philip Roth put this basic human lesson another way, when he observed that 'we all need to remember to forget'. This necessity has sometimes been played out, to seismic effect, upon the global stage. The Good Friday Agreement of Easter 1998 – accords that deliberately employed vague language in places, by way of 'constructive ambiguity' – arguably succeeded in bringing peace to Northern Ireland by harnessing the power of an entire people to, by degrees, 'forgive and forget'.

That is not to say such slates are wiped clean. The oppositional forces of history in Ireland were explicitly acknowledged – by both side's representatives – in the wording of the treaty and thus remembered. Elie Wiesel – whose

---

* The obverse of Shereshevsky's case is the landmark, unforgettable story of American Henry Molaison (known until his death as patient 'H. M.'), who lost the ability to form any new memories after his hippocampi, amygdala and other key neurological centres of memory were excised during an operation to cure his epilepsy. The transformative impact of his unique and troubling case on the field of memory research is described in Suzanne Corkin's study *Permanent Present Tense*.

childhood memories appear herein – observed that 'justice without memory is incomplete'.

Similarly, the battleground of apartheid in South Africa was, in Nelson Mandela's estimation, 'the pitting of memory against forgetting'. Mandela – perhaps partly thinking of his own father again – recognised that memory is 'the fabric of identity' and accordingly put his movement's victory down to its remembering 'our ancestors, our stories, our values and our dreams'.* This indomitable will to remember evolved into the 'Truth and Reconciliation' Commission. There, again, a nation's *collective memory* was invoked. History was made.

As with the difference between the words 'origin' and 'beginning', the key distinction here is agency. History (as collected in public *historials* and museums) resides always in the past tense, whereas *memory* is forever present (*memorials* being artistic representations and not informational resources).†

In these ways, a society's future is often shaped by the sense of its own memory: just as the seat of memory in a human brain – where those engrams synapse our stories – is the very same neurological centre within which conceptions of the future are forged.

Today, in this twenty-first century, social media has offered new means for cataloguing memory. Online platforms serve as our photo albums. Height charts on walls give

* From *A Prisoner in the Garden: Opening Nelson Mandela's Prison Archive* (2005).
† For a fuller discourse on this distinction, see *Thinking the Twentieth Century* (2012), by Tony Judt and Timothy Snyder.

way to timelines. Indeed millennials' memories can seem, to more forgetful older generations, instantaneous. The likes of Instagram and Twitter may not always be forward-thinking. Yet – as seen during the Arab Spring – they can bring about great change, for better and for worse.

There were 68.5 million people displaced from their homes by conflict and disaster in 2017.* Over twenty-five million of these unfortunates were refugees, people seeking sanctuary after their home became 'the mouth of a shark'.†

Almost 100,000 of the 1.3 million people who sought asylum in Europe during 2015 were lone children. These refugees traverse continents. Other than the clothes they are wearing, they have no possessions. Except for their dreams and memories: nostalgia for the parents and siblings left behind and those spaces where they once ran free.

For some refugee children, even this is too much. Many are born inside the camps. Other kids are simply too young to remember anywhere else. Traumatised by displacement, recollections of home disappear. How else am I to explain why the three-year-old Syrian child in the 'Olive Grove' camp in Moria, Lesvos, told me that he was from Moria – even though he had arrived there only two months previously?

Eva Hoffman, a Second World War child refugee whose first memories also appear later in this section, recognised such baptisms of hellfire:

* The Global Trends Report for 2017, published by UNHCR.
† As vividly imagined by Warsan Shire in her 2009 poem 'Home'.

In the beginning was the war. That was my childhood theory of origins.*

Today's refugee crisis is the largest flow of people fleeing for their lives since the Second World War, of which Hoffman writes. The plight of those Jewish child refugees of the 1930s scorches these pages. Even as their generation passes away, its remembrances live on.

Shlomo Breznitz's father was killed at Auschwitz. Shlomo was hidden during the Holocaust in a Roman Catholic orphanage before escaping to Israel with his mother in 1949. When he remembers those times, now a distinguished professor, Breznitz views them in childish terms:

The fields of memory are unbounded. Locations are their servants, and time is their playground.

The innocent-sounding lanes of memory through which Breznitz skips are the same pathways as his compatriot Günter Grass would dance down. For Grass, memory was perennially 'a game of hide-and-seek'.† By chasing after it, he implied, we scour a child's secret garden. Such is our inner nature. And yet these particular writers, of course, comprise a grotesque pairing: Nobel laureate Grass infamously served in the Waffen-SS (a youthful experience revealed only towards the end of his life). What unites both men, though, is memory. There, at least, they inhabited the

---

* From *After Such Knowledge: Memory, History and the Legacy of the Holocaust* (2004).
† In his memoir *Peeling the Onion* (2006).

same hinterland. With their observations, each indirectly corroborated Nietzsche (whose own writings were tainted by Nazi revisionism) and his maxim that human maturity can only be attained once we rediscover the seriousness of the child at play.

The memories and epiphanies in this collection should encourage us to seize the day and live in the moment. In turn, this section – 'Rights of Passage' – rallies a call to alms. We, the fortunate, need to take more responsibility for today's needy. If all those people who have been forced to leave their homes due to persecution, conflict or violence came together, a population greater in size than that of the United Kingdom's would be formed. These people are no different from us. After all, *everyone*'s most prized possessions are their memories and dreams. We are all in the same boat.

It is only with the help of the more fortunate that the destitute can forge for themselves a new identity and arrive at a better beginning. If only all today's refugees might come to understand what Eva Hoffman experienced when she discovered a new, safe homeland. Her beginning may have been 'the war' but when sanctuary arrived, it offered a biblical rejoinder:

The sense of the future returns like a benediction, to balance the earlier annunciation of loss.*

---

* From *Lost in Translation* (1989), p. 279.

When we speak of child refugees, often we actually mean teenagers. Having visited the remarkable Children's Section of the Refugee Council, in Croydon, I was caught out myself by how grown-up its charges are. In my naivety, as a parent of young 'children', I was surprised to find the place full of young adults. The Tuesday night I went by, the place was rocking. A seminar was about to start up but it was still breaktime. Laughter bounced off the colourful walls. Pool balls clacked. The air was full of the brio of adolescence. My surprise at their maturity moved from quiet embarrassment on to joy, as I observed some of society's most bereft finding sanctuary.

Others take a different view. When the UK accepted a paltry busload of child refugees from the Jungle camp in Calais, during the days before its demolition, hateful headlines greeted their arrival. National newspapers did not celebrate this modest gesture of solidarity but instead impugned the guests' eligibility, querying their true ages. The refugees were demonised. Decency and humanity were brushed aside in favour of salacious stories. Predictably, the plight of these most vulnerable, desperate individuals – and the countless others like them trapped in painful limbos all over the world – was soon forgotten amid a bluster of mob outrage. Never mind the fact that over 10,000 such migrant and refugee children reportedly went missing during 2014–17 in Europe.

The UK has agreements with European countries (under the Dublin Regulation) allowing it to forcibly return anyone who has previously claimed asylum in another EU state. This is also the case with the US and Canada, where – under the terms of the Safe Third Country Agreement – a refugee must seek asylum in the first nation that they enter after flight. Of course, many try to bypass such formalities. They trail through forests, down motorways, along train tracks and rivers – towards a country of greater safety, one that promises more permanent refuge (in these past few years in Europe, this has generally meant Germany or Sweden).

Refugee children arriving into a new state for the first time will not usually have a passport or identity card, let alone a birth certificate (such documentation is often not issued in countries such as Afghanistan). Lacking papers of origin, these wanderers must submit to having their age estimated. These tests take various forms. In Germany, some kids are forced to undergo medical analysis. Outer genitalia and pubic hair can offer guide indications of a teenager's likely age. In Sweden, officials commonly examine teeth and knee joints. In the relevant Greek islands, volunteers continue to bus young refugees on a daily basis to overworked local hospitals so that their age can be scrutinised.

I caught up in Lesvos, Greece, with one Syrian boy who had recently turned eighteen. He and his mates were out late in the capital, Mytilene. The police had earlier rounded them up. They had locked them in a cell – apparently without cause – making them miss the night bus back to the hellishly overcrowded camp in Moria. The trio was trudging back, along the quayside, beneath a striking crescent moon. Bright stars – themselves astral memory traces of yesteryear – pin-holed the sky. The eighteen-year-old was anxious.

While most of us celebrate this landmark birthday with a party, he had a case of the jitters. He was concerned that his newly minted adulthood would jeopardise his chances of being reunited with his parents in Germany.* My travel companion Ghias, an activist originally from Syria but now a Brit, offered some reassuring words. He put the lads in a taxi to get them back safely to Moria. We watched it curve off into the moonlight, cresting the local Statue of Liberty.

The 'unaccompanied minors' who make it to the UK today are not given medical tests. The British authorities take a more 'holistic' approach. The subject's appearance, behaviour and background are assessed. Their overall demeanour is analysed. The authorities profile the youthful refugee, a routine that leads many youngsters seeking refuge in Britain – a country that accepts shamefully few of them – to feel assailed upon arrival. They soon learn that it is no Promised Land. *How did you get here? Who brought you here? What happened to your parents? Where did you grow up? Can you describe your home?*

In other words, what the authorities want first are the child's earliest memories.

Here, we honour such recollections. I don't wish to ghettoise voices but it would be churlish to pretend that a child refugee's earliest epiphanies and watershed realisations are not set apart from those of most other children. The consciousness of a child refugee is, in many ways, different

---

* This ordeal is explored vividly in *Turning 18*, an audio series put together in 2012 by the Refugee Council and Penguin Books in which a range of refugees and asylum seekers described the mixed emotions they felt at reaching their eighteenth birthday.

to that of other kids. Their song lines are the exilic pathways of dis*place*ment, dis*location*, dis*orientation*.

Didier Drogba, one of Africa's greatest ever footballers, was not a refugee but he was forced to leave his parents and native Ivory Coast at an early age. 'I was only five years old, yet I have an almost perfect recollection of that day,' he now recalls. The experience remains raw. The colossus who bestrode the world's greatest stadia is still, in some respects, the five-year-old sobbing as he sees 'destiny slipping away from him'. That childhood pain, those earliest memories of annexation, drove the man to achieve extravagant sporting glory.

> You need to have experienced expatriation, even at a less tender age (than 5) to understand. The pain, the images, always stay with you. Leaving your country, your very skin, to seek your future elsewhere – what could be less natural? Most involuntary exiles have experienced the feeling of a rupture in their life, the loneliness, the attempt to forget. But you never forget your roots, you never wipe out your history. It was this fissure that made me the man I am.*

Home only really exists for us, then, in its truest sense, when children. Like so much of life, during infancy, it is untrammelled and whole. A place – for most – of safety,

---

* From his *Autobiography* (2008), written with Hervé Penot, translated by Paul Morris

comfort and warmth. Hence when parental units dislocate, it is the 'home' that is deemed 'broken', not – as might be argued more apposite – the 'family' or even, dare I say, the 'child'.

As we grow older, however, most of us come to realise that in fact there really is no place like home. 'Home', for an adult, is a state of mind, not a location. Indeed we must be at our most *mindful* to relocate it. T. S. Eliot put it best:

> Home is where one starts from. As we grow older
> The world becomes stranger, the pattern more
>   complicated
> Of dead and living. Not the intense moment
> Isolated, with no before and after.
> But a lifetime burning in every moment . . .*

Yet what if we never had a true home to think back on? What of that child refugee who never had roots? Just as the word 'refugee' is formed by a person fleeing back upon themselves†, so when a child is bereft of a true sense of belonging, they not only grow up unnaturally fast but often end up homeless in their heart. A maddening nostalgia can envelop such wanderers – a lonesome yearning for somewhere they've never been.

---

* From 'East Coker' (1940), *Four Quartets*.
† In the sense that 'refugee' derives from the Latin word *fugere*, meaning 'to flee'. The addition of the prefix 're' renders this 'to flee back somewhere'; making, in turn, 'a refuge' somewhere that a person has fled back towards, a place of safety or haven (from OE *haefn*, implying self-possession) or sanctuary (from *sanctum*, so a sacred place). Where else could be more secure and holy than somewhere deep within ourselves?

The biggest camp in Lesvos, at Moria, is currently home (at the time of writing) to around 9,000 refugees. It was originally intended as a temporary staging post for at most 3,100 people. Some of its residents have been stuck there for years.

On my first morning in Lesvos, Ghias and I took a taxi there from Mytilene. A defiant mantra was graffitied along the coastal roadside: *No Human Is Illegal.* Right on cue, as we headed for a camp notorious for its inhumane conditions, the radio piped out The Killers' catchy anthem 'Human'. I found myself humming along with its searching refrain, *'are we human?'*

I gazed out at the castle ruins overlooking the Aegean. Those ramparts have long borne witness to exoduses.[*] On the glittering horizon, islands hovered like dozing dragons. Continually, new arrivals pitch up in Lesvos: those who have made it through Homer's 'unharvestable sea'. Their captains have made their passengers outlandish promises. Those stumbling ashore often ask to be pointed towards Athens (which, to their shock, in fact lies hundreds of nautical miles away). Two boats arrived the same day that I did. Yet, as of writing, the statistics are nothing like the astounding peak numbers of 2015.[†]

---

[*] Not least following Lesvos' absorption into the Greek state in 1912, which led to the arrival of many refugees; notably, following the destruction by Turkey of Smyrna in 1922.

[†] At the peak of the arrivals in late 2015, some 8,000 people arrived in Lesvos during a single day. Over 750,000 people arrived there during 2015, mostly from Syria. By January 2018, numbers were down to approx. 1,000 for the month. The reduction is in large part due to the EU's deal with Turkey. Some 39 per cent of those making the journey during January 2018 were children.

The volunteer islanders whom I spoke with on the ground – the likes of Melinda McRostie of Starfish Foundation, a local NGO devoted to spreading aid strategically to where it is needed – feel 'forgotten'. Just as half their relatives and friends no longer speak to them because of their helping the refugees (thus supposedly encouraging them to come to Lesvos, in turn damaging the tourism that funds 90 per cent of the local economy), so has the media coverage of their work withered. The image of the body of three-year-old Alan Kurdi washed onto Lesvos' northern beach during September 2015 prompted momentary moral outrage. However, the media has a short memory when it comes to humanitarian crises.

I am old enough to recall a time when the word 'refugee' denoted someone courageous, a person most deserving of respect and charity. These noble connotations can partly be traced back to 1951's UN Refugee Convention. This defined a refugee as someone who has left their homeland due to a 'well-founded fear of being persecuted for reasons of race, religion, nationality, membership of a particular social group or political opinion'. Who could argue with such motivations? Migration today, however, is prompted by a more amorphous rumble of motivations – the lines between a migrant, asylum seeker and refugee becoming genuinely blurred. This, in part, helps explain the hysterical level of suspicion that has engulfed the issue.

Ghias and I entered the fenced-off Moria camp in Lesvos with the help of two of its residents. They got us in (the place had only recently been closed to outsiders, some say due to a spate of children disappearing). This impressive duo had been living there for over a year. One of them – a sparky lad called Bassel – had even made it to Athens for a while, only to be arrested and sent back to Moria after some anarchists in his squat fell foul of the law.

The ramshackle township's pathways were caked in mud. The air reeked, in pockets, of urine and sewage. Lopsided tenting was cocooned in every corner, the tents rubbing up against wire and shanty shelters. While an Algerian man clambered into the light to speak to sympathetic Ghias, an eyeball peeked out at me from behind a spidered window pane.

We moved on, through a hole in the fence. A Somali youth stood cleaning another cabin doorway. The cramped silhouettes of his seven roommates ghosted behind him. He waved at us. When we asked how he was doing, the guy simply shrugged back, lost for words.

Some families had recently departed the camp's gated, barbwired perimeter – even from Sector C, the protected area for 'vulnerable families'. Unable to take the squalor or dangers, they decamped to an adjacent, more makeshift turf known simply, for obvious reasons, as 'Ellaion' or 'The Olive Grove'. Corridors of UNHCR canvas, slung together, skirted the tree lines. We chatted among the tenting with a mother and her girls, as they wrung out washing and hung it over nearby branches. Their father poked at a crackling campfire with a stick. A girl of five tapped mischievously on my knee with a balloon. The sight of it was incongruous. Then, from nowhere, a scamp appeared with a cheeky laugh. In pursuit of a dog, he swiftly darted between our knees and stumbled after the unwitting animal – giving chase in mud-caked, oversized boots that were on the wrong way round.

The boy's grandmother confided that his mother, Maria (her daughter), had been bleeding and was in pain. She needed to see a doctor. Unable to raise one there, on site, despite the proximity of the reputedly very good Médecins Sans Frontières teams, we grabbed another taxi. Ghias rode shotgun. I and the family bundled into the backseat: Maria was in the middle beside me, little Mohammad on her lap.

As we headed back towards the island's capital, Maria's mother – a striking woman not much older than me – spoke in Arabic to Ghias of their abandoned life in Baghdad. Apparently, her husband had disappeared three years previously. She still has no idea, only suspicions, what happened to him. Once he had vanished, she became the subject of neighbourhood recriminations. She was targeted for not wearing a veil and beaten repeatedly in the streets.

She then pulled a photo from her person. It was a surprisingly large print of Mohammad. She held it up, adjacent to his cheek. Side by side, he and the boy in the picture looked markedly different. Not so much because he was chubbier in the photograph but because his visage was purple. A patchwork of livid bruises smouldered the kid's features. His entire forehead was covered by bandaging. Big eyes gazed blankly at the camera. Adjacent to them, those very same irises were now staring directly at me. Mohammad's face remained just as adorable – same saucer-wide eyes, dimpled chin, fair hair wanting a tousle – and yet he had grown serious and wan. I noticed that scars from his injuries lined his forehead. They thatched those bushy little eyebrows. Mohammad may have been chasing the dog when we first encountered him back among the olive trees, but his mother now confided that her son had grown scared to play with other children since being attacked in Iraq.

Struck by her story and feeling remiss, being the one who couldn't speak their language, I introduced myself belatedly to this brave matriarch. I hadn't caught her name. I asked her it, via Ghias – 'Ahlam' she replied. I remarked on how beautiful it was. She smiled and thanked me for the compliment.

'It means "Dreams",' Ghias said from the passenger seat.

Seeing as we were handling introductions, Mohammad then – unbidden – grabbed my hand and jerkily shook it with a cheeky grin. I gave him five in return. He upped the ante and, to everyone's delight, blew kisses my way, even though I was squeezed up right next to him.

As the taxi continued to wend its way through the hazy winter sunshine towards the hospital, the Greek driver prattling on his mobile throughout, Mohammad kept glancing excitedly out of the window. He commentated in a pitter-patter all his own, pointing out scenery: the sea (thálassa, I explained, showing off my elementary Greek); the gargantuan cruise ship; the toy dinosaur in the shop window. As we dawdled at a red light near the centre, however, his pidgin commentary dropped away.

Mohammad was gazing past me onto a primary school playground. It was break time and the yelps of the playing

Greek children wafted through the open window. His liquid eyes bulged. I peered into them for a split second. They were deep as centuries, absorbing so much. Suddenly I felt struck by how this put-upon, adorable boy was hitting just the age at which first memories most often ripen. Mohammad had turned three just a couple of months previously (and one month before the family's arrival by skiff to Europe).* These times might well be lodging somewhere within him for keeps (maybe not this taxi ride, admittedly, even if I shall always remember it). I peered for a tiny moment longer at those wheels turning furiously inside the child, while the stationary taxi waited for green. I considered the grown man suspended somewhere in the boy's future. The adult who one day would stare out from behind those same big, brown eyes. Who he would be. Where he might end up.

The cab moved off. I turned back to face front. From the corner of my eye, though, I saw Mohammad continue to peer past me. The child's sightline had remained fixed. He was looking away from the road ahead, back towards the playground scene already fading into memory.

* The late Alan Kurdi was also three when he arrived in Lesvos.

Stefan Zweig (1881–1942)

I am aware of the unfavourable circumstances, characteristic though they are of our time, in which I am trying to shape my reminiscences. I write them in the midst of war, in a foreign country, and without the least aids to my memory. None of my books, none of my notes, no friends' letters are at hand in my hotel room. Nowhere can I seek information, for in the whole world the mails from country to country have been disrupted or hampered by censorship. We live cut off from one another as we did a hundred years ago, before steamships, railroads, planes, and mails were invented. I have nothing more of my past with me than what I have retained in my mind. All else at this moment is unobtainable or lost. But the good art of not pining over that which is lost has been thoroughly learned by our generation, and it is quite possible that the loss of documentation and detail may actually be an advantage for my book. For I look upon our memory not as an element which accidentally retains or forgets, but rather as a consciously organizing and wisely exclusionary power. All that one forgets of one's life was long since predestined by an inner instinct to be forgotten. Only that which wills to preserve itself has the right to be preserved for others. So choose and speak for me, ye memories, and at least give some reflection of my life before it sinks into the dark! . . .

It was not a century of suffering in which I was born and educated. It was an ordered world with definite classes and calm transitions, a world without haste. The rhythm of the new speed had not yet carried over from the machines, the automobile, the telephone, the radio, and the aeroplane, to mankind; time and age had another measure. One lived more comfortably, and when I try to recall to mind the figure of the grown-ups who stood about my childhood, I am struck with the fact that many of them were corpulent at an early age. My father, my uncle, my teacher, the salesmen in the shops, the members of the Philharmonic at their music stands were already, at forty, portly and 'worthy' men. They walked slowly, they spoke with measured accent, and, in their conversation, stroked their well-kept beards which often had already turned grey. But grey hair was merely a new sign of dignity, and a 'sedate' man consciously avoided the gestures and high spirits of youth as being unseemly. Even in my earliest childhood, when my father was not yet forty, I cannot recall ever having seen him run up or down the stairs, or ever doing anything in a visibly hasty fashion. Speed was not only thought to be unrefined, but indeed was considered unnecessary, for in that stabilized bourgeois world with its countless little securities, well palisaded on all sides, nothing unexpected ever occurred. Such catastrophes as took place outside

321

on the world's periphery never made their way through the well-padded walls of 'secure' living. The Boer War, the Russo-Japanese War, the Balkan War itself did not penetrate the existence of my parents. They passed over all reports of war in the newspapers just as they did the sporting page. And truly, what did it matter to them what took place outside of Austria, what did it change in their lives? In their Austria in that tranquil epoch there were no State revolutions, no crass destruction of values; if stocks sank four or five points on the exchange, it was called a 'crash' and they talked earnestly, with furrowed brows, about the 'catastrophe.' One complained more as a habit than because of actual conviction about the 'high' taxes, which actually, in comparison with those of the post-war period, were no other than small tips to the state. Exact stipulations were set down in testaments, to guard grand-children and great-grandchildren against the loss of their fortunes, as if security were guaranteed by some sort of invisible promissory note by the eternal powers. Meanwhile one lived comfortably and stroked one's petty cares as if they were faithful obedient pets of whom one was not in the least afraid. That is why when chance places an old newspaper of those days in my hands and I read the excited articles about some little community election, when I try to recall the plays in the Burgtheater with their tiny problems, or the disproportionate excitement of our youthful discus-sions about things that were so terribly unimportant, I am forced to smile. How Lilliputian were all these cares, how wind-still the time! It had better luck, the generation of my parents and grandparents, in that it lived quietly, straight and clearly from one end of its life to the other.

From *The World of Yesterday* (1942)

Stefan Zweig was born in Vienna but took British nationality after fleeing Austria following Hitler's accession to power. During his lifetime, Zweig was one of the most popular writers in the world. His novels include *Passion and Pain* (1924) and *Beware of Pity* (1939). The house in Brazil in which he lived and died during 1942 – from a barbiturate overdose, together with his wife Lotte, propelled by their despair at the situation in Europe – is now a cultural centre named in his honour.

Walter Benjamin (1892–1940)

For a long time, life deals with the still-tender memory of childhood like a mother who lays her newborn on her breast without waking it. Nothing has fortified my own memory so profoundly as gazing into courtyards, one of whose dark loggias, shaded by blinds in the summer, was for me the cradle in which the city laid its new citizen. The caryatids that support the loggia on the floor above ours may have slipped away from their post for a moment to sing a lullaby beside that cradle – a song containing little of what later awaited me, but nonetheless sounding the theme through which the air of the courtyard has forever remained intoxicating to me. I believe that a whiff of this air was still present in the vineyards of Capri where I held my beloved in my arms and it is precisely this air that sustains the images and allegories which preside over my thinking, just as the caryatids, from the heights of their loggias, preside over the courtyards of Berlin's West End.

The rhythm of the metropolitan railway and of carpet-beating rocked me to sleep. It was the mold in which my dreams took shape – first the unformed ones, traversed perhaps by the sound of running water or the smell of milk, then the long-spun ones: travel dreams and dreams of rain. Here, spring called up the first shoots of green before the grey façade of a house in the back; and when, later in the year, a dusty canopy of leaves brushed up against the wall of the house a thousand times a day, the rustling of the branches initiated me into a knowledge to which I was not yet equal. For everything in the courtyard became a sign or hint to me. Many were the messages embedded in the skirmishing of the green roller blinds drawn up high, and many the ominous dispatches that I prudently left unopened in the rattling of the roll-up shutters that came thundering down at dusk.

What occupied me most of all in the courtyard was the spot where the tree stood. This spot was set off by paving stones into which a large iron ring was sunk. Metal bars were mounted on it, in such a way as to fence in the bare earth. Not for nothing, it seemed to me, was it thus enclosed; from time to time, I would brood over what went on within the black pit from which the trunk came. Later, I extended these speculations to hackney-carriage stands. There, the trees were similarly rooted, and similarly fenced in. Coachmen were accustomed to hanging their capes on the railing while they watered their horses, first clearing away the last remnants of hay and oats in the trough by drawing water from the pump that rose up out of the pavement. To me, these waiting-stations, whose peace was seldom disturbed by the coming and going of carriages, were distant provinces of my backyard.

Clotheslines ran from one wall of the loggia to another; the palm tree looked homeless — all the more so as it had long been understood that not the dark soil but the adjacent drawing room was its proper abode. So decreed the law of the place, around which the dreams of its inhabitants had once played. Before this place fell prey to oblivion, art had occasionally undertaken to transfigure it. Now a hanging lamp, now a bronze, now a china vase would steal into its confines. And although these antiquities rarely did the place much honor, they suited its own antique character. The Pompeian red that ran in a wide band along its wall was the appointed background of the hours that piled up in such seclusion. Time grew old in those shadowy little rooms which looked out on the courtyards. And that was why the morning, whenever I encountered it on our loggia, had already been morning for so long that it seemed more itself there than at any other spot. Never did I have the chance to wait for morning on the loggia; every time, it was already waiting for me. It had long since arrived – was effectively out of fashion – when I finally came upon it.

Later, from the perspective of the railroad embankment, I rediscovered the courtyards. When, on sultry summer afternoons, I gazed down on them from my compartment, the summer appeared to have parted from the landscape and locked itself into those yards. And the red geraniums that were peeping from their boxes accorded less well with summer than the red feather mattresses that were hung over the windowsills each morning to air. Iron garden chairs, made in imitation of winding branches or wickerwork, comprised the seating arrangements of the loggia. We drew them close together when, at dusk, our reading circle would gather there. Gaslight shone down, from a red- and green-flamed calyx, on the pages of the paperback classic. Romeo's last sigh flitted through our backyard in search of the echo that Juliet's vault held ready for it.

In the years since I was a child, the loggias have changed less than other places. This is not the only reason they stay with me. It is much more on account of the solace that lies in their uninhabitability for one who himself no longer has a proper abode. They mark the outer limit of the Berliner's lodging. Berlin – the city god itself – begins in them. The god remains such a presence there that nothing transitory can hold its ground beside him. In his safekeeping, space and time come into their own and find each other. Both of them lie at his feet here. The child who was once their confederate, however, dwells in his loggia, encompassed by this group, as in a mausoleum long intended just for him.

From *Berlin Childhood around 1900* (1950), translated by Howard Eiland

Walter Benjamin was a critic, essayist and philosopher. He translated and also wrote essays about Proust. In Paris during the 1930s he befriended fellow Jewish German refugees, such as Hannah Arendt, Herman Hesse and Kurt Weill. He published his influential essay 'Theses on the Philosophy of History' in 1940, while in exile. Later that year, Benjamin took an overdose of morphine in Portbou at the French–Spanish border, choosing death over capture by the Nazis.

Eva Hoffman (1945–)

I am lying in bed, watching the slowly moving shadows on the ceiling made by the gently blowing curtains, and the lights of an occasional car moving by. I'm trying hard not to fall asleep. Being awake is so sweet that I want to delay the loss of consciousness. I'm snuggled under an enormous goose-feather quilt covered in hand-embroidered silk. Across the room from me is my sister's crib. From the next room, 'the first room,' I hear my parents' breathing. The maid – one of a succession of country girls who come to work for us – is sleeping in the kitchen. It is Cracow, 1949, I'm four years old, and I don't know that this happiness is taking place in a country recently destroyed by war, a place where my father has to hustle to get us a bit more than our meagre ration of meat and sugar. I only know that I'm in my room, which to me is an everywhere, and that the patterns on the ceiling are enough to fill me with a feeling of sufficiency because . . . well, just because I'm conscious, because the world exists and it flows so gently into my head. Occasionally, a few blocks away, I hear the hum of the tramway, and I'm filled by a sense of utter contentment. I love riding the tramway, with its bracing but not overly fast swaying, and I love knowing, from my bed, the street over which it is moving; I repeat to myself that I'm in Cracow, Cracow, which to me is both home and the universe. Tomorrow I'll go for a walk with my mother, and I'll know how to get from Kazimierza Wielkiego, the street where we live, to Urzędnicza Street, where I'll visit my friend Krysia – and already the anticipation of the walk, of retracing familiar steps on a route that may yet hold so many surprises, fills me with pleasure.

Slowly, the sights and sounds recede, the words with which I name them in my head become scrambled, and I observe, as long as possible, the delicious process of falling asleep. That awareness of subsiding into a different state is also happiness.

Each night, I dream of a tiny old woman – a wizened Baba Yaga, half grandmother, half witch, wearing a black kerchief and sitting shriveled and hunched on a tiny bench at the bottom of our courtyard, way, way down. She is immeasurably old and immeasurably small, and from the bottom of the courtyard, which has become immeasurably deep, she looks up at me through narrow slits of wise, malicious eyes. Perhaps, though, I am her. Perhaps I have been on the earth a long, long time and that's why I understand the look in her eyes. Perhaps this childish disguise is just a dream. Perhaps I am being dreamt by a Baba Yaga who has been here since the beginning of time and I am seeing from inside her ancient frame and I know that everything is changeless and knowable . . .

My father almost never mentions that war; dignity for him is silence, sometimes too much silence. After a while, he finds it difficult to talk about many things, and it is not until the events have receded into the past that he recounts a few stories from those years – by that time so far removed that they seem like fables again, James Bond adventures. How will I ever pin down the reality of what happened to my parents? I come from the war; it is my true origin. But as with all origins, I cannot grasp it. Perhaps we never know where we come from; in a way, we are all created *ex nihilo*.

Before they had to hide in their forest bunker, my father had a narrow escape. This was when the roundups of Jews were intensifying in his town, and the Wydra brothers – there were three of them – were considered a prize catch because they kept eluding the gestapo so successfully. So when a German truck with Jews being transported to a nearby concentration camp passed my father on the road one day, one of the people on it couldn't contain himself and stupidly shouted out, 'There's a Wydra!' The German in charge of course stopped and ordered my father to get on. None of the people on that truck came out of the war alive. My father did because, as the Germans stopped the truck for the night and herded people into some house reserved for this purpose, he noticed a door that was a crack open and slid through it. Then he was out in the back and he started to run, toward the forest ahead. Within minutes, there were loud barks of dogs pursuing him. But he ran fast, and once he was in the forest, he managed to throw the animals off his track. The area was unfamiliar, and he wandered through the snow until dawn, when he found himself on the edge of the woods again. Approaching him was a figure of a peasant. My father couldn't know whether the presence of the peasant meant rescue or death – but by that time, he couldn't walk anymore anyway. The peasant turned out to be all right; he took my father into his house – situated next to the concentration camp to which the transport was being taken. Then, word was sent to my mother of my father's whereabouts, and she came to fetch him in a cart. For the next few days, she told me, my father had a cold.

When they hid in their bunker, my father had to come out each night to forage for food. Sometimes, he would make his way to the village church, where the priest would give him some bread. But one night on the way back, he was grabbed by two young Ukrainians – strong and drunk – who told him they were going to take him to the gestapo. They each took him by the arm. But as they were crossing the bridge of a local river, my father – 'strong as a bull' – threw them off violently, letting them fall against the bridge's railings (he makes a violent gesture with his powerful arms as he tells me this), and then jumped into the river, though it was half iced over at this time of the year. He stayed in the freezing water, diving under the ice repeatedly for an hour or so, until he was quite sure that his pursuers had given up and gone away. 'Ach,' my father finishes, making an impatient gesture with his hands, as if to throw off these memories. What does it matter? It happened, it happened, what can you make of it?

My mother wants me to know what happened, and I keep

every detail of what she tells me in my memory like black beads. It's a matter of honor to remember, like affirming one's Jewishness. But I don't understand what I remember. To atone for what happened, I should relive it all with her, and I try. No, not really. I can't go as near this pain as I should. But I can't draw away from it either.

When I am much older, I try to get away more. Surely, there is no point in duplicating suffering, in adding mine to hers. And surely, there are no useful lessons I can derive from my parents' experience: it does not apply to my life; it is in fact misleading, making me into a knee-jerk pessimist. This is what I tell myself, and for a while I have a policy of keeping my mother's stories at a long arm's length. But once, years later, in a noisy cafeteria in New York, I meet somebody who knew my parents in their town before the war. It is the only such person I've ever met – she has located my parents, on this other continent, by a series of flukes, and now she wants to talk to me. It is also the first time I get some glimpses of how my parents – whose history has always made them archetypal in my eyes – have a peculiarity, even within this metastory. This woman is different from my mother: divorced, working on her own, tougher. Her daughter is as different from me as I can imagine – a saleswoman who takes dance lessons and doesn't care a whit about the past – and this also comes as a surprise. We should be more like each other; we have been molded by the same Thing. The mother has a photograph of herself and other young women – including my mother's sister. They stand on a tiny bridge in a frozen landscape, in coats with fur collars, looking older than their age, their heads cocked in an innocent gesture of coquetry. So that's what she looked like; yes, a little like Alinka. But the image adds so little information; there is no way to penetrate the veil this way either. My parents' old friend, though, tells me a story while we're having lunch in the Union Square cafeteria that I have never heard: when my parents finally had to run for the bunker, she recounts, my mother, who had had a miscarriage, was too weak to walk through the snow all the way. My father ended up carrying her on his back, kilometer after kilometer. Another image for me to store, another sharp black bead added to the rest. As I listen, I lower my head in acknowledgment that this – the pain of this – is where I come from, and that it's useless to try to get away.

From *Lost in Translation* (1989)

Eva Hoffman grew up in Cracow, Poland, before emigrating in her teens to Canada and then the United States. She is the author of six works of non-fiction – including *After Such Knowledge: Memory, History and the Legacy of the Holocaust* (2004) – and two novels, *The Secret* (2002) and *Illuminations* (2008).

Elie Wiesel (1928–2016)

I search my mind for my earliest memory and I see a little boy sitting on his bed, calling for his mother. At the age of three, four, or five, I felt unhappy and harassed by my classmates at *heder*. I would count the minutes that separated me from my mother. I didn't understand why she couldn't spend all morning and afternoon with me. Had she been present, I would have learned the Hebrew alphabet and the Pentateuch – the first five books in the Scriptures – in no time flat and vanquished all the enemies of Israel. My dream was never to leave her. I would cling to her skirts even when she went to the ritual baths. I would sit on the stairs, hold my breath, and wait for her. 'How come I can't go in?' I would ask. 'Because it's forbidden,' she replied. 'Why?' I persisted. 'It says so in the Torah.' That stopped me. The Torah demanded silence and a kind of sacred respect. All prohibitions came from the Torah.

With time, however, study became a true adventure for me. My first teacher, the Batizer Rebbe, a sweet old man with a snow-white beard that devoured his face, pointed to the twenty-two holy letters of the Hebrew alphabet and said, 'Here, children, are the beginning and the end of all things.

Thousands upon thousands of works have been written and will be written with these letters. Look at them and study them with love, for they will be your links to life. And to eternity.'

When I read the first word aloud – *Breshit*, 'in the beginning' – I felt transported into an enchanted universe. An intense joy gripped me when I came to understand the first verse. 'It was with the twenty-two letters of the *aleph-beth* that God created the world,' said the teacher, who on reflection was probably not so old. 'Take care of them and they will take care of you. They will go with you everywhere. They will make you laugh and cry. Or rather, they will cry when you cry and laugh when you laugh, and if you are worthy of it, they will allow you into hidden sanctuaries where all becomes . . .' All becomes what? Dust? Truth? Life? It was a sentence he never finished.

There was something terrifying and fascinating about reading ancient texts, something that filled me with awe. Without moving I could ramble through words visible and invisible. I was in two places at once, a thousand places at once. I was with Adam at the beginning, barely awakened to a world streaming with light, with Moses in Sinai under a flaming sky. I seized upon a phrase, a word, and distances vanished.

Yet reading isolated me. My classmates were no longer beside me. I no longer saw or heard them, for I was elsewhere, in far-off kingdoms ruled by the word alone. Even my mother remained behind, as if on the far side of a river. To rediscover her at home was always a joy, but how could

I ease that wrenching feeling that preceded my return? I found a solution: take her with me. All I needed was determination and imagination. When I went to see Adam, Eve wore my mother's sensitive face. When I followed Moses in the desert, his sister Miriam became my mother. Now nothing could separate us. Even at *heder*, I had only to open a book and I would see her. Only when I paused, when there was no book before me, did I feel alone and abandoned.

Once, however, we made each other suffer. But the suffering came neither from her nor from me, but from Rabbi Israel of Wizhnitz when he came to Sighet.

I was eight years old. As usual, my mother took me with her to seek the Rabbi's blessing: good health for her family, success and respect for the head of the family, good husbands for her daughters, fear of God for her son. A large crowd thronged the antechamber, spilling out into the corridor and onto the street. As the daughter of Reb Dodye, my mother did not have to wait in line. She herself, not the secretary, wrote out her request to the Rabbi, who talked with her about countless family matters as I stood holding my mother's hand, not understanding everything they said, focused as I was on the beaming face of this rabbi, whose *ahavat Israel* (love for Israel, and therefore for every being in Israel) was legendary. I was captivated by his eyes, his eyebrows, his beard. Suddenly the Rabbi told me to approach. He put me on his lap and asked me tenderly about my studies. I answered his easy questions as best I could, stammering, almost incoherent. At which point the Rabbi asked my mother to leave us alone. 'Good,' the Rabbi said when she closed the door behind her. 'Now we can speak calmly.' About everything: the sidra of the week (a portion of the Torah read on Shabbat), the Rashi commentary, the chapter of a Talmudic tractate I was studying at the time. We were alone a few minutes. Or was it a few hours? At last he kissed me on the forehead and told me to wait outside. 'Tell your mother to come back,' he said. When she re-emerged from talking with him, what seemed like days later, I froze. I tried to run to her, but my legs would not obey. She was a changed woman. Violent sobs shook her body. People stared at her in commiseration. The Rabbi must have said terrible things to her, terrifying, painful things – about me. I must have shamed her with my bad behaviour, or by giving wrong answers to the Rabbi's questions. 'Why are you crying?' I asked. She refused to answer. I repeated my question again and again, but in vain. I tried the next day too, and the day after that, to no avail. All I got were those same tears. I persisted stubbornly, desperate to know what evil I might have done to cause such sorrow. It went on for weeks, until finally I gave up, exhausted. By then she had stopped crying.

One day, some twenty-five years later, I got an urgent phone call from a distant relative who told me my cousin Anshel Feig was gravely ill. He needed an operation, but had refused to sign the consent form until he could see me. Fearing the worst, I jumped in a cab. Anshel had owned a fish market on Amsterdam Avenue near Eighty-sixth Street, close to where I lived. Whenever I had seen him, he was modest and happy. A kipa on his head. He spoke in Manhattan just as he had in Sighet: in song.

'Thank you for coming,' Anshel said. 'I need you. I need your blessing.'

'Are you out of your mind?' I asked, trying to hide my concern. 'You want *me* to bless *you*? Your standing up above is surely a lot stronger than mine.'

Anshel, in fact, had retained his old Hasidic fervor, carefully observing all the commandments of the Torah, going to synagogue morning and evening, whereas I . . . But he insisted. 'What are you waiting for?' his doctor – the relative who had called me – whispered in my ear. 'His life is at stake.'

So I took the patient's hand and gave him my blessing, the same one I had received when I was sick as a child: May everything turn out for good, may God bring a swift and total cure.

A few days later I went to visit Anshel. The operation had been a success and I could now speak to him freely. I asked him why he had insisted on receiving my blessing. He did not seem surprised by the question.

'Do you remember the last time the Rabbi of Wizhnitz visited Sighet?' he asked.

'Like yesterday,' I replied. 'How could I forget?' The painful image of my mother's sobbing surged back. 'It's funny,' I told Anshel, 'but I never found out why she came away from the Rabbi in tears.'

'I know why,' Anshel said with the hint of a smile.

'You know?' I jumped. Stunned, I felt like grabbing him

by the shoulders and shaking him, even if it sent him back to the O.R. 'You knew all along and you never told me?'

His eyes clouded, and he spoke as if in a dream. 'I was one of the people waiting in the antechamber to see the Rabbi, but when I saw your mother crying I left to see her home. You were walking ahead of us and that was when she swore me to secrecy and told me what Rabbi Israel of Wizhnitz, may his memory protect us, had said to her. He said: "Sarah, know that your son will become a *gadol b'Israel*, a great man in Israel, but neither you nor I will live to see the day. That's why I'm telling you now." And now you know why she cried.'

I stared at him. Neither of us spoke until finally he sighed deeply and said, 'That's why I wanted your blessing. If the Rabbi of Wizhnitz had such faith in you, your blessing must mean something in heaven.'

As for me, the only blessing that meant anything was my mother's. Away from her I felt lost, surrounded by enemies. In my child's imagination, my first teacher viewed me with scorn. To please him I had to work infinitely harder. There was another melamed who wore a heavy coat winter and summer. I was troubled by his cold and indifferent air, and tried to win him over by redoubling my efforts to explain a page of the Talmud. I was convinced that my classmates detested me, and I decided to mollify them with bribery. At first I shared my buttered bread, fruit, and snacks, and later I let them divide it all among themselves while I stood apart and watched. They would laugh and devour my treats without so much as thanking me, as though I didn't exist.

I should have been bolder, devised other ways of asserting myself, but years went by before I dared. Until my bar mitzvah, whenever I received a present, I gave it away to my classmates. Sometimes – though it shames me to recall it – I even dipped into the till at the store, not out of generosity but out of insecurity. I feared exclusion and isolation, but as much as I yearned to be part of the group, to be like the others and with the others, I always remained apart. My mother was my sole ally and support. She alone understood me. Yet I never gave *her* a present.

From *All Rivers Run to the Sea* (1994), translated by Marion Wiesel

Elie Wiesel authored fifty-seven books, mostly in French and English, including *Night* (1960), a work based on his experiences as a prisoner in the Auschwitz and Buchenwald concentration camps.

He campaigned for victims of oppression in areas throughout the world, from South Africa to Nicaragua to Kosovo. He won the Nobel Peace Prize in 1986, the Nobel Committee calling him a 'messenger to mankind'.

Isabel Allende (1942–)

I think Tata was always sorry I wasn't a boy; had I been, he could have taught me to play jai alai, and use his tools, and hunt. I would have been his companion on the trips he made every year to Patagonia for the sheepshearing. In those days one travelled south by train, or by automobile over twisting dirt roads that could turn into quagmires, immobilizing cars until a team of oxen pulled them free. Lakes were crossed by rope-drawn ferries, and mountains on muleback. Those were demanding expeditions. My grandfather slept beneath the stars, wrapped in a heavy Castilian blanket; he bathed in raging rivers fed by snowmelt from the peaks and ate garbanzo beans and tinned sardines until he reached the Argentine side of the mountain. There a crew was waiting for him with a truck and a lamb roasting over a slow fire. Rough men, they hunkered around the fire in silence. They lived in a vast, forsaken landscape where the wind tore the words from their mouths. With gaucho knives they sliced off great hunks of meat and devoured them, their gaze fixed on the glowing coals. One of them might strum a plaintive song on his guitar while the maté passed from hand to hand, the aromatic brew of bitter green yerba they drink there

341

like tea. I treasure indelible memories of the one trip to the south I made with my grandfather – even though I was so carsick I thought I would die, a mule threw me twice, and then as I watched them shearing the sheep I was struck dumb, unable to speak until we returned to civilization. The sheepshearers, who were paid by the animal, could zip off a fleece in less than a minute, but, however careful they were, they often sliced off strips of skin with the wool, and I saw more than one wretched lamb split open, its guts stuffed back any which way in its belly before being stitched up with an upholstery needle and returned to the flock with the hope it would survive and produce wool.

My love for heights, and my relationship with trees, originated with that trip. I have returned several times to the south of Chile and I always feel the same indescribable love for the landscape. Crossing the cordillera of the Andes is engraved in my soul as one of the true epiphanies of my existence. Now, and during other critical moments when I try to remember prayers and cannot evoke the words or the rituals, the only vision I can turn to for consolation is that of those misty paths through the chill forest of gigantic ferns and tree trunks rising toward the heavens, the sheer mountain passes, and the sharp profile of snow-covered volcanoes reflected in emerald lakes. To be one with God must be very much like being in this extraordinary realm. In my memory, my grandfather, the guide, and the mules have disappeared. I am alone, walking in solemn silence through that temple of rock and vegetation. I am breathing clean air cold and wet with rain. My feet sink into a carpet of mud and rotted leaves; the scent of the earth is a sword piercing my bones. Effortlessly, I walk and walk along the narrow, misty paths, yet never leave that undiscovered world surrounded with century-old trees, fallen trunks, strips of aromatic bark, and roots bursting through the earth like mutilated, vegetal hands. On the path, my hand is brushed by strong spiderwebs, lace tablecloths pearled with drops of water and phosphorescent-winged mosquitoes. Here and there I glimpse the brilliant scarlet and white of copihues and other flowers that live at these heights tangled among the trees like glittering beads. You can feel the breath of the gods, throbbing, absolute presences in this resplendent domain of precipices and high walls of black rock polished by the snow to the sensual perfection of marble. Water, and more water. Thin crystalline serpents slip through fissures of rock into the hidden depths of the mountains and join together in small brooks and sounding waterfalls. Suddenly I am startled by the scream of a bird or thud of a rock rolling from above, but the enveloping peace of this vastness descends again, and I realize I am weeping with happiness. That trip, with all its obstacles and hidden dangers, its desired solitude and breathtaking beauty, is like the journey of my own life. This memory is sacred to me; this memory is my country. When I say Chile, this is what I think of. Time and time again I have tried to recapture the emotion that forest stirs in me, a feeling more intense than the most perfect orgasm, than the longest ovation.

From *Paula* (1994)

Isabel Allende – then a prominent journalist – fled Chile in 1975 with her husband and two children. Their exile followed the military coup led by General Pinochet, during which Chile's elected president, her cousin Salvador Allende, was assassinated.

Her acclaimed debut novel *The House of the Spirits* (1982) – a Chilean family saga that spans the 1920s through to the coup – grew out of a farewell letter written to her dying grandfather, in which Allende revisited her childhood memories of his home.

She has since written twenty-two more works and now lives in California.

Gillian Slovo (1952–)

I was two when [my mother] Ruth went to China [on a study trip] and, while she was away, I learned to walk. It had taken me a long, long time. My parents and my grandparents had watched over me, since I turned one, in anticipation of my first steps. To no avail. I seemed to be developing normally – I learned to talk early in fact – but still I didn't seem able to walk.

My speech was fluent by the time they carted me off to the specialist. Nothing organic wrong, was the doctor's verdict: she'll walk eventually. And so back home I was carried, as always contained by some adult's arms. And then one day, when Ruth was in China, I was sitting in the kitchen and I was hungry.

'I want that,' I said, pointing at a packet of coveted biscuits on the counter, knowing that my black nanny would bring them to me.

'Fetch them yourself,' she said.

Was that all that I'd been waiting for? Someone to tell me to stand up on my own two feet? Perhaps it was: I obeyed. I stood up and I walked.

It was my grandmother who, late in life, told me this

story. If I hadn't known her, and known how her life had limited the stretch of her imagination, I would have assumed she'd made it up. It was too apocryphal of white South African life, the white toddler unable to move without the black servant's chiding.

Looking back, I guess the story was invented and that it contained a message. With her reputation of unbearable honesty, my grandmother did sometimes bury her meaning deep. I remember how, on another occasion, in 1984, when she had just returned from a visit to South Africa, she chose to describe at length, and with seeming admiration, the beautiful cast-iron fretwork in one of her relatives' Jo'burg home. Only after I had kissed her parchment skin and walked away, did I realise that what she had described were the bars her hosts had erected to keep servants and black intruders out at night.

Perhaps when she told me the story of how I had learned to walk, what she was really saying was that, once again, it was time for me to get up and stand on my own two feet. Thinking back to the moment she had chosen to tell me the story, and of how angry I had been at the time at something she had chosen to do, I think that this is precisely what she meant. But in those early days, in the fifties, my grandmother was always there and there were no bars separating us from the world. Walk I did, in time for my mother's return. A shadow was lifted. My parents could once again be framed by their own dazzling optimism: with their help, all humanity's problems would soon disappear.

They made choices, brave choices, that others in their

country did not make. For this they were heroic. But they were also lucky. There were few commonplace restraints to hem them in. If they had opted for ordinary white lives in South Africa, they could certainly have made much more money yet even though they chose a highly dangerous course, they were still white and well off. Ruth was a working mother and an activist but she had no need to occupy the kitchen: she had domestic workers to do the cooking, the cleaning and the childcare. She also had her parents, ever generous, to supply the extras which included a constant stream of new Citroëns that were my grandfather's obsession. She and Joe worked hard but they played hard too. People fought to get an invitation to their parties: they were, in their circles at least, the king and queen of Jo'burg.

Our family albums are full of those years of gracious living. There's the house we lived in – a three-bedroomed new-built bungalow in one of Johannesburg's middle-class suburbs, without a swimming pool but with a big garden overlooking an open *veld* and a huge spreading broad-leafed plane tree that we three sisters used to climb . . .

There are other photographs as well of that period of our lives, each telling a different part of the story. One, taken in 1956, is of us three chubby-cheeked sisters around a table, eating rice crispies. It was our second breakfast of the day. The newspapers had come to snap us eating because the night before both our parents were among 156 others, rounded up and taken to a police station to be charged with treason. Six-year-old Shawn was our spokesperson:

'Mummy's gone to prison,' she said, 'to look after the black people.' . . .

We children played out fantasies in the garden while around us the world moved fast. The images of those times come to me sporadically: the sound of neighbourhood dogs barking as black dustbin men hefted huge trash cans on their backs and ran down the road after the dustbin lorry whose driver's white skin stopped him from slowing down for them; the sticky crimson blood oozing out of the black newspaper deliverer's skull, seeping on to strewn newspapers as we waited for the black ambulance to come and pick him up; the black women who ran up our driveway seeking sanctuary from the men who had robbed them in the *veld*, the fear in their eyes turning to dulled acceptance as the police, hearing that the victims were black, refused to come round.

And all the time while this was happening we were lifted in our freshly pressed uniforms to school, sitting in small whites-only classes, directed by kind white teachers whose ample bosoms were cossetted in fluffy, wool twinsets. And then we were driven back again to that garden of our imagination to feel the first, faint echoes of what was to come.

From *Every Secret Thing* (1997)

Gillian Slovo, the daughter of famed anti-apartheid activists Joe Slovo and Ruth First, was born in South Africa but has lived in London since 1964. Her parents' perilous life of exile, imprisonment and armed resistance culminated with her mother's assassination by South African forces in 1982. Her father subsequently became the first white member of the ANC's National Executive in 1986. Slovo has published fourteen novels, two plays and two memoirs. She has also served as president of English PEN.

Ayaan Hirsi Ali (1969–)

'Who are you?'

'I am Ayaan, the daughter of Hirsi, the son of Magan.'

I am sitting with my grandmother on a grass mat under the talal tree. Behind us is our house, and the branches of the talal tree are all that shields us from the sun blazing down on the white sand. 'Go on,' my grandmother says, glaring at me.

'And Magan was the son of Isse.'

'And then?'

'Isse was the son of Guleid, was the son of Ali. Was the son of Wai'ays. Was the son of Muhammad. Ali. Umar.' I hesitate for a moment. 'Osman. Mahamud.' I catch my breath, proud of myself.

'Bah?' asks my grandmother. 'Which consort?'

'Bah Ya'qub, Garab-Sare.' I name the most powerful of Osman Mahamud's wives: daughter of Ya'qub, she of the highest shoulder.

My grandmother nods, grudgingly. I have done well, for a five-year-old. I have managed to count my forefathers back for three hundred years – the part that is crucially important. Osman Mahamud is the name of my father's subclan, and thus my own. It is where I belong, who I am . . .

I used to try to imagine my father when he was little. My mother, when I asked her, only told me that we had never met. *Afwayne*, who was a real monster, not like the kind in my grandmother's stories, had put my father in jail. *Afwayne*, Big Mouth, was what everyone called the president, Siad Barré. There were huge portraits of him in every shop and every public space in Mogadishu; he had a huge mouth, with big, long teeth. Sometimes *Afwayne*'s special police burst into houses and took people away. They tortured them into admitting something terrible, then they killed them. Even I knew that. The adults in my house all went suddenly still when we heard the executioner's rifle in Tribunka Square.

Siad Barré had become the vice commander of Somalia's army at the time of independence, in 1960, and later became an advocate of Marxism after training with Soviet officers. He was a Marehan, a small subclan of the Darod, and of very humble background. The exact circumstances of the coup are not very well known; it's not clear whether Barré ordered the assassination of the president, or whether he simply took power in the aftermath of the president's assassination. His regime was a classic Soviet client state, with a single party, single trade union, a women's organization, and young pioneer groups. A great deal of money was spent on weaponry rather than on development, but still, there was a conscious investment in schools, whether to educate children to adore the regime or simply to educate them.

Every night till I was six, as my mother stood over the charcoal brazier, we children knelt in a semicircle and begged Allah to free our father. At the time, this didn't make an enormous amount of sense. My mother never took the time to really tell us about God; he just *was*, and he minded the prayers of little children most of all. But although I tried my best to pray hard, it didn't seem to be working. When I asked Ma why Allah hadn't set my father free yet, she just urged us to pray more.

Our mother could visit our father in prison, but only my brother, Mahad, was allowed to go with her. Haweya and I had to stay at home with Grandma. We were too little to go out with my mother, and we were girls; Mahad, in every way, came first. Our brother was always angry when he came back from these visits, and my mother made him promise not to tell us anything about them: we might stupidly let some information out, and the secret police might hear.

Once, as he was walking out of the jail with my mother, Mahad attacked the huge cardboard portrait of *Afwayne* hung at the entrance. He must have been about six. 'He was throwing stones at it and yelling,' Ma told my grandmother when she came home that night. 'Thank Allah, the prison guard was from our clan.' Ma sounded as if she couldn't help admiring Mahad's warrior spirit. But the guard could have accused her of teaching her son to oppose the government, to be an 'anti'. I knew that were it not for Allah and the protection of the clan, Haweya and I could have been sitting alone under the tree that night with my grandmother, begging Allah to free our mother and brother from prison, too.

Allah was a mystery to me. One of my first memories, from when I was perhaps three years old, is of watching my grandmother engaged in an inexplicable performance. She was crouching face-down on a mat in her bedroom with her nose on the floor. I thought that she was playing some kind of game with me, so I pranced around and made faces at her, poking. She ignored me, and continued bending up and down, muttering things that sounded maddeningly strange. I couldn't understand it. Finally, when she had finished, she turned around to me with a very scary look on her face. 'Bastard child!' she cursed, hitting me and biting my arms. 'Let Almighty Allah take you away! May you never even *smell* Paradise!'

My cousin Sanyar, the thirteen-year-old daughter of my mother's twin, extricated me from my grandmother's fierce grasp and took me outside. Sanyar helped my grandmother look after us when Ma was out. She was kind and explained that I had disturbed my grandmother in prayer, which was like talking to God, the most important moment of an adult's life.

I was startled: I knew for sure there had been nobody but Grandma and me in that room. But Sanyar said I was too little to understand. When I grew up, I would feel Allah's presence.

From *Infidel* (2006)

Ayaan Hirsi Ali was born in Mogadishu, Somalia, but today is a Dutch-American activist and writer. Raised as a devout Muslim, she is now an atheist. In 2004, Ali was forced into hiding in the Netherlands following the assassination by a radical Islamist terrorist of director Theo van Gogh, with whom Ali had collaborated on the short film *Submission*.

Ali continues to attract considerable controversy for her outspoken views. She followed her memoir *Infidel* with the books *Nomad: From Islam to America* (2010) and *Heretic: Why Islam Needs a Reformation Now* (2015). Through her AHA Foundation, Hirsi Ali campaigns against the denial of education for girls, female genital mutilation, forced marriage and honour violence.

Eric R. Kandel (1929–)

Memory has always fascinated me. Think of it. You can recall at will your first day in high school, your first date, your first love. In doing so you are not only recalling the event, you are also experiencing the atmosphere in which it occurred – the sights, sounds, and smells, the social setting, the time of day, the conversations, the emotional tone. Remembering the past is a form of mental time travel; it frees us from the constraints of time and space and allows us to move freely along completely different dimensions.

Mental time travel allows me to leave the writing of this sentence in my study at home overlooking the Hudson River and project myself backwards sixty-seven years and eastward across the Atlantic Ocean to Vienna, Austria, where I was born and where my parents owned a small toy store.

It is November 7, 1938, my ninth birthday. My parents have just given me a birthday gift that I have craved endlessly: a battery-operated, remote-controlled model car. This is a beautiful, shiny, blue car. It has a long cable that connects its motor to a steering wheel with which I can control the car's movement, its destiny. For the next two days, I drive that little car everywhere in our small apartment – through

355

the living room, into the dining area, under the legs of the dining room table where my parents, my older brother, and I sit down for dinner each evening, into the bedroom and out again – steering with great pleasure and growing confidence.

But my pleasure is short-lived. Two days later, in the early evening, we are startled by heavy banging on our apartment door. I remember that banging even today. My father has not yet returned from working at the store. My mother opens the door. Two men enter. They identify themselves as Nazi policemen and order us to pack something and leave our apartment. They give us an address and tell us that we are to be lodged there until further notice. My mother and I pack only a change of clothes and toiletries, but my brother, Ludwig, has the good sense to bring with him his two most valued possessions – his stamp and coin collections.

Carrying these few things, we walk several blocks to the home of an elderly, more affluent Jewish couple whom we have never seen before. Their large, well-furnished apartment seems very elegant to me, and I am impressed with the man of the house. He wears an elaborately ornamented nightgown when he goes to bed, unlike the pajamas my father wears, and he sleeps with a nightcap to protect his moustache. Even though we have invaded their privacy, our appointed hosts are thoughtful and decent. With all their affluence, they also are frightened and uneasy about the events that brought us to them. My mother is embarrassed to be imposing on our hosts, conscious that they are probably as uncomfortable to have three strangers suddenly thrust upon them as we are to be there. I am bewildered and frightened during the days we live in this couple's carefully arranged apartment. But the greatest source of anxiety for the three of us is not being in a stranger's apartment; it is my father – he disappeared abruptly and we have no idea where he is.

After several days we are finally allowed to return home. But the apartment we now find is not the one we left. It has been ransacked and everything of value taken – my mother's fur coat, her jewelry, our silver tableware, the lace tablecloths, some of my father's suits, and all of my birthday gifts, including my beautiful, shiny, remote-controlled blue car. To our very great relief, however, on November 19, a few days after we have returned to our apartment, my father comes back to us. He tells us that he had been rounded up, together with hundreds of other Jewish men, and incarcerated in an army barracks. He won his release because he was able to prove that he had been a soldier in the Austro-Hungarian army, fighting on the side of Germany during World War I.

The memories of those days – steering my car around the apartment with increasing assurance, hearing the bangs on the door, being ordered by the Nazi policemen to go to a stranger's apartment, finding ourselves robbed of our belongings, the disappearance and reappearance of my father – are the most powerful memories of my early life. Later, I would come to understand that these events coincided with Kristallnacht, the calamitous night that shattered not just the windows of our synagogues and my parents' store in Vienna, but also the lives of countless Jews all over the German-speaking world.

In retrospect, my family was fortunate. Our suffering was trivial compared with that of millions of other Jews who had no choice but to remain in Europe under the Nazis. After one humiliating and frightening year, Ludwig, then age fourteen, and I were able to leave Vienna for the United States to live with our grandparents in New York. Our parents joined us six months later. Although my family and I lived under the Nazi regime for only a year, the bewilderment, poverty, humiliation, and fear that I experienced that last year in Vienna made it a defining period of my life.

It is difficult to trace the complex interests and actions of one's adult life to specific experiences in childhood and youth. Yet I cannot help but link my later interest in mind – in how people behave, the unpredictability of motivation, and the persistence of memory – to my last year in Vienna. One theme of post-Holocaust Jewry has been 'Never forget,' an exhortation to future generations to be vigilant against anti-Semitism, racism, and hatred, the mind-sets that allowed the Nazi atrocities to occur. My scientific work investigates the biological basis of that motto: the processes in the brain that enable us to remember.

From *In Search of Memory* (2006)

Professor Eric R. Kandel won the 2000 Nobel Prize in Physiology or Medicine for his research on the physiological basis of memory storage in neurons.

Madeleine Albright (1937–)

The national memory of any people is a mixture of truth and myth. For Czechs, 1620 is the year they lost their independence and 1918 the year they regained it. The Ides of March 1939 is when they had their liberty snatched away again. Within days, there were red-bordered posters with an eagle and swastika plastered all around Prague. Storm troopers loitered with fastened bayonets on the streets of Old Town, around Wenceslas Square, in front of cathedrals, and on old Hradčany. The Gestapo set up headquarters. German-language street signs appeared on every corner. According to a March 19 dispatch from the U.S. Embassy:

> There are several thousand . . . political refugees and their families here in hiding and in danger of their lives. Many of the women and children are spending their days and nights in the woods in the vicinity of Prague, notwithstanding that the ground is covered by snow. All relief organizations have been forcibly disbanded . . . the German secret police here are making hundreds and perhaps thousands of arrests in the usual Nazi manner; the Jewish population is terrified; as are . . . those persons closely associated with the former regime.

My parents were among those who had one question uppermost in their minds: how to get out? In the words of my mother:

To leave Czechoslovakia immediately was technically impossible. There was complete chaos in Prague. Communication was stopped, banks were closed, friends were detained. We learned from competent sources that Joe's name was on the list of people who should be arrested. After leaving Madeleine with my family, Joe and I moved out of our apartment and began sleeping each night with friends, spending the days in Prague streets and in restaurants. It was mostly during the nights that the Gestapo captured people.

After more than a week of living on the run, my parents obtained the necessary paperwork. My mother wrote later that a little bit of petty bribery might have been involved, which would not have been surprising in those days. The Nazis had established an office to process exit visas with an eye to preventing known enemies from leaving, but they were dependent at the outset on Czech inspectors who ignored instructions and allowed hundreds of politically active countrymen to escape.

On March 25, my mother collected me from Grand-mother Růžena and, in the afternoon, sat with me in a coffee shop while my father went to the police for the final stamp of approval. When he returned, about five o'clock, we had time to pack two small suitcases before heading to the railroad station. My guess is that Růžena, Arnošt, and Olga were all there to see us off, because in my mother's letter she noted with sadness that that was the last time we saw them alive.

It was ten days after the Nazi invasion. The southwest-bound Simplon Orient Express came through Prague only three times a week; on that day, the waiting platform must have been jammed and the carriages packed. To my parents, the sight of swastikas everywhere would have removed any doubts about their choice. They pushed their way in and handed their tickets to the conductor. The whistle blew, and our seventeen-hour journey began. The sleeping cars consisted of wood-paneled compartments, each with two beds, one above the other, and a tiny washbasin. During the day, the beds could be put up and the space converted into a small sitting room. There being no separate seat for me, I must have been handed back and forth while being encouraged to settle in and sleep. The first border we came to was that of the newly independent Slovakia. Next was the crossing into Hungary, where I imagine every passenger, including every political activist and most particularly every Jew, held his or her breath until travel documents were returned and the train began again to move. After Hungary came Yugoslavia, then on to Greece where we boarded a boat for England. Our destination: freedom.

From *Prague Winter* (2012), written with Bill Woodward

The daughter of Czechoslovak diplomat Josef Korbel, **Madeleine Korbelová (later Albright)** emigrated with her family to the United States in 1948, becoming a US citizen in 1957. She went on to become the first US ambassador to the United Nations to have been born outside the USA (1993–96) and, subsequently, also the first woman to serve as United States Secretary of State, from 1997 to 2001.

Gulwali Passarlay (1994–)

Before I died, I contemplated how drowning would feel.

It was clear to me now; this was how I would go: away from my mother's warmth, my father's strength and my family's love. The white waves were going to devour me, swallow me whole in their terrifying jaws and cast my young body aside to drift down into the cold, black depths.

'*Morya, Morya,*' I screamed, imploring my mother to come and snatch up her twelve-year-old son and lift him to safety.

The journey was supposed to be the beginning of my life, not the end of it . . .

'I found you in a box floating down the river.'

I eyed my grandmother suspiciously.

Her deep brown eyes danced mischievously, set within a face that was deeply lined and etched by a lifetime's toil in the harsh Afghan sun.

I was four years old, and had just asked the classic question of where I'd come from. 'You are joking with me, *Zhoola Abhai.*'

Calling her 'old mother' always made her smile.

'Why would an old woman lie? I found you in the river, and I made you mine.' With that she gave a toothless chuckle and wrapped me in her strong arms – the one place in all the world where I felt most safe, loved and content. I was my grandparents' second grandchild, born after my older brother, but I felt like I was their favourite, with a very special place in their hearts.

We are from the Pashtun tribe, which is known for both its loyalty and its fierceness. Home was the eastern Afghan province of Nangarhar, the most populated province in Afghanistan, and also a place of vast deserts and towering mountains. It is also a very traditional place, where local power structures run along feudal and tribal lines.

I was born in 1994, just as the Taliban government took control of Afghanistan. For many Afghans, and for my family, the ultra-conservative Taliban were a good thing. They were seen as bringing peace and security to a country that for over fifteen years had suffered a Russian invasion, followed by a brutal civil war.

For much of their marriage, my grandparents had lived in a refugee camp in the north-western Pakistani city of Peshawar. The refugee camp was also where my parents had met and been married. By the time I was born, Afghanistan was not at war, and relatively stable under Taliban rule.

My earliest memory is of being four years old and running with my grandfather's sheep high in the mountains. Grandfather, or *Zoor aba* ('old father'), as I called him in my native language of Pashtu, was a nomadic farmer and shepherd. He was a short man, made taller by the traditional grey turban he always wore. His hazel-flecked green eyes shone with a vital energy that belied his years.

Each spring he walked his flock of thickly fleeced sheep and spiral-horned cattle to the furthest reaches of the mountains in search of fresh and fertile pasture. My grandparents' home, a traditional tent made from wooden poles and embroidered cloth, went with them. Two donkeys carried the tent on their backs, along with the drums of cooking oil, sacks of rice, and the flour my grandmother needed to bake naan bread.

I would watch transfixed as my grandmother spread and kneaded sticky dough along a flat rock before baking it over the embers of an open fire. She cooked on a single metal pan which hung from chains slung over some branches balanced over the fire. I loved helping her gather armfuls of wild nettles which she boiled to make a delicately scented, delicious soup. I don't know how she did it, but everything she created in that pan tasted of pure heaven to a constantly hungry little boy like me.

Every year, as the leaves began to turn into autumn's colours, they would head back down to lower ground, making sure to return to civilization before the harsh snows of winter descended and trapped them on the mountains' slopes. There they joined the rest of their family, their six children and assorted grandchildren, in the rambling house that was home to our entire extended family. Our house then was a very simple but lovely, single-storey stone-built structure perched above a clear, flowing river.

I was my grandparents' shadow so I was thrilled when, aged three, they took me with them the next time they returned to the mountains. Their youngest daughter, my auntie, Khosala ('happy'), was also with us. She was fifteen and like a big sister to me.

For the next three and a half years I shared my grandparents' nomadic lifestyle, at night falling asleep beneath a vast, star-filled mountain sky, safely tucked up inside the tent nestled between the pair of them.

Grandfather loved his family with a fierce passion, and laughter came easily to both him and my grandmother. I don't think I ever saw him angry. One time I accidentally almost took his eye out with a catapult. Blood was streaming down his cheek from where my badly aimed flying rock had cut it. It must have really hurt but he didn't chastise me. Instead, with characteristic humour, he managed to make a joke of it: 'Good shot, Gulwali.'

My grandmother was sturdily built and bigger than my grandfather. She was definitely the boss, but I could see they adored each other. Love isn't something people really discuss in Afghanistan. Families arrange marriage matches according to social structure, tribal structure or even to facilitate business deals; no one expects or even wants to be in love. You just do as your parents demand and make a marriage work the best you can – you have to, because divorce is forbidden for women.

It was explained to me once – by my grandfather – that a woman is too flighty and unsure of her own mind to understand the consequences of leaving her marriage. Besides, who would look after her if she did? Men do have the right to divorce their wives, but it is still very frowned upon. I knew of only one woman whose husband had divorced her. She'd been taken in by her brother but this was a great shame to her family. She had been lucky that he had accepted her and hadn't turned her away on to the streets.

My grandparents would never have dreamt of breaking up, even if they could have done. They had married when she was fifteen and he eighteen, meeting for the first time on the day of their wedding, as is still often the norm. But anyone could see that their years together had given the pair a special bond.

By the time I was five I was already a skilled shepherd, able to shear off a fleece all on my own. I recognized every animal individually and loved how they knew the sound of my whistle. I particularly enjoyed watching my grandfather's two sheepdogs working. One was a large, thick-headed beast and the other a small, wiry terrier-type dog. They would run rings around the flock, corralling them into order. And when the local vet, a man who traversed the furthest reaches of the mountains to service his clients, came to treat the sheep, I remember thinking how brilliant it might be to be a vet myself when I grew up. I was fascinated by him and the various implements he used.

It was about as wonderfully simple and rural a life as you can possibly imagine.

From *The Lightless Sky* (2015), with Nadene Ghouri

Gulwali Passarlay left Afghanistan in 2006, embarking on an extraordinarily torturous journey across eight countries. He reached the UK a year later and is currently reading Politics and International Relations at the University of Manchester. In 2012, he was invited to carry the Olympic torch. Today he remains a torchbearer for all those to whom his memoir is dedicated: 'the 60 million or so refugees and internally displaced people who are out there somewhere in the world today, risking their lives to reach safety'.

Ocean Vuong (1988–)

Reading and writing, like any other crafts, come to the mind slowly, in pieces. But for me, as an E.S.L. student from a family of illiterate rice farmers, who saw reading as snobby, or worse, the experience of working through a book, even one as simple as *Where the Wild Things Are*, was akin to standing in quicksand, your loved ones corralled at its safe edges, their arms folded in suspicion and doubt as you sink.

My family immigrated to the U.S. from Vietnam in 1990, when I was two. We lived, all seven of us, in a one-bedroom apartment in Hartford, Connecticut, and I spent my first five years in America surrounded, inundated, by the Vietnamese language. When I entered kindergarten, I was, in a sense, immigrating all over again, except this time into English. Like any American child, I quickly learned my ABCs, thanks to the age-old melody (one I still sing rapidly to myself when I forget whether 'M' comes before 'N'). Within a few years, I had become fluent – but only in speech, not in the written word.

One early-spring afternoon, when I was in fourth grade, we got an assignment in language-arts class: we had two weeks to write a poem in honor of National Poetry Month. Normally, my poor writing abilities would excuse me from such assignments, and I would instead spend the class mindlessly copying out passages from books I'd retrieved from a blue plastic bin at the back of the room. The task allowed me to camouflage myself; as long as I looked as though I were doing something smart, my shame and failure were hidden. The trouble began when I decided to be dangerously ambitious. Which is to say, I decided to write a poem.

'Where is it?' the teacher asked. He held my poem up to the fluorescent classroom lights and squinted, the way one might examine counterfeit money. I could tell, by the slowly brightening room, that it had started to snow. I pointed to my work dangling from his fingers. 'No, where is the poem you plagiarized? How did you even write something like this?' Then he tipped my desk toward me. The desk had a cubby attached to its underside, and I watched as the contents spilled from the cubby's mouth: rectangular pink erasers, crayons, yellow pencils, wrinkled work sheets where dotted letters were filled in, a lime Dum Dum lollipop. But no poem. I stood before the rubble at my feet. Little moments of ice hurled themselves against the window as the boys and girls, my peers, stared, their faces as unconvinced as blank sheets of paper.

Weeks earlier, I'd been in the library. It was where I would hide during recess. Otherwise, because of my slight frame and soft voice, the boys would call me 'pansy' and 'fairy' and pull my shorts around my ankles in the middle of the schoolyard. I sat on the floor beside a tape player. From a box of cassettes, I chose one labelled 'Great American Speeches.' I picked it because of the illustration, a microphone against a backdrop of the American flag. I picked it because the American flag was one of the few symbols I recognized.

Through the headset, a robust male voice surged forth, emptying into my body. The man's inflections made me think of waves on a sea. Between his sentences, a crowd – I imagined thousands – roared and applauded. I imagined their heads shifting in an endless flow. His voice must possess the power of a moon, I thought, something beyond my grasp, my little life. Then a narrator named the man as a Dr. Martin Luther King, Jr. I nodded, not knowing why a doctor was speaking like this. But maybe these people were ill, and he was trying to cure them. There must have been medicine in his words – can there be medicine in words? 'I have a dream,' I mouthed to myself as the doctor spoke. It occurred to me that I had been mouthing my grandmother's stories as well, the ones she had been telling me ever since I was born. Of course, not being able to read does not mean that one is empty of stories.

My poem was called 'If a Boy Could Dream.' The phrases 'promised land' and 'mountaintop' sounded golden to me, and I saw an ochre-lit field, a lushness akin to a spring dusk. I imagined that the doctor was dreaming of springtime. So my poem was a sort of ode to spring. From the gardening shows my grandmother watched, I'd learned the words for flowers I had never seen in person: foxglove, lilac, lily, buttercup. 'If a boy could dream of golden fields, full of lilacs, tulips, marigolds . . .'

I knew words like 'if' and 'boy,' but others I had to look up. I sounded out the words in my head, a dictionary in my lap, and searched the letters. After a few days, the poem appeared as gray graphite words. The paper a white flag. I had surrendered, had written.

Looking back, I can see my teacher's problem. I was, after all, a poor student. 'Where is it?' he said again.

'It's right here,' I said, pointing to my poem pinched between his fingers.

I had read books that weren't books, and I had read them using everything but my eyes. From that invisible 'reading,' I had pressed my world onto paper. As such, I was a fraud in a field of language, which is to say, I was a writer. I have plagiarized my life to give you the best of me.

This essay, 'Surrendering', first appeared in the *New Yorker* (2016)

Saigon-born poet and essayist **Ocean Vuong** spent a year in a refugee camp aged two before moving to the United States. His collection *Night Sky with Exit Wounds* (2016) won both the Forward Prize for Best First Collection and T. S. Eliot Prize, among other awards.

George Szirtes (1948–)

This is the story of a love affair that began when I was eight. You are not really serious when you are seventeen, wrote Arthur Rimbaud in 'Romance', his poem about adolescent love, and he was right. But it is different at eight. Everything is serious then, and later, when love goes, there still remains the memory of the romance.

Let me begin with the sunshine on the high wall that bounds our yard. The light constantly changes but the wall is always the same, still flint, still centuries old, still with the remnants of what must have been a low sloping roof embedded in it. Pigeons, blackbirds, blue tits, robins and various finches have perched on it. A pair of collared doves have watched their fledgling – born flightless with one stunted wing – scuttle around underneath and take shelter by huddling against it.

There is, according to the romance, something peculiarly English about both the light and the wall, especially the light. Returning from visits abroad it seems a clear yet soft light, a light to walk into. It is harder to define once you are in it and you really need to have been away at least a month and to have arrived by plane to notice it at all, but it is local light: neither Mediterranean nor mid-continental. It is an island-light built out of sea.

Almost thirty years ago we spent most of the year in my landlocked birthplace, Hungary, and when we returned to the UK there was the same light and a smell I can only conjure rather than experience now. 'I smell the sea,' I declared on the tarmac at Heathrow. I can't have of course but it was as if what I knew of the sea was in the air, perceptible to heightened senses. There was clearly a difference in the light and the smell, and the difference had to be the sea.

Those heightened senses were an echo of the eight-year-old boy's first experience of the sea. When we arrived in England in the December of 1956 the authorities placed us, along with a lot of other Hungarian refugees, in off-season boarding houses on the Kent coast. Hundreds, maybe thousands of us were being accommodated in such places elsewhere. It was in the depth of winter, cold and dull, but we could take walks along the prom and gaze at the sea, a great alien body of water the like of which none of us had seen before. It was as grey as everything else around us at that time but its noise was denser, a hiss, a low growl and sort of clattering surge that served as both threat and safeguard. Surely the sea was the best of all possible walls against those who would, elsewhere, have harmed us. No invading army had marched along this promenade for many centuries. We were in a strong place. Strong army, strong navy, strong sea. The sea was almost strong enough by itself. It was tangible, almost solid. If we wrapped up well and kept watching we would finish up tasting of salt. Our fingers had a clear salty taste. And as the year moved towards spring and colours brightened we got sharp salty winds and moved through what we began to think of as salty light.

The sea was the earliest definition of English life but it was soon joined by what faced it: rows of terraces, houses with gables and front gardens, hotels, shops selling seaside mementos like rock and funny hats, and amusement arcades blasting rock 'n' roll. For us as children there were the English comics we soon had our hands on, full of wild pictures with talks- and thinks-bubbles. *Beano, Beezer, Dandy, Tiger, Lion* were the magical names and, most wonderful of all, the *Eagle* with Dan Dare, Digby and The Mekon.

All this was induction, as was the scout hut on the cliff path in Westgate where the cubs would meet, the Winter Gardens in Margate, the wrestling night, the English breakfasts, the fish and chips, the cups of tea, the pounding of English children's feet down the street into our heads and the blossoming of soft clear light into April and May.

This was England. We were not going back, now or ever.

(2017)

George Szirtes' first book of poetry *The Slant Door* won the Geoffrey Faber Memorial Prize in 1980. His numerous other collections include *Reel* (2004), which won the T. S. Eliot Prize. Szirtes' translations of Hungarian literature include works by Sándor Márai, among numerous others.

Aso Saber (1970–)

My most precious memory from childhood is of flying a kite after a long day at nursery. It might even be my first memory.

The city is surrounded by mountains. A shallow, murky river flows through them. It is mid-autumn and the wind is strong enough to break the branches of trees. I am a small kid running up and down the hills, jumping over streams with a wide smile. During early autumn we children climb the trees and play among their golden, crisp leaves. The clouds overlap each other and fight to push the blue sky away. In the foothills, it is perfect weather for flying. Many children's kites appear among the clouds.

My kite is big and colourful with a long, strong string. It is beautiful. My father bought it for me in our capital city, Baghdad. It is a sunny, windy afternoon, the first time that I fly my new kite. I am full of joy. I hold the kite tightly and throw it into the air. My kite flies into the deep blue sky, far away from me. I sing, laugh and shout as it soars.

The wind and my cheerful cries, however, soon mix with the sound of airplanes. They start to bomb the land. My kite means the world to me, though, and so I'm not worried at first about being in a battlefield. I simply think, 'These things belong to men, and I am just a kid with his kite. I haven't anything to do with the war.' But the fire from the land mixes with the smoke of the aircraft above and soon entirely covers the blue sky. Before long, my kite has disappeared into the dark. All that remains is its handle and a shred of its long string. When I realise I have lost my beautiful toy, I run home and cry. All the people in my town are bereft because of the war and I join them now, weeping for my kite.

Seeing that I am very sad, my father tells me: 'When the war ends your kite will be back.' I believe my daddy's promise. Yet one day soon afterwards, while I await its return, the smoke of war swallows my father too.

I remember dreaming one night around then that I am flying through a clear blue sky, into the whitest clouds, searching for my father and kite. The next morning, my mother tells me that I can't fly away. She promises me though that once the war ends I will, sure enough, see my father and my kite again.

My mother was clever. Although, like my father, she didn't herself see the end of war, I came to discover everything just as she promised.

Happiness returned. I did see my own father again — inside myself. I also realised that my little daughter is just like my beautiful kite, flying free.

The war is over now. Those winds still blow over there — only without the smoke. There are a lot of children flying their kites once again, in exactly the same place in the foothills and with the same happiness.

(2017)

377

Aso Saber, a Kurdish Iraqi, was born in Sulaymaniyah, in northern Iraq. Saber worked as a magazine editor in Iraq but his political views and journalism led to his being persecuted and then tortured by Saddam Hussein's regime. He moved to London as a refugee in 2005.

Jade Amoli-Jackson (1971–)

As a reverend, my dad would receive many clothes from abroad, so he had a good few pairs of shoes. A number of them were very colourful but not all were to be admired. In fact, I found some downright embarrassing.

One particularly awful pair was made of car tyres. Another was a pair of wooden shoes. He really loved these ones and would wear them whenever he could: especially during the evenings, after his duties at school were done, and over the weekend. He had smart shoes for work and even smarter ones reserved for whenever visits from the school inspectors were due. As well as a reverend, he was the local headmaster and had to show them that he could set an example for the teachers and students, both in school and at home. School children had to be smart at all times – even if we had no shoes to wear and walked barefoot. He also took pride in wearing those smart shoes to the Sunday church services.

To be frank with you, though, I hated Dad's wooden shoes because they were really noisy when he walked and, if you were dozing off, the sound of them would make you jump back awake. The noise of those shoes is one of my very earliest memories. It would often keep us up at night. He didn't take them off until he went to bed himself, not even when bathing. It was a relief when he sat down to mark his pupils' schoolwork or listened to the news on his small radio, for then the shoes would be momentarily silenced.

It was not only us children who were fed up with the sound of his wooden shoes. Whenever he passed her by while wearing them, my stepmother would roll her eyes. One day she decided to take action and throw them into the fire. Yet just as she was about to fling them into the flames, my dad walked in and caught her in the act! She tried to lay the blame on me! I did not attempt to defend myself but her lie backfired when my little sister, her daughter, said, 'But Mum, you already made Dad's sandals into firewood to cook our dinner!' I crept away, leaving them to sort it out.

When my dad was shot dead, together with my twin sister, all his shoes were stolen. None of us know where his shoes disappeared to. My brother would have inherited them – but the devils had other ideas. They were my dad's pride and joy. He had so many shoes but the ones I miss most are the annoying ones – that embarrassing pair made of tyres and, especially, those wooden shoes that kept us awake every night.

(2017)

Jade Amoli-Jackson worked as a journalist and broadcaster in her country of origin but, after the murder of her family by government soldiers, and with her own life in danger, she fled to the UK as a refugee in 2001. She published her first collection of poetry, *Moving a Country*, in 2013.

Yusra Mardini (1998–)

Five minutes to go. It's cold. I shudder at the sight of the glinting water. I pull the training jacket closer around my slight frame and hug my shoulders. I jump on the spot and shake out both my legs. I catch my breath. It's a huge honour. At just ten years old, I'm the youngest swimmer here. I might look small, but I know I'm good enough to beat these teenagers. I'm fast, I've been breaking records. And now here I am, about to swim for my country, Syria, for the first time.

I reach down into the kitbag at my feet and rummage for my phone. I need Dad. I need to hear his voice. Dad is my swimming coach, my mentor. He's the one who started all this, who put me in the pool when I was just three years old and showed me how to kick. He can't be here in person, but his voice will be with me for every stroke of the race, pushing me, driving me on towards the finish line. I dial the number and hold my breath as the ringtone purrs in my ear.

Dad comes on the line and begins going over the plan one last time. As if I'd forget. His race strategy is lodged in my head and etched in my muscle memory. Still, I listen hard, soaking up the calming sound of his voice so I can replay it later in the water. Keep it steady in the first one hundred and fifty metres, he says, don't rush, take your time. Whatever the others do, don't panic, hold your nerve, save it all for the last fifty-metre sprint. Call me back when it's done. Yes, coach. I hang up.

I feel less alone now. It's like Dad's here, watching, willing me on, shouting silent instructions from the poolside. I take off my training jacket and adjust my swimming cap and goggles. I look down the line at the other swimmers. They're huge. I gaze at their muscular arms and long, powerful legs. They stare back at me; the skinny, quiet little girl with the wide eyes. Doubt rises for a second and I shiver. I must seem so tiny to them, like nothing. Dad's voice returns, and I remember. I'm not nothing, I'm with Dad. And we have a plan.

Thirty seconds to go. My mind grows quiet as my body takes over. I step up onto the block, my right foot forward, toes curled around the edge. Gripping the block with both hands, I gaze at my knees, tense my body and lean back. Beep. I launch forward into the water and begin rolling my torso and legs in a dolphin kick. I break the surface, gasping for air. My shoulders whirl. I dive, my hands crash over my head and pull towards my core, sketching a keyhole shape in front of my chest.

I play Dad's voice in my head. Keep it steady, he says. Don't panic. Save your power for the sprint. I glimpse the dark, churning shapes of my rival swimmers in the water beside me. We're level, but something tells me they're

383

pushing too hard. They'll burn out before the end. The thought spurs me on. I reach the poolside, dive and whirl into a somersault turn. As I roll my legs into the second dolphin kick, I'm sure the others have peaked too soon. Dad's voice is tense. Wait, hold it, get ready.

Fifty metres to go. Dad's voice shouts in my head. Now. Sprint. Give it everything you have. I push harder, reach higher, kick stronger and my tiny frame flies through the water. I inch out in front, shifting up a final gear just as the others are beginning to flag.

Twenty-five metres to go. It's only me and one other swimmer, pounding towards the finish line. Reach. Crash. Reach. Crash. Arms out, I slam the touchpad, grab the side and straighten up in the water. I tear off my goggles and gaze at the scoreboard. Yusra Mardini. Silver.

Before I know it, I'm on the podium, jittery with euphoria as an official places the medal over my head. My one thought is that this is only the beginning. Squinting into the distance, it feels like I can see every race, competition and medal laid out before me. The World Championships. The Olympics. The world is going to know my name.

When I fled Syria, I lost the photo of me, grinning wide, with my first international medal around my neck. But before both photo and medal were buried in the rubble of my family home, I used to look at them a lot. I'd laugh and remember how tiny I was. Just ten years old, up there with those teenagers, showing the world I wasn't as small as I looked.

And I'd remember how, as the butterflies fluttered in my

stomach, something clicked into place. Suddenly, I truly wanted to swim, not for Dad, but for me. And nothing, not a revolution, or a catastrophic war, or even a sinking dinghy, was going to stop me.

Written with Josie Le Blond (2018)

Yusra Mardini grew up in Damascus. She fled Syria with her sister in August 2015, eventually arranging to be smuggled onto a boat for Greece. However, after the over-crowded dinghy's motor stopped working in the Aegean Sea, Mardini and her sister got into the water and swam the boat onward for over three hours – until it reached Lesvos. They then travelled through Europe to Germany, where they settled in Berlin.

Mardini went on, the following year, to represent the Refugee Olympic Athletes Team in the pool at the 2016 Olympics in Rio de Janeiro. In 2017, she was appointed a UNHCR Goodwill Ambassador and in 2018 published a memoir, *Butterfly*.

Alf Dubs (1932–)

Until I left Prague for the UK on the *Kindertransport* in June 1939, I lived in Prague with my parents.

My earliest memories start in the summer of 1937. That summer, my mother took me on holiday to Austria – where she was from – and I remember hearing gunshots ringing out across the Wörthersee lake which we were visiting. I was four years old. When I asked my mother what was happening she told me that Nazi thugs were doing shooting practice.

Even before the invasion of Czechoslovakia by the Nazis the country was on high alert – Czech soldiers were being mobilised after the Sudetenland fell to the Nazis and I recall tear gas being dropped in the centre of Prague. Perhaps the soldiers were rehearsing for the conflict that was to come. In the summer of 1938 my mother and I didn't go on holiday to Austria which was by then under Nazi control.

The Germans occupied Prague in March 1939. My father, who was Jewish, disappeared immediately and fled to the UK. Shortly after the invasion I remember that we were told at school that we had to tear out the picture of the Czech president Beneš from our school books and replace it with a picture of Hitler.

After the invasion, Hitler visited Prague as part of a victory parade. Children from my school – and many others – were told to go to Wenceslas Square to welcome Hitler. My mother objected and refused to allow me to go.

My mother put me on a *Kindertransport* train in June 1939 with a knapsack of food for the journey. I can still clearly see her in my mind standing on the platform waving me off, surrounded by German soldiers in uniforms and swastikas. Of course, for many of the parents waving their children off that day, it was the last time they ever saw them.

The children travelled in carriages of six to eight. We had hard wooden seats to sit and sleep on. It was no great hardship for us – we were children and didn't mind sleeping on the benches.

It took one day to get to the Dutch border by train and two days to get to Liverpool Street. The journey seemed interminably long to me. When we reached Holland I remember the older children on the train cheering – I didn't know why – I was one of the youngest, if not the youngest child on the train and was looking out for windmills and wooden shoes, which was all I knew about Holland. Only afterwards did I understand that they were cheering because we had reached safety from the Nazis.

From the border, the train took us to the Hook of Holland; from there, we took a boat to Harwich; and then came via train to Liverpool Street.

The children all had dog tags to identify them and

we were allocated a family or foster parents to meet us at Liverpool Street station. I was lucky; my father was waiting for me. When I got to London I realised that I hadn't touched the food my mother had packed for me two days before.

One of my earliest memories of England was seeing women soldiers – possibly from the ATS – marching in Hyde Park. I thought that was marvellous. The only soldiers I'd seen until then had been men – mainly German occupiers. And I remember the barrage balloons.

I was six when I arrived. I only spoke German and Czech, so my father enrolled me in a school so I could learn English. I was so much more fortunate than many of the other children who I travelled with, as my mother was able to escape and join us. She arrived in London the day before the war broke out.

So began my life in the UK.

(2018)

Alf Dubs was one of the 669 Czech-resident, mainly Jewish, children saved from the Nazis by Nicholas Winton and others on the *Kindertransport*.

Dubs went on to serve as an MP from 1979 to 1987, then as chief executive of the Refugee Council (1988–95) and, in 1994, he was made a life peer.

In 2016, amid the deepening European migrant crisis, Lord Dubs sponsored an amendment to the Immigration Act that would offer unaccompanied refugee children in Europe safe passage to Britain. Originally rejected by the House of Commons, the amendment was accepted by the government following a second vote in favour by the Lords. However, in February of 2017, the Home Office restricted the scheme to 480 children.

That same year, it is estimated that 20,000 child refugees arrived in Europe.

Endnote

Home. Name. Time. Our touchstones for living. The corner-stones of this collection. Threaded together, they even echo and half-rhyme. Yet each is rendered meaningless, nothing at all, unless it coalesces with that other human construct; the one that allows us to live as sentient beings. They are all – home, our names, time itself – mere homilies to memory.

'As we travel through life it is hard to find a truer friend,' wrote Shlomo Breznitz of memory.

We should perhaps qualify the observation, however acute: our *childhood* memories are the truest companions of all. A strong early memory allows us, momentarily at least, to forgo time and remember ourselves. Visitations such as these – recollecting where we came from – let us rediscover our place in the world.

Yet childhood memories are really more like lifelong *imaginary* friends. They dance alongside our adult selves, second shadows, reminding us that it is never too late to start consciously living – with them – in the here and now. There, we will find ourselves alongside Nietzsche's

grown-up and Picasso's artist: at play in a state of grace.*
For, in order to stay truly alive as grown-ups and enjoy our
short stay here on Earth – before we head home for the
last time – we need to keep *growing young*. Like Peter Pan
himself; or, rather, the children we once were (remember
the time when you couldn't imagine ever being grown-up?
That's the kid I mean).

We should all now and again, by whatever means, seek
them out. Not only will we then create valuable new mem-
ories, but we'll also discover those Neverland spaces among
which we can be 'surprised by joy' or ambushed by wonder.
It is in these clearings that we can each welcome home –
with the open arms that every displaced young person
deserves – our prodigal inner child.

Only then, like memory itself, will we truly be living in
the present.

---

* Pablo Picasso famously declared not only that '*all children are artists*' but also that it
took him '*four years to paint like Raphael but a lifetime to paint like a child*'. Sure enough,
his later works – famed drawings of doves, flowers and such – gleam with a pristine,
childlike simplicity.

Afterword

In mining the deep-lying seams of memory, this compelling anthology reminds us of the all-too-familiar imprecision and subjectivity of our childhood recollections.

In choosing to connect with refugees, by sharing their memories in this book, and by supporting the Refugee Council, Ben Holden has also alighted on a fundamental dysfunction of our asylum system in the UK and in many other countries worldwide: the failure to take account of the damaging impact of trauma on the ability to retrieve and relate consistent and objectively accurate personal narratives.

To be entitled to the protection afforded by the Refugee Convention, you must first convince the authorities in the country in which you've sought asylum that you are who you say you are. You must demonstrate to them that your story is true and that your fear of the persecution or harm you would face were you to be returned to your country of origin is well founded.

In assessing this future risk, often in the absence of any compelling corroborative evidence, authorities rely on the account you give of your identity, your background, the harm or the threats you've experienced, and why you fear being sent back to the place you fled.

Therefore, your memories – and, moreover, the consistency of those recollections – play a huge part in establishing your credibility and determining your need for protection. Officials will test your recall of: the geography or culture of the country or region in which you grew up; how many men raped you while you were being held in detention; which countries you passed through on your journey to exile and how long you stayed in each; the fundamental tenets of the outlawed faith you follow; the precise date your parents were murdered.

You will likely be required to give your account of events repeatedly as you navigate the bureaucratic minefield of the asylum process: when you are screened on arrival; when you apply for asylum accommodation; when you are interviewed by your legal representative; when you are at your substantive asylum interview with the authorities and the tribunal where your appeal against an initial refusal of protection is heard. Any inconsistency or contradiction in your account will call your credibility into question and reduce your chances of being granted asylum.

Insufficient regard will be given to the disruptive impact of traumatic experiences on your chronological memory – despite the extensive and authoritative body of academic literature establishing the connection – and to the difficulties of disclosing painful and long-suppressed memories to sceptical, if not openly hostile, officials. The risk of retraumatisation, triggered by the recalling and retelling of deeply disturbing events, again well documented, will be discounted. Your psychological condition – as you grapple with isolation, depression, loss, guilt and anxiety about those left behind, not to mention your fear of the consequences of being disbelieved – will be of little concern.

Your ability to concentrate may have been undermined by recurrent nightmares or by the medication you take to combat them. The overwhelming sense of shame you feel about what was done to you may also have rendered any detailed memory largely irrecoverable, particularly on demand in a hostile, adversarial setting.

The long delays in decision making and the inadequacy of the asylum support system combine to lock you into a new, damaging cycle of torpidity, squalor, illness and destitution. This, alongside the ever-present threat of arbitrary detention hanging over you, will compound your troubled state of mind. Yet the system will continue to regard anything less than perfect recall of all that might have happened to you as clear evidence of falsehood.

For young refugees – particularly those who made their long, hazardous journeys alone, during which their trust was subject to betrayal and exploitation at every turn by their smugglers or traffickers – the subsequent impact of an adversarial system that assumes from the outset that they are lying, particularly about their age, is even more acute. It is no surprise that, by the time we get to see them at the Refugee Council, many of the young people we help are isolated emotionally, with limited recall of the detail of even recent events. Our first challenge is to find a way to re-establish their trust in adults.

What we need is an asylum process rooted in respect and

empathy for the individual, embodying in all its actions the spirit, not just the letter, of the Refugee Convention. We need a way of determining eligibility for refugee protection that understands that people flee for their lives because staying put is not an option and recognises, in a far more holistic assessment of credibility, the disruptive impact of traumatisation on memory.

We know that this alternative future is possible because we see the transformational change that occurs daily when our beneficiaries access the personalised advice, guidance, advocacy, tuition, therapeutic care or employment support that we provide. It is this knowledge that drives our lobbying and campaigning for a new refugee protection vision and culture, in which people seeking asylum are treated as human beings first, immigration cases second, and whereby providing protection is always a higher priority than preventing abuse. If we are successful, then refugees will be able to look ahead with confidence, coming to terms with their traumatic pasts by recovering memories of happier times also.

Getting there will require a shift in political priorities that only a change in public mood and opinion can generate. Thanks to Ben, this fine anthology is well primed not just to raise awareness, but also to trigger the calls for humanity and understanding that will make such change far more likely.

Maurice Wren
Chief Executive, Refugee Council

Further Reading

Below are just some of the books that have proven crucial during the curation of this anthology.

Memory

In Praise of Forgetting: Historical Memory and Its Ironies by David Rieff (Yale)

In Search of Memory: The Emergence of a New Science of the Mind by Eric R. Kandel (Norton)

Living Psychoanalysis: From Theory to Experience by Michael Parsons (Routledge)

Memory: A Very Short Introduction ed. Jonathan K. Foster (Oxford)

Moonwalking with Einstein: The Art and Science of Remembering Everything by Joshua Foer (Penguin)

Permanent Present Tense by Suzanne Corkin (Basic)

Pieces of Light: The New Science of Memory by Charles Fernyhough (Profile)

Searching for Memory by Daniel L. Schacter (Basic)

Mythology and Origins

An Odyssey: A Father, a Son and an Epic by Daniel Mendelsohn (William Collins)

Creation by Adam Rutherford (Penguin)

The Mighty Dead: Why Homer Matters by Adam Nicolson (William Collins)

The Origin of (almost) Everything by Graham Lawton and Jennifer Daniel (*New Scientist*)

The Refugee Crisis

Human Cargo: A Journey Among Refugees by Caroline Moorehead (Picador)

The New Odyssey: The Story of Europe's Refugee Crisis by Patrick Kingsley (Guardian/Faber)

Rescue: Refugees and the Political Crisis of Our Time by David Miliband (TED / Simon & Schuster)

Acknowledgements

First, heartfelt thanks are due to Suzanne Baboneau: a wonderful publisher and editor, who – alongside Ian Chapman – has become a cherished friend, through the rough and the smooth. This has proven another memorable collaboration. Thank you to the rest of the team at Simon & Schuster and Scribner also, notably Suzanne King and Judith Long.

For her encouragement and inimitably adroit advice, I again owe a debt of gratitude to Anna Webber – whose clear-eyed account of her earliest memory has lingered in my own mind, ever since our initial conversation about this project!

The late John David Morley claimed to remember the circumstances of his birth. *If anyone could . . .* Seventy years later, at this enterprise's outset, J's vote that I was 'onto something' was a boon. I remain thankful for it and him.

As well as our parents, I thank my brothers: Joe Holden, for emptying a bin into my cot, and Sam Holden, for his suggestion a few years subsequently that I put that piece of chalk up my nose, thus prompting perhaps my earliest memory (at least I *think* it was you, Sam)! Thanks for your support during this project too, particularly the ideas about approaching the Refugee Council and 'Rights of Passage'.

Ditto the rest of the family: Ursula, Rosemary and Aurelia; Cindy, Ben, Marce, Artie, Siena, Chris, Violet and Aya; and the Leventis clan.

At the Refugee Council, profound thanks go to Maurice Wren, Maxine Saca McMinn, Helen Johnson, Alice Crawford, Amy Neale, Judith Dennis and Helen Lakeland.

For various reasons, I'm also indebted to: Ghias Aljundi, Tom Davies and other friends at Amnesty International; Melinda and Omar of the Starfish Foundation; Michael Parsons and Melanie Hart; Angelica Ronald and Josh Hyams; Emily Jones; Alan Samson; Lucy Popescu; Hasani; Kathleen Riley; Lorraine Jerram; and the staff of Kensington Central Library.

Professor Martin Conway – a pioneer of our understanding of memory, particularly the autobiographical variety – generously offered feedback on some key elements of the manuscript. Any errant scientific mistakes are of course mine.

I will for ever be grateful to my generous contributors for sharing such personal and sometimes painful memories, as well as to the other great individuals – living and deceased – whose memoirs are extracted here. Thanks also to the contributors' support staff where applicable, not to mention the countless agents and rights teams around the world who helped with permissions. Apologies for not mentioning more specific names. And to anybody whom I might have forgotten. My memory ain't what it used to be.

Finally, thank you to my first and last; start and finish; beginning, middle and end: Salome, George and Ione.

Copyrights and Credits

The extracts from the below-referenced memoirs, like the essays original to this collection, appear in this book with the permission of the following parties.

1. My First Memory

Lines from *Four Quartets* by T. S. Eliot reprinted by permission of Faber and Faber Ltd.

Iris by John Bayley: copyright © 1998, John Bayley. Used by permission of Gerald Duckworth & Co Ltd.

My Early Life by Winston Churchill: copyright © The Estate of Winston S. Churchill. Reproduced by permission of Curtis Brown, London, on behalf of the Estate of Winston S. Churchill.

The Secret Life of Salvador Dalí, copyright © 2019, Salvador Dalí, Fundació Gala-Salvador Dalí, Figueres.

Memoirs of a Dutiful Daughter by Simone de Beauvoir, published by Penguin Classics, copyright © 1958, Librarie Gallimard; translation copyright © 1959, The World Publishing Company. Reproduced by permission of Penguin Books Ltd. All rights reserved.

Cider with Rosie by Laurie Lee, published by the Hogarth Press,

2. The Sense of a Beginning

405

Index

Achebe, Chinua 225–7
Afghanistan: Gulwali Passarlay
    363–8
Albright, Madeleine 359–62
Ali, Ayaan Hirsi 350–4
Ali, Muhammad 157, 202–5
Allende, Isabel 301, 341–4
Alzheimer's disease 9, 27, 113
amnesia 23
    childhood amnesia 16
Amoli-Jackson, Jade 379–81
amygdala 12, 124–5, 292
Angelou, Maya 246–8
animals, memories of
    Allende, Isabel 342
    Bolt, Usain 252–3, 255
    Dalai Lama 209
    Gosse, Edmund 40
    Layard, Austen 139
    Lessing, Doris 93–4
    Maxwell, Gavin 190–2
    Passarlay, Gulwali 367
    Sacks, Oliver 110
    Sutcliff, Rosemary 86

Thatcher, Margaret 96
apperception 10
Arab Spring 306
archaeological terminology
    23–4
Arendt, Hannah 327
Astaire, Fred 157, 187–9
asylum system 392, 392–5
auditory cues 22, 23
Augustine of Hippo 7–8, 100
Auster, Paul 81–3

babies and memory 14–15
    see also intra-uterine
    memories
Banville, John 275–8
Barnes, Julian 151
Barré, Siad 351
Barry, Sebastian 116–18
Baudelaire, Charles 276
Bayley, John 27–8
Beauvoir, Simone de 60–1
Benjamin, Walter 324–7
Big Bang theory 144, 145

409

Bolt, Usain 157, 249–56
Bombay: Rudyard Kipling 54–5
Borges, Jorge Luis 304
Bragg, Melvyn 119–22
brain
    amygdala 12, 124–5, 292
    dentate gyrus 15
    hippocampus 12, 15
    medial temporal lobes 12, 15
    memory functions and 9, 11,
        12, 292
    occipital cortex 12, 23
Brando, Marlon 91–2
Breznitz, Shlomo 307, 390
Brierley, Saroo 152–3, 257–61
buried memories 19
Byatt, A. S. 23

Carreras, José 208
Carter, Jimmy 4–5
Casanova, Giacomo 31–4
Cash, Johnny 215–18
childhood amnesia 16
Christmas, memories of
    Hurston, Zora Neale 175–6
    Roosevelt, Eleanor 169
church, memories of
    Bragg, Melvyn 120
    Morpurgo, Michael 131
Churchill, Winston 24, 48–9
Cicero 7
clothes, memories of
    Amoli-Jackson, Jade 379–80

Bragg, Melvyn 120
Fox, Paula 219, 220
Greenfield, Susan 112, 114
Smith, Dodie 76
Washington, Booker T.
    161–2
Wharton, Edith 50
Woolf, Virginia 65
Coetzee, J. M. 25
Cohen, Leonard 156–7
Coleridge, Samuel Taylor 11–12
collective memory 302, 305
colour, memories of
    Beauvoir, Simone de 60–1
    Dalí, Salvador 56
    Hitchens, Christopher 102
    Marías, Javier 128
    Maxwell, Gavin 191–2
    Woolf, Virginia 65, 66
creation myths 142, 144, 146–7
Czechoslovakia: Alf Dubs
    386–7

Dalai Lama 209–12
Dalí, Salvador 13, 18, 56–7
Darwin, Charles 35–6
Davis, Miles 89–90
De Quincey, Thomas 276
death, memories of
    Gorky, Maxim 44–7
    Roosevelt, Eleanor 169–70
dentate gyrus 15
Descartes, René 9

diaries and journals 26–7
  see also memoirs
Didion, Joan 26, 149
digital memory aids 7
Djibouti: Mo Farah 262–3, 264
Domingo, Plácido 208
dreams and visions
  Casanova, Giacomo 32–3
  Hoffman, Eva 329
  Mankell, Henning 267
  Saber, Aso 377
Drogba, Didier 312
Dublin: Winston Churchill
  48–9
Dubs, Alf 386–9

Eagleman, David 288–93
Einstein, Albert 144, 145,
  181–2
Eliot, T. S. vii, 313
English Heritage 303
engrams 11, 12, 22, 305
epics 297–8
episodic (autobiographical)
  memory 9, 15
explicit recall 15

false memory syndrome 18,
  98–9
Farah, Mo 262–5
fathers, memories of
  Achebe, Chinua 225–6
  Albright, Madeleine 360–1

Ali, Ayaan Hirsi 351
Ali, Muhammad 204
Amoli-Jackson, Jade 379–80
Astaire, Fred 187
Auster, Paul 82
Bolt, Usain 250–1, 253–5
Bragg, Melvyn 119–20
Cash, Johnny 215–16,
  217–18
Farah, Mo 263
Fox, Paula 221, 222–3
Gorky, Maxim 44–7
Hoffman, Eva 330–1, 333
Hurston, Zora Neale 175–6
Jung, Carl 70
Kandel, Eric R. 357
King, Martin Luther, Jr
  194–6
Lessing, Doris 93–4
McGahern, John 238–9, 240
Malcolm X 73
Mandela, Nelson 147–8
Mardini, Yusra 382, 383, 384
Murdoch, Iris 27
Neruda, Pablo 200
Obama, Barack 145–6
Pankhurst, Emmeline 166
Pavarotti, Luciano 206, 207
Pelé 243, 244
Poitier, Sidney 228, 230
Roosevelt, Eleanor 168,
  169–70
Saber, Aso 377

fathers, memories of – *continued*
    Sacks, Oliver 110
    Slovo, Gillian 346–8
    Springsteen, Bruce 272
    Wharton, Edith 50–2
    Zweig, Stefan 321–2
fear, memories of
    Bragg, Melvyn 120
    Davis, Miles 89
    Freud, Sigmund 38, 39
    Hawking, Stephen 108
    Humphrey, Nicholas 124–5
    Washington, Booker T. 161
    see also traumatic memories
First, Ruth 346–8, 349
food, memories of
    Bolt, Usain 252
    Jung, Carl 68
    Passarlay, Gulwali 365
    Smith, Dodie 75
forget, the need to 303, 304
Foster, Jonathan K. 16
Fox, Paula 219–24
Franklin, Eileen 17–18
Franklin, George 17–18
Freud, Sigmund 7, 19, 37–9,
    57, 72
friends, memories of
    Ali, Muhammad 202–3
    Farah, Mo 263
    Hadley, Tessa 283–5
    Hurston, Zora Neale 172–3,
        174–5

King, Martin Luther, Jr 194
Knausgaard, Karl Ove 105–6

Gogh, Theo van 354
Good Friday Agreement
    304
Gorky, Maxim 44–7
Gosse, Edmund 40–1
grandparents, memories of
    Ali, Ayaan Hirsi 350, 352,
        353
    Allende, Isabel 341–2
    Casanova, Giacomo 31–2, 33
    Gorky, Maxim 44–7
    Humphrey, Nicholas 124,
        125
    King, Martin Luther, Jr 193
    Passarlay, Gulwali 363–7
    Roosevelt, Eleanor 168
    Slovo, Gillian 345–6
    Smith, Dodie 75
    Springsteen, Bruce 272, 273
Grass, Günter 307
Greene, Graham 17
Greenfield, Susan 112–15
Guthrie, Woody 178–80

Hadley, Tessa 283–7
Hawking, Stephen 108–9, 144
Hesse, Herman 327
Hill, Archibald 124
hippocampus 12, 15
Hitchens, Christopher 102–4

Hitler, Adolf 387
Hoffman, Eva 306–7, 308,
    328–33
Holden, Ben 3–30
Holocaust, memories of the 307
    Albright, Madeleine 359–61
    Dubs, Alf 386–7
    Hoffman, Eva 330–3
    Kandel, Eric R. 355–7,
        355–8
homecoming narratives
    298–301
homes, childhood, memories of
    Achebe, Chinua 226
    Beauvoir, Simone de 60–1
    Brando, Marlon 91
    Brierley, Saroo 257
    Cash, Johnny 215, 217
    Farah, Mo 262
    Fox, Paula 221–2
    Guthrie, Woody 179
    Hoffman, Eva 328
    Holden, Ben 5–6
    Jung, Carl 68
    Knausgaard, Karl Ove 107
    Lee, Laurie 63
    Leigh Fermor, Patrick 77
    Lessing, Doris 93
    Morpurgo, Michael 133–4
    Neruda, Pablo 199
    Passarlay, Gulwali 365
    Smith, Dodie 75–6
    Springsteen, Bruce 271, 273

Thatcher, Margaret 95
Twain, Mark 42
hospitals, memories of
    Barry, Sebastian 116–17
    Roosevelt, Eleanor 168–9
Humphrey, Nicholas 123–6
Hurston, Zora Neale 171–7

illness, memories of
    Astaire, Fred 188
    Auster, Paul 82
    Barry, Sebastian 116–17
    Casanova, Giacomo 31–4
    Jung, Carl 70
    see also death; hospitals
implicit memory 15
infantilism 25
intra-uterine memories 13
    Dalí, Salvador 13, 56–7
involuntary memory 23
Iraq: Aso Saber 376–8

James, Henry 55
James, William 7, 9, 10
journeys, memories of
    Achebe, Chinua 225
    Albright, Madeleine 361
    Cash, Johnny 216–17
    Dubs, Alf 387–8
    Hitchens, Christopher
        102–3, 104
    Knausgaard, Karl Ove 106
    Lee, Laurie 63–4

journeys, memories of – *continued*
  Marías, Javier 128
  Nabokov, Vladimir 58
  Pelé 243–4
  Presley, Elvis 155–6
  Thatcher, Margaret 95–6
  Woolf, Virginia 65
Jung, Carl 20–1, 23, 68–72, 152

Kandel, Eric R. 355–8
Kermode, Frank 149–50, 157
Keynes, Maynard 125–6
Kindertransport 386, 387–8
King, Martin Luther, Jr 193–7, 371
Kipling, Rudyard 54–5
Knausgaard, Karl Ove 105–7
Korbel, Josef 362
Kristallnacht 357
Kurdi, Alan 315

Lambert, Constant 145
landscape and nature, memories of
  Allende, Isabel 342–3
  Brando, Marlon 91
  Hitchens, Christopher 102
  Jung, Carl 68, 69, 71
  Knausgaard, Karl Ove 105, 106–7
  Lee, Laurie 62
  Lewis, C. S. 183

McGahern, John 237–8, 241
Mantel, Hilary 100–1
Woolf, Virginia 65–7
language acquisition, memory and 15
Layard, Austen 139–42
Le Guin, Ursula K. 279–82
Lee, Laurie 62–4
Leigh Fermor, Patrick 29, 77–80
Lessing, Doris 25, 93–4
Lewis, C. S. 28, 183–6
Library of Ashurbanipal 142
loci method 7
London, memories of
  Morpurgo, Michael 131–2
  Thatcher, Margaret 95–6
Love, Gladys 156

McAdams, Dan 302
McCartney, Paul 155
McGahern, John 237–42
McIndoe, Archibald 135
'madeleine moment' 22
Malcolm X 73–4
Malta: Christopher Hitchens 102–4
Mandela, Nelson 147–8, 305
Mankell, Henning 149, 266–70
Mantel, Hilary 98–101
Mardini, Yusra 382–5
Marías, Javier 127–30
Marlborough, Duke of 48

Maxwell, Gavin 190–2
medial temporal lobes 12, 15
memoirs 20, 21, 24, 25, 154,
    158
memorials 305
memory
    average age for first
        memories 12–13
    brain chemistry and 9, 11,
        12, 292
    collective memory 302, 305
    episodic (autobiographical)
        memory 9, 15
    explicit recall 15
    false memory syndrome 18,
        98–9
    implicit memory 15
    involuntary memory 23
    primary memory 9
    procedural memory 8, 9
    reconsolidation 10
    recovered memories 18
    repression 19
    revisionist 8
    secondary memories 10, 13,
        292
    semantic memory 8, 9, 15
    slow-motion perception
        289–92
    subjectivity of 8
memory palaces 6–7
Messiaen, Olivier 23
Miles, Caroline 16

Miller, Arthur 25, 88
mnemonics 7
Molaison, Henry 304
Morpurgo, Michael 131–6
mothers, memories of
    Albright, Madeleine 360–1
    Ali, Ayaan Hirsi 352
    Ali, Muhammad 204
    Auster, Paul 82
    Barry, Sebastian 117
    Bolt, Usain 250, 251, 255
    Bragg, Melvyn 119, 120, 121
    Brierley, Saroo 257–8, 259,
        260
    Cash, Johnny 216–17
    Darwin, Charles 35
    Dubs, Alf 386, 387, 388
    Freud, Sigmund 37, 38, 39
    Gorky, Maxim 44–7
    Guthrie, Woody 179
    Hitchens, Christopher 104
    Hoffman, Eva 332–3
    Humphrey, Nicholas 123,
        124, 125
    Jung, Carl 70
    Kandel, Eric R. 356
    Kipling, Rudyard 55
    McGahern, John 241
    Malcolm X 73
    Mantel, Hilary 100
    Marías, Javier 128
    Miller, Arthur 88
    Morpurgo, Michael 132, 133

mothers, memories of – *continued*
   Murdoch, Iris 27
   Neruda, Pablo 198
   Pamuk, Orhan 234–5
   Pavarotti, Luciano 206
   Pelé 243
   Poitier, Sidney 228–9, 230–1
   Saber, Aso 377
   Slovo, Gillian 346–8
   Springsteen, Bruce 272–3
   Sutcliff, Rosemary 84–5,
     86–7
   Washington, Booker T. 162
   Wiesel, Elie 334, 335–6,
     337, 338–9, 340
   Woolf, Virginia 65, 66
Murdoch, Iris 27–8
museums 302, 305
music, memories of
   Cash, Johnny 215
   Pavarotti, Luciano 206–8
   Presley, Elvis 156

Nabokov, Vladimir 22, 23,
   58–9
names and identity 152–4
   Brierley, Saroo 152–3
   Washington, Booker T. 163
Neruda, Pablo 198–201
neurogenesis 15
New Deal 215–16
New York: Edith Wharton
   50–2

Nietzsche, Friedrich 308
Nimrud 140–1
nostalgia 5, 298, 303, 306

Obama, Barack 145–7
occipital cortex 12, 23
Odyssey 297, 298–301
Omaha: Fred Astaire 187–8
oppression, memories of
   Ali, Ayaan Hirsi 351–3
   see also Holocaust; race and
     segregation
origin stories 142, 143–9
Orwell, George 55

Pamuk, Orhan 232–6
Pankhurst, Emmeline 165–7
Parkinson's disease 9
Parks, Rosa 213–14
Passarlay, Gulwali 363–8
Pavarotti, Luciano 157, 206–8
Pelé 157, 243–5
perspective 25, 158
Picasso, Pablo 391
Poitier, Sidney 154–5, 228–31
prams, memories of
   Mantel, Hilary 100
   Sutcliff, Rosemary 86
   Thatcher, Margaret 95
Presley, Elvis 155–6
primary memory 9
procedural memory 8, 9
Proust, Marcel vii, 22, 23

race and segregation, memories of
  Angelou, Maya 246, 247
  King, Martin Luther, Jr
    193–7
  Malcolm X 73
  Parks, Rosa 213
  Slovo, Gillian 348
  Washington, Booker T.
    160–4
Reagan, Ronald 25
reconsolidation 10
recovered memories 18
refugee children and memories
    306–19, 392–5
  Albright, Madeleine 361
  Drogba, Didier 312
  Dubs, Alf 386–9
  Mardini, Yusra 382–5
  Passarlay, Gulwali 368
  Szirtes, George 373–5
  Vuong, Ocean 369
Refugee Olympic Athletes team
    385
relativity theories 144–5
repression 19
revisioning memories 8
Ribot, Théodule 11
Rieff, David 303
Rimbaud, Arthur 373
Roosevelt, Eleanor 168–70
Roth, Philip 304

Saber, Aso 376–8

Sacks, Oliver 110–11
Said, Edward 150–1, 158
St Ives, Cornwall: Virginia
    Woolf 65–7
Sartre, Jean-Paul 61
Schacter, Daniel 16, 24
schools and teachers, memories
    of
  Bragg, Melvyn 121
  Greenfield, Susan 112
  Hawking, Stephen 108–9
  McGahern, John 241
  Mankell, Henning 269
  Marías, Javier 128–9
  Morpurgo, Michael 131
  Pankhurst, Emmeline
    165–6
  Vuong, Ocean 369–72
  Washington, Booker T.
    161–3
  Wiesel, Elie 334–5, 339–40
secondary memories 10, 13,
    292
self-consciousness 113
self-mythology 157
semantic memory 8, 9, 15
sensory receptors see colour;
    smells; taste
servants, memories of
  Freud, Sigmund 38
  Jung, Carl 71
  Kipling, Rudyard 54
Shereshevsky, Solomon 303–4

siblings, memories of
  Ali, Ayaan Hirsi 352
  Angelou, Maya 246–7
  Astaire, Fred 188
  Barry, Sebastian 116–17
  Beauvoir, Simone de 60
  Freud, Sigmund 37–8
  Le Guin, Ursula K. 279
  Lee, Laurie 63
  Lewis, C. S. 183
  Poitier, Sidney 229, 230
Simonides 6–7
Slovo, Gillian 345–9
Slovo, Joe 346–8, 349
slow-motion perception 289–92
smells, memories of 22
  Jung, Carl 23, 68
  Lessing, Doris 93–4
  Morpurgo, Michael 131
Smith, Dodie 75–6
social media role in cataloguing
  memory 305–6
spatial awareness, memory
  consolidation and 15
Spielberg, Steven 13–14
sports, memories of
  Ali, Muhammad 203–5
  Bolt, Usain 253
  Mardini, Yusra 382–5
  Pelé 244–5
Springsteen, Bruce 155, 271–4
Steinbeck, John 29
superhero film genre 142–3

Sutcliff, Rosemary 84–7
synaesthesia 23
Szirtes, George 373–5

Taliban 364
taste, memories of: Marcel
  Proust 22, 23
Thatcher, Margaret 95–7
Tolstoy, Leo 16–17
toys and games, memories of
  Hadley, Tessa 283–7
  Kandel, Eric R. 355–6
  Le Guin, Ursula K. 280–1
  Saber, Aso 376–7
train journeys, memories of
  Marías, Javier 128
  Nabokov, Vladimir 58
  Pelé 243–4
  Thatcher, Margaret 95–6
traumatic memories 19, 28–9,
  393–4
  Fermor, Patrick Leigh 79
  Gorky, Maxim 44–7
  Humphrey, Nicholas 123
  Kandel, Eric R. 356–7
  Malcolm X 73
  Steinbeck, John 29
Trump, Donald 147
Truth and Reconciliation
  Commission 305
TV and cinema, memories of
  Farah, Mo 262–4
  Mankell, Henning 268

Poitier, Sidney 229
Springsteen, Bruce 271–2
Twain, Mark 42–3

violence, memories of
 Bragg, Melvyn 120–1
 Malcolm X 73
 see also traumatic memories
Vuong, Ocean 369–72

Washington, Booker T. 160–4
Washington, Denzel 154
Waugh, Evelyn 154
Weill, Kurt 327
Wesley, John 96
Wharton, Edith 26, 50–2
Wiesel, Elie 304–5, 334–40
Williams, Tennessee 10

Wilson, Harold 96
Wilson, Woodrow 179
Winton, Nicholas 388
Wittgenstein, Ludwig 277
Wolfe, Thomas 247
Woolf, Virginia 65–7
Wordsworth, William 158–9
World War I, memories of:
 Patrick Leigh Fermor 77–9
World War II, memories of
 Bragg, Melvyn 119–20, 122
 Humphrey, Nicholas 123–4
 Morpurgo, Michael 132,
  134–5
 see also Holocaust

Zweig, Stefan 320–3